D1447059

In the Service
of the State

THE CINEMA OF

ALEXANDER DOVZHENKO

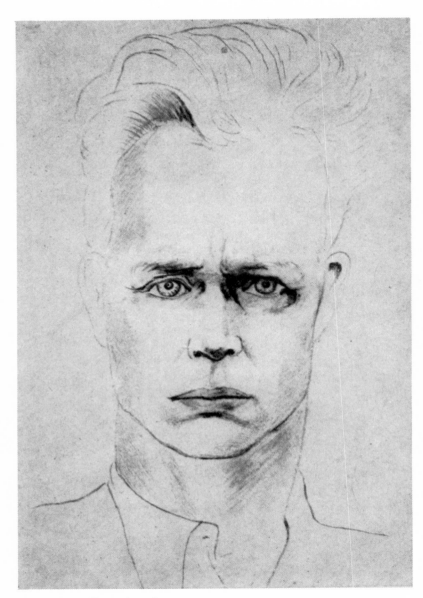

A Dovzhenko self-portrait, 1948

In the Service
of the State

THE CINEMA OF

ALEXANDER DOVZHENKO

Vance Kepley, Jr.

The University of Wisconsin Press

Published 1986

The University of Wisconsin Press
114 North Murray Street
Madison, Wisconsin 53715

The University of Wisconsin Press, Ltd.
1 Gower Street
London WC1E 6HA, England

First printing

Printed in the United States of America

For LC CIP information see the colophon

ISBN 0-299-10680-2

Chapter 4 appeared in an earlier version in *Film Criticism* 6, no. 1 (1982): 37-46.

Chapter 5 appeared in an earlier version in *1978 Film Studies Annual,* © copyright by
Purdue Research Foundation, West Lafayette, Indiana 47907. Reprinted with
permission.

Chapter 8 appeared in an earlier version in *Post Script: Essays in Film and the Humanities*
2, 2 (Winter 1983): 37-54.

Chapter 10 appeared in an earlier version in *Journal of Popular Film and Television* 8, no. 2
(1980): 19-26. Reprinted with permission of the Helen Dwight Reid Education
Foundation. Published by Heldref Publications, 4000 Albemarle Street, NW,
Washington, DC 20016. Copyright 1980.

For Betty

Contents

Acknowledgments

I OWE A VARIETY of debts to a variety of individuals and agencies. Grants from the research boards of the University of Delaware and the University of Wisconsin advanced the research and writing of this book. Particular thanks are in order for two department chairmen who proved to be wise and gracious bosses: Zack Bowen of the University of Delaware English Department and Lloyd Bitzer of the University of Wisconsin Communication Arts Department.

The staffs of several film archives made the original research for this book far more pleasant than I had any right to expect. I probably could not name all the individuals who extended me various courtesies during my research visits, but each works for one of the following institutions: The Museum of Modern Art, Anthology Film Archives, the Oesterreichisches Filmmuseum, and the Staatliches Filmarchiv der D.D.R.

Friends and associates have lent advice, support, and assistance: David Bordwell, Robert Carringer, Steven P. Hill, Herb Eagle, Dudley Andrew, Kristin Thompson, Ronee Messina, Gail Cagney, Peter Givler, Carolyn Moser, Betty Steinberg, Carol Olsen, and Jack Kirshbaum.

This book—indeed, my entire career—reflects the personal and professional influence of Russell Merritt, mentor and valued friend. Finally, my wife, Betty, has more than earned a dedication page. My gratitude to her is not of the sort customarily expressed at a typewriter.

A Note on Transliteration

CERTAIN PROBLEMS of transliteration are posed by the fact that this book will be read both by students of film, who are used to many conventional English equivalents of Russian names (e.g., Eisenstein), and by specialists in Soviet studies, who might prefer more exact forms of transliteration (Eizenshtein). The matter is complicated by the frequent differences between Russian and Ukrainian spellings.

In the scholarly apparatus I use the Library of Congress form of transliteration, omitting diacritics. This is System II of J. Thomas Shaw's *Transliteration of Modern Russian for English-Language Publication* (Madison: University of Wisconsin Press, 1967). In the text proper, however, I often revert to familiar equivalents; thus, Dovzhenko's first name appears in the text as Alexander rather than Aleksandr (Russian) or Oleksandr (Ukrainian). The Soviet newspaper is *Izvestia* in the text and *Izvestiia* in the apparatus. When I introduce into the text Russian terms for which no English equivalent exists (e.g., *partiinost'*), I employ an exact transliteration form. For the names of characters in Dovzhenko's films, I simply reproduce the spellings that are most common in those prints of the films available in the American market.

What my tactics lack in absolute consistency of spelling, I trust they will compensate in a certain clarity for potential readers.

In the Service
of the State

THE CINEMA OF

ALEXANDER DOVZHENKO

I

Introduction

ALEXANDER DOVZHENKO is consistently characterized as the great folk artist of cinema. His films on his native Ukraine, considered to be among the most lyrical works of the Soviet cinema, derive much of their beauty from a Ukrainian pastoral tradition and from an abiding faith in peasant custom. So closely are Dovzhenko's films identified with such lyricism that Soviet writer Victor Shklovsky once mused, "The trees distinctly rustled in his silent films."[1]

Yet Dovzhenko is also firmly a part of the strident, revolutionary cinema of the Soviet Union, ranking among the foremost of the so-called heroic school of Soviet cinema. This political and polemical film movement emphasized modern trends and proselytized for the abandonment of old Slavic traditions in favor of the revolutionary transformation of Soviet society. Such a didactic strain would seem to be fundamentally incompatible with the pastoral tradition which so informs Dovzhenko's work. That tension resides at the center of Dovzhenko's cinema. He is at once the lyrical poet and the modern polemicist, the spokesman for tradition and the advocate of revolutionary change.

As such, Dovzhenko presents fascinating challenges to the scholar. Yet three decades after Dovzhenko's death, we still lack full English-language studies of his films. Although Western scholars in recent years have shown considerable interest in the major Soviet filmmakers and have greatly expanded the critical literature on Eisenstein, Vertov, and others, and although the bibliography on Dovzhenko in Russian (and Ukrainian) and French is quite extensive, English-language criticism of Dovzhenko's work consists of only a few scattered essays of uneven quality.[2]

The relative paucity of scholarly work on Dovzhenko might be explained partly by the greater difficulty, relative to the other Soviet masters, that Dovzhenko poses for Western scholars. Dovzhenko's historical

3

situation was fundamentally different from that of the other major Soviet directors, and it has proven somewhat harder to recover. To begin with, Dovzhenko was born a Ukrainian peasant, while Eisenstein and his associates emerged from Russian urban settings and worked largely in the cultural spotlight of Moscow. Dovzhenko was not directly associated with the celebrated Moscow-based movement which became such a vital part of early Soviet art. While we can readily trace many of the important influences on the Muscovite circle of filmmakers—we are aware of the importance of formalist literary theory, for example, and of constructivist art and theater, and we know that the Muscovites borrowed heavily from American and West European films—Dovzhenko's sources are linked to his peasant background and to his Ukrainian national heritage. Unlike his more cosmopolitan contemporaries, he took material from such esoteric sources as regional folklore, a fact which may have helped to discourage substantive critical studies of his work.

If we may trace a dominant theme in those English-language articles that have appeared, it emerges from the conception that Dovzhenko remained an unabashed romantic artist with somewhat mystical assumptions about his own work. Dovzhenko professed to an expressive notion of creativity, maintaining that there were forces, even voices, within him which spontaneously emerged to shape his films. He identified his art with private impulses, claiming, for instance, that he used his own personality and his early experiences as direct sources for his fictional characters: "Who are my heroes? Father, Mother, Grandad [sic], and myself. I am Vasyl, Shchors, Bozhenko, and Michurin. It is my grandad who dies in *Earth*. Shkurat is my father. I am the boy who sits with the girl by the house."[3] Dovzhenko's assertion that his films represent the direct cinematic transcription of personal visions certainly leaves the impression that the accumulated fictional worlds of his work constitute a private, imaginary idyll, a mythical terrain as fully subject to sole ownership and proprietorship as Faulkner's Yoknapatawpha County.

A similar conception of expressivity informs much of the English-language criticism of Dovzhenko. His English and American admirers emphasize the pastoral nature of his work and seize on the image of a sensitive lyric poet whose art reflects an individual sensibility. This is stressed to the near exclusion of the social and political conditions of the Soviet system in which Dovzhenko worked, a critical convention which obviates the necessity of searching out the more arcane sources for his films. Excusing Dovzhenko as well from some presumed taint of Soviet propaganda, such critics ascribe much to the films' "poetic qualities" and to a special but vaguely defined "vision." We read, for example, that "in every one of his films he was expressing his own view, his own apprehension of life"; that he was "the most poetic" of Soviet directors and that in his films "every image is a source of mystery and wonder"; that as "the screen's greatest lyric poet," his work has nothing to do with Soviet party-line ideology; that he drew his strength from a "mythopoeic vision"; and that "he saw nature and human nature as one."[4]

While we cannot dismiss such observations out of hand, we can certainly identify them as narrow and incomplete, for in stressing the notion that Dovzhenko's fictions define some idealized, pastoral world, such critics lose sight of the countless historical references that permeate the films. Far from creating a never-never land of grass, trees, rivers, and characters drawn from personal musings, Dovzhenko produced films which constantly allude to their historical settings. In fact, few filmmakers, Soviet or otherwise, fashioned a more topical cinematic corpus. His nine fiction films all took up issues of immediate concern to Soviet audiences. All but one, *Diplomatic Pouch,* were set in the USSR, and that one exception dealt with characters in transit abroad whose actions still directly affected the USSR. All save four—*Zvenigora, Arsenal, Shchors,* and *Michurin*—involved stories set in the time of the films' productions, and those four exceptions were historical dramas treating formative aspects of Soviet social and political history.

It hardly compromises Dovzhenko to recognize that his films were created in and shaped by a particular social matrix. Indeed, it does little service to an artist to cut him off from the society in which he worked by assigning him a place in some special, ahistorical realm identified somewhat vaguely as "the poetic." We are, I submit, better advised to grasp the topical nature of Dovzhenko's fiction films and to explore just how the films might have drawn much of their richness from specific historical circumstances. I propose, then, to examine Alexander Dovzhenko's extant fiction films in a series of historical readings,[5] to look at the various film narratives Dovzhenko created and to determine how they borrowed and organized material from the society in which they were created. I intend primarily to explicate the films' narratives, but I will do so with an eye to their historical contexts. I do not present a full biography or complete chronicles of the making of the films, although biographical and production information will frequently come into play as appropriate contexts. I am principally interested in how Dovzhenko seized on topical political and social issues and fashioned narratives that spoke to the timely interests of his Soviet audience. With these qualifications in mind, we may turn to the fundamental question of this study: How might we position Dovzhenko's fictional films in their original historical contexts? This task of situating films historically suggests other, more pointed questions: From what particular issues of the moment did Dovzhenko draw, and how did he organize such material into dramatic form?

The answers would seem to lie in the refracted relationship between text and context that is in the nature of narrative, particularly topical narrative. The evidence of that relationship can be examined in a series of historical readings, the methods of which derive from some recent work of the French literary theorist Pierre Macherey and his English disciple Terry Eagleton,[6] who advocate that the "task of criticism is to analyze the complex of historical articulations to [the] structures which produce the text."[7] In a critical methodology which rejects the notion that an artwork remains complete unto itself, a well-wrought urn that should be admired in pristine isolation, Macherey and Eagleton argue that looking beyond the text is crucial to understanding the text itself. An artistic text is not a sealed, hermetic item, they would argue, but the possessor of a larger "historical possibility,"[8] a greater social reality which the critic must identify in the process of explicating the text itself. Any artistic text was, after all, created in a particular historical setting. It includes, willy-nilly, the traces of that setting among its purely fictional constructs. Historical reading, as defined by Macherey and Eagleton, takes note of how those traces function within the text and what they reveal about the text's origins.

At least two tenets of Macherey and Eagleton's complex theories provide useful tools for this study. One is their position that historical reading involves more than what the text explicitly "says." The critic must look beyond the manifest sequence of signs which make the text meaningful. He or she must also attend to what Macherey calls the "unspoken," the text's significant omissions and silences. What the text omits can prove as efficacious in historical readings as what it includes. Frequently, its most significant omissions betray the workings of social ideology on the text.[9] Ideology constitutes a crucial artistic determinant, according to Macherey and Eagleton, in part for the way it mediates between the text and social reality, preventing the text from addressing certain aspects of that reality. Ideology is traditionally defined as that body of ideas and beliefs propagated to assure, in Eagleton's apt phrase, that the "situation in which one class has power over the others is either seen by most members of society as natural or not seen at all."[10] In this capacity, ideology frequently acts to suppress knowledge of social reality, and it can often be measured in artistic texts by the inability of the text to deal fully and frankly with certain aspects of its social setting. The text remains silent on those areas of its own historical situation which are not entirely "knowable" within the dominant ideology, and the critic must attend to the "unspoken" to identify this process. "History then certainly 'enters' the text," says Eagleton, "not the least the 'historical text'; but it enters precisely as ideology, as a presence determined and distorted in its measurable absences."[11]

Such absences would include gaps in the logic of the narrative, issues set up but not developed, and realms of activity and experience arbitrarily denied the characters. Equally important are those historical sources which inform the narrative but which are not fully acknowledged in the text proper. Their status resembles that of the strings in the marionette show, invisible to the casual spectator but betrayed by the puppet's awkward movement. Historical criticism treats such extrinsic elements as part of the overall domain of text explication, seeking to articulate what the text leaves unsaid, to ask what issues are left untreated and why. As we shall see in the case of Dovzhenko, particular sets of background issues only cryptically acknowledged in the texts themselves provide both the crucial determinants for the films and the fields of study for historical criticism: for *Love's Berry* (1926) , the "new Soviet morality" of the 1920s and lingering sexual inhibition; for *Diplomatic Pouch* (1927), the role Soviet leaders saw themselves playing in international socialism; for *Zvenigora* (1928) and *Arsenal* (1929), the popular mythology of the 1917 revolution in the aftermath of the USSR's tenth anniversary; for *Earth* (1930), the rigors of rural collectivization; for *Ivan* (1932), the nature of industrial labor under the first Five-Year Plan; for *Aerograd* (1935), the Stalinist xenophobia of the 1930s and the effect of the purges; for *Shchors* (1939), the image of the hero as part of Stalin's personality cult; and for *Michurin* (1948), the Lysenko movement in Soviet science.

Macherey and Eagleton offer a second valuable tenet through their explanation of the role of contradiction in artistic texts. The system of the text often contains tensions which bespeak larger social contradictions. Rejecting organic unity as a standard of artistic value, Macherey claims, "To explicate texts is first of all to recognize in them the terms of the contradictions." In borrowing from social reality, the fictional narrative may incorporate social ingredients which are in conflict with each other. The text then becomes laced with tensions which derive from the preexisting contradictions of society. The text "expresses these conflicts and adds to them an imaginary resolution," the resolution of dramatic conflict that is traditional to narrative forms.[12] The process of historical reading calls upon one to see through this "imaginary resolution" in order to understand how the text grasps and transposes the contradictions of its society. The text's internal conflicts provide a form of access to larger, formative social contradictions.

The Soviet Union of the 1920s and 1930s, the period of Dovzhenko's greatest productivity, was characterized by pronounced social contradiction. In fact, it conforms to Louis Althusser's definition of an "overdetermined" society, one where a fundamental contradiction is represented in various social formations which in turn contain their own lesser, internal tensions. This was certainly true of revolutionary Russia, described by Althusser as "the most advanced and the most backward nation of Europe," one in which a modern, revolutionary political system was imposed on a largely conservative, tradition-bound population.[13] The definition of social contradiction applies as well to the USSR's troubled process of change from an almost medieval agrarian society to an industrial power, a process which lasted through the Stalin years and which saw the term *revolution* being applied not just to the events of 1917 but to the USSR's ongoing transformation. Isaac Deutscher lucidly describes the determining social contradiction of the Soviet revolution, one evidenced in Dovzhenko's films, by noting that the USSR "was caught up in the contradictions inherent in any socialist revolution occurring in an underdeveloped country."[14] The Russian empire had not fully experienced the familiar hardships—oppression of labor, worker alienation, social dislocation—commonly identified with capitalist industrial development. Instead, the revolution preceded industrialization. But that fact only postponed the requisite developmental hardships, as a determined, often ruthless Soviet political leadership had to force a reluctant, largely peasant population through the arduous process of industrialization. All the antagonisms and struggles of industrial development were experienced during the building of socialism rather than constituting its precondition. Out of this basic social contradiction emerged other problems. Intensive industrialization was supposed to represent a means to an end, that end being the material betterment of the population; but, as Deutscher observes, "means and ends were perpetually confused." Worship of work quotas took priority over the comfort of the workers themselves, and the "ideal image of a classless society was dragged down to the miseries of the period of transition and to the crude necessities of a primitive accumulation of wealth."[15] Through it all, the social values and routines which had provided a sense of continuity to generations were in flux and in seeming danger of being sacrificed to the new religion of industrial production.

Such overdetermination—in which policies of social change struggled against the inbred conservatism of the population, in which the necessity of modernization came into conflict with the urge for social continuity, in which the long-range interests of the population were advanced by the political oppression of that population—shaped every element of the Soviet superstructure, including, at some level of remove, the films of Alexander Dovzhenko. And in turn, Dovzhenko, the lyricist and polemicist, the spokesman for both tradition and change, dealt with such pervasive contradictions in his work, incorporating them into a series of topical stories and striving through the "imaginary resolution" of narrative to reconcile them. In so doing, he followed a consistent but hardly rigid narrative strategy. In several of his films, a small group of characters, constituting a limited social unit, must confront and cope with rapidly changing social conditions. The group typically starts out as an integrated social entity—a family *(Zvenigora, Earth)*, a ship's crew or military unit *(Diplomatic Pouch, Shchors)*, a village commune *(Ivan)*—in which the members share community values. The forces of change threatening such values may derive from any number of sociopolitical realms, including sexual relations *(Love's Berry)*, international politics *(Diplomatic Pouch, Aerograd)*, industrial relations *(Earth, Ivan)*, and even science *(Michurin)*. The test for the characters is to adapt their values to new conditions in such a way as to accommodate change without doing extreme violence to their traditions. In a larger sense, Dovzhenko used such social microcosms to explore how the Soviet Union might preserve its cultural heritage while fundamentally altering social and economic relations, how it might find a measure of continuity in the midst of its revolutionary upheaval.

A historical reading of the films promises at least to qualify the emphasis placed on the lyricism of Dovzhenko's films and to add an appreciation of their topicality. There is much, however, that this study does not presume to achieve. The individual explications of the films deal largely with narrative, drawing as they do from methods of narrative analysis borrowed from literary study. They offer no systematic discussion of Dovzhenko's cinematic style. A reader will derive little sense of how these films "look" from this study; neither Dovzhenko's stylistic contribution to Soviet cinema nor the evolution of his cinematic techniques are at issue here. Nor do I deal with Dovzhenko's four documentaries, two of which are not available for study and two of which were made in World War II under military commission and for which Dovzhenko merely edited footage shot by others. I do not take up Dovzhenko's several scripts and unfinished projects, some of which were produced after his death by his wife and long-time assistant director Julia Solntseva, although I do not doubt that they manifest concerns similar to those of his finished features. And I do not analyze any of his nonfilm creative efforts; I am personally somewhat in awe of this versatile figure, who made important contributions to Soviet painting, drawing, theater, prose fiction, poetry, and rhetoric, but I am content for now to hope that some more ambitious scholar will someday do justice to Dovzhenko's many creative achievements in a full biography. The effort to situate Dovzhenko's films historically seems task enough for the moment. And perhaps the problems encountered in that effort will testify, in some way at least, to the subtlety of Dovzhenko's work.

II

The Formative Years

IN A FAMOUS PASSAGE from his autobiography, Dovzhenko describes his decision to abandon an art career for the cinema. "In June 1926 I sat up all night in my studio, assessed my thirty-two unsuccessful years of life, and in the morning I picked up my cane and suitcase, leaving behind my canvasses and painting supplies, and departed, never to return. I went to Odessa to get a job in the film studio as a director."[1] This description suggests that, in making the move to cinema, Dovzhenko broke with all past ties, and that his work in cinema would represent a completely new beginning, distinct from his first "thirty-two unsuccessful years."

On the contrary, far from marking a clean break with the past, his entry into cinema represented the culmination of a search for a significant role to play in the emerging Soviet system, and a review of his background will help us understand the nature of that role. By the time he became a filmmaker, he had already lived more than half of his eventual sixty-two years, had labored in the fields as a peasant, had worked as a teacher, had pursued an interest in art, had fought for the Soviet revolution, and had formed many of the convictions that would shape his films. Born of conservative peasant stock, he came to maturity during the upheavals of revolution, and the dual foci of his film work, tradition and change, would owe much to his complex historical situation, a situation that had been largely determined by the time he had experienced that sleepless night in 1926.

If Dovzhenko's films are not to be explained as the projections of an isolated imagination, neither should they be represented as perfect reflections of contemporary society. They are highly mediated representations of reality, as indeed are all artistic texts, according to Macherey and Eagleton. Two mediations between text and context given special emphasis by Macherey and Eagleton are the particular historical situation of the author—his or her background and position in society—and the mode of artistic production in which the author works.[2] In Dovzhenko's case we can trace the influence of his class origins, his education, his political commitment, and his associations within Ukrainian artistic circles to define the former mediation and characterize the Soviet film industry he entered and worked in, including the industry's organization and the government policies affecting its operation, to define the latter.

Tension between tradition and modernity, so important to Dovzhenko's work, was felt by other important Ukrainian cultural figures as they sought to preserve a distinct cultural identity while accepting the social changes effected by the new regime in Moscow. For Dovzhenko and many of his Ukrainian contemporaries, the problem became tied up with conflicting loyalties between national origin and submission to a government centered in Moscow and controlled by Great Russians, loyalties that predated the revolution and grew out of the Ukraine's neocolonial status. On the one hand, unity with Russia under the old Russian empire provided the Ukraine with security from various aggressive enemies and a sense of belonging to a cross-cultural holy tradition under the aegis of the Orthodox church. On the other hand, Ukrainians had to guard their cultural identity, laboring, for example, to preserve a distinct language and literature in the face of tsarist policies of "Russification" of the Ukraine. Frequently that impulse for cultural preservation gave rise to determined efforts to win full political independence—the most spectacular of which proved to be the Ukrainian independence movement which followed the Bolshevik revolution.[3]

A similar dichotomy appears in much of the Ukrainian artistic activity of the late nineteenth and early twentieth centuries. Numerous writers, for example, struggled with the question of whether to project a distinctly national flavor in their work by taking subjects from Ukrainian folklore and history, or whether to look to the Russian masters such as Pushkin for inspiration. The two poles were represented in literature by the two most important writers to emerge from the nineteenth-century Ukraine, Nikolai Gogol and Taras Shevchenko: Gogol, despite celebrated exceptions such as *Taras Bulba*, would reject a distinctly Ukrainian flavor in his work, move to St. Petersburg, and write about Nevsky Prospect; by contrast, Shevchenko would flirt with Russian sources and then return to native ground to become the most celebrated proponent of a Ukrainian peasant heritage.[4]

Ukrainian artistic leaders faced similar dilemmas after the revolution, although the Russian influence was now represented by the Moscow-based Bolshevik party and its policies. The particular nature of Dovzhenko's background defined the problem even more sharply in his case. If his class origins left him with a respect for Ukrainian peasant tradition and lore, his eventual commitment to political activity during the revolution compelled him to advocate the Soviet policies of modernization which originated in Moscow.[5]

He was born in 1894 in the Chernigov region of northeast Ukraine into a peasant family which lived at a subsistence level, their estate covering only about nineteen acres of the rather arid farmland along the Desna River. Conditions proved sufficiently harsh that of the fourteen children born to Alexander Dovzhenko's mother, most died in infancy, and only two, Alexander and a sister, survived to lead full adult lives. Like many peasant families of the tsarist period, the Dovzhenko family found its lot harder at the turn of the century than in the years just after the 1861 emancipation of the serfs; an increased peasant population consumed relatively scarce tillable land, and conservative agricultural methods—the rejection of such techniques as deep plowing, full fertilization, and crop rotation already practiced in Western Europe—kept harvests down. Such problems were aggravated by social stratification, as wealthy, industrious kulaks bought up land to establish large estates and gain disproportionate economic power. In the process, the kulaks won the undying enmity of peasants from lower strata, including the Dovzhenko household.[6]

The Dovzhenko clan was no strong yeoman farm family. They knew hardship in the present and held no expectation of economic advancement in the future: the bond that sustained them was a link to the past. Four generations lived in the same hut, and the past survived in a set of oral legends of Cossack exploits passed between generations. The overall social organization of the peasant household bred conservatism; in such extended families children were cared for, not by parents, who had to work in the fields, but by grandparents, so that the most rigid, conservative minds shaped the most flexible young imaginations.[7] In the Dovzhenko household young Alexander's first mentor was his great-grandfather, who entertained the boy with Cossack legends and lyrical tales "about the Desna, the grass, and the mysterious lakes." Clinging to the past also represented the family's way of dealing with the hardships of the present. Although the Dovzhenko family would have been listed in the economic stratum of "middle peasants," owners of small estates, they lived with the pejorative label "muzhik." More than an economic designation, the muzhik status represented something of a social stigma, identifying one with lethargy and ignorance. The response of the Dovzhenkos was to claim a proud ancestry, including descent from Don Cossacks. "Muzhiks you could call us," Alexander Dovzhenko remembered his father complaining. "Yes, just muzhiks, that's all. Once they say we were Cossacks, but now that's the only name left."[8]

The danger for such members of the peasant class was to succumb to the muzhik mentality, an aimless existence and passive acceptance of hardship and injustice. One form of escape in the tsarist system—an option not open to all peasants, by any means—was through education. A set of fortuitous circumstances, including the recent expansion of the empire's provincial school system and financial sacrifice on the part of the Dovzhenko family, permitted Alexander to become the first member of his household to receive a full education. He attended elementary and secondary school in his village and eventually entered the regional teachers' institute to study for a possible career in education. Although an undistinguished student, he graduated in 1914 and began teaching school in a village in central Ukraine. With little opportunity to specialize afforded by such village schools, Dovzhenko taught physics, natural sciences, geography, history, and gymnastics, an experience that doubtless broadened his hitherto limited intellectual horizons. It was here as well that he developed his initial interest in art, sketching landscapes and caricatures in his spare time and harboring ambitions to leave teaching in order to study painting.[9]

Excused from military service during World War I for medical reasons, he moved to Kiev in 1917 in the hope of entering a major university, but inferior examination scores relegated him to the lesser academic setting of the city's Commercial Institute in economics, a field in which he took no particular interest. Indifferent as his classroom training may have been at the institute, his experiences there proved formative in an important respect, for he became caught up in the events of the 1917 revolution and drawn into political activism. The period in Kiev represented this rather provincial peasant's first significant exposure to metropolitan culture, and significantly, he found himself in the city that was the center of Ukrainian political life at the moment of that nation's greatest political upheaval, as the Ukraine entered a three-year civil war that would be characterized by factionalism and shifting loyalties. As various armies moved through Kiev, capturing and losing control of the city in response to the tides of war, civilians found themselves changing sides simply to survive, and protean political movements formed, dissolved, and reorganized, reflecting the latest fortunes of one or another military organization.

Dovzhenko was pulled into political activism by the forces around him, forces of almost bewildering complexity. It is necessary to summarize these chaotic events, not only to establish the reasons for Dovzhenko's eventual commitment to the Soviet revolution, but also to understand the many historical incidents to which he would refer time and again in his films.[10]

Much of the Ukrainian leadership welcomed the fall of Tsar Nicholas, believing that the February revolution would lead to the establishment of an autonomous Ukraine. As soon as the Provisional Government assumed authority from the tsar, a group of leading Ukrainian radicals and progressives met to establish the Central Rada, the Ukrainian equivalent of the Russian Supreme Soviet and the new ruling body for the Ukraine. Rada officials hoped that the Provisional Government in far-off Petrograd would recognize the autonomy of the Rada and grant Ukrainian independence, but the Provisionals failed to act.

Matters became more complicated after the October revolution and the Bolshevik seizure of power. Ambiguity and at times duplicity marked the Bolshevik policy toward independence for the various nationalities of the old empire. The Bolsheviks were faced with the embarrassment of having denounced tsarist imperialism while at the same time hoping to preserve much of the empire intact after 1917. Marx had not prepared the Bolsheviks for the fact that nationalist aspirations would become entangled in a proletarian revolution, having assumed that revolution would originate in Western Europe, where nationalist sentiment would be replaced by international proletarianism. Marx failed to anticipate the true nature of revolutionary sentiment in those Slavic countries which had been subjected to foreign rule and where national independence rather than the dictatorship of the proletariat would represent the driving revolutionary ideal. One theory advanced to overcome this problem was brought to Lenin's attention by the Austrian Social Democrats, who advocated that the international proletarian revolution grant cultural autonomy to various peoples—respecting separate languages, literatures, religions, and the like—without permitting a political division into small national units. The Bolsheviks considered this position prior to 1917 and then rejected it. Despite Lenin's personal conviction that nationalism had no place in proletarian revolution, he opted for a policy of complete political and cultural independence for the nationalities for pragmatic reasons: he had to satisfy members of his own party who were from the minority states of the tsarist empire and who sought absolute self-determination. He authorized an attack on the Austrian position of cultural autonomy and proclaimed that complete self-determination represented the only acceptable course. But despite this public stance, he had no intention of letting the empire he had inherited dissolve completely, and he issued a caveat that it was not the entire population of a nation that had the right to decide on self-determination but only the proletariat. He did not feel compelled to honor what he called "bourgeois-inspired" separatist movements. This proved to be a handy provision; since Lenin professed to believe that the proletariat was innately inclined toward internationalism, he could then dismiss any national independence movement as bourgeois. He had, through a cunning maneuver, erased both cultural autonomy and genuine self-determination, a move that would have important repercussions for the Ukraine.[11]

The Ukrainian Rada had at first been sympathetic to the Bolshevik takeover, hoping to hold Lenin to his stated position on self-determination, but by the beginning of 1918, Rada leaders realized that Lenin would not recognize the Ukraine as an independent state. In January 1918, Lenin's commissar of nationalities, one Joseph Stalin, declared that the Soviet government would support the efforts of the toiling masses to resist bourgeois separatist movements. Translated, this meant that the Red Army was on its way to the Ukraine. The Bolsheviks proved prepared to pay a military price to retain control of the Ukraine, with its important agricultural and mining resources and its Black Sea coast. Clashes between Ukrainian and Red Army troops led to the Rada's formal declaration of independence on 22 January 1918. In the meantime, pro-Bolshevik Ukrainians in Kiev rebelled against the Rada and seized Kiev's fortresslike "Arsenal" munitions plant, initiating bitter street fighting between Bolshevik sympathizers and Rada troops. By February, Red Army troops from the north had captured Kiev and put the Rada on the defensive.

The military setback forced the Rada into a desperate course, as it joined forces with German troops on the eastern front of the continuing World War. The Germans not only repelled the Red Army advance; they overthrew the Rada, established a puppet government under the reactionary Ukrainian Paul Skoropadsky, and began expropriating Ukrainian grain harvests. With the end of the World War and the withdrawal of German troops from the Ukraine, the Rada managed to depose Skoropadsky and his right-wing regime; and Simon Petliura, military commander of the Rada, assumed effective control of the government and promptly renewed the conflict with the Bolsheviks. This clerk-turned-soldier proved a tenacious opponent of Moscow and a champion of Ukrainian separatism. But while Petliura fought Red Army troops to the north, his situation was complicated by the presence of foreign troops to the west and south. The Poles, traditional enemies of the Ukraine, invaded from the west as a part of a general offensive, while French forces landed on the Black Sea coast during the Allied intervention of 1919. Petliura, faced with the prospect of fighting a two-front war against both Bolsheviks and Poles, appealed to the Allies for aid, assuming that the French would offer military support. After much indecision, the French decided not to intervene, but their continued presence in the Ukraine merely compromised Petliura in the eyes of many Ukrainians who opposed his efforts at collaboration with foreign invaders. By April 1919 the Allies had finally withdrawn from the Ukraine, and the Bolsheviks had recaptured Kiev and other key locations. For the rest of 1919 and 1920 Petliura fought a retreating campaign until he was finally forced into exile, and by the end of 1920 the Bolsheviks had consolidated authority throughout the Ukraine.

Dovzhenko came to political maturity in this period of near anarchy. In such a kaleidoscopic political setting, Dovzhenko, like countless other Ukrainians, flirted with different nationalist and socialist factions, but as the civil war ran its course, he moved steadily to the left, eventually making a full commitment to Bolshevism and to political unity with Russia. His initial instincts, he admitted in his autobiography, were nationalistic. He first learned of the tsar's abdication during the February revolution while he was still teaching in the provinces, and he welcomed the news as an opportunity for Ukrainian independence. His eventual move to Kiev brought him into direct contact with the civil war's various competing factions and drew him into the struggle. Dovzhenko's reaction to the Skoropadsky regime—which professed to represent Ukrainian nationalism but only made a mockery of the ideal by collaborating with the German invaders—was to commit to political activity. In 1919 while still at Kiev's Commercial Institute, Dovzhenko organized an anti-Skoropadsky rally and a march to the official residence, a demonstration that ended tragically when Skoropadsky's guards fired on the group, killing twenty students. The experience pushed Dovzhenko to greater militancy. There is evidence he may have fought briefly with the Rada, apparently as part of the Rada's anti-Skoropadsky offensive of 1918. When the Rada eventually became tarnished by foreign alliances and anti-Semitism—including tolerance of several pogroms—many leftist Ukrainians were driven into the arms of the Bolsheviks, and Dovzhenko joined them, enlisting in one of several Ukrainian regiments of the Red Army. He fought in the civil war in 1919 and 1920, serving under Red Army hero Nikolai Shchors, whom Dovzhenko would eventually honor in his 1939 film.

Dovzhenko established his first official political affiliation in 1920 by joining the Borotbist party, an organization of Ukrainian leftists. When the Borotbists merged with the pro-Bolshevik Ukrainian Communist party to consolidate power, Dovzhenko joined that expanded organization and committed himself to support of political union with Russia under the new Soviet system. During the course of the civil war he moved from tepid nationalism, to leftist militancy, and ultimately to full-scale Bolshevism, an evolution determined in large part by the force of events.

In reward for Red Army and party service, the party assigned Dovzhenko to administrative duties, and in 1920 he entered the diplomatic service through the Ukrainian Commissariat of Foreign Affairs. While marking time as a party functionary, he maintained the hope of continuing his study of painting and following through on his previous ambition of becoming a professional artist, and a fortuitous posting advanced his plans. Assigned to the Soviet consulate in Berlin in 1922, he managed to make contact with that city's vital artistic community, and he even acquired a small scholarship to study with Erik Heckel, one of the central figures of the Bruecke movement. During his brief posting in Berlin, Dovzhenko met the leftist cartoonists Heinrich Zille and Georg Grosz, and his exposure to their militant drawings persuaded Dovzhenko that his vocation of political activity and his avocation of art could prove mutually enriching.

The lesson served him well when he returned to the Ukraine in 1923. Released from government service and removed from party affiliation, Dovzhenko struck out on the career he had long dreamed of by moving to Kharkov to begin work as a painter and cartoonist. That city was witnessing a flourish of activity in the arts and letters in the wake of the 1917 revolution. Dovzhenko found a home among the poets, playwrights, and journalists who flocked to Kharkov and established it as the intellectual capital of the Soviet Ukraine, and his Kharkov period proved to be seminal.

The art of Dovzhenko's contemporaries at Kharkov generally defined two strains: excitement over the possibilities of the new Soviet system and admiration for prerevolutionary Ukrainian art and literature.[12] Although the Kharkov writers were true Soviet revolutionaries, many of whom had fought with the Red Army in the civil war, they nevertheless considered their literary roots to be firmly in their national literature, and they expressed this conviction in their regard for Shevchenko, the nineteenth-century poet and national hero who wrote only in Ukrainian to protest Russification and who regularly took sources from Ukrainian folklore. One Kharkov literary group, for example, chose to illustrate its dual loyalty to Ukrainian nationalism and Soviet-style socialism by holding semiannual general meetings on two dates invested with symbolic weight—the anniversaries of Shevchenko's birth and of the October revolution.

In the early 1920s the Kharkovites enjoyed a brief interval of artistic freedom, and new literary and political journals began appearing almost daily. The initial creative activity in Kharkov centered on two literary organizations, Pluh (The Plow) and Hart (Tempering). Pluh was established in 1922 and consisted largely of peasant-born writers, while Hart was founded the following year and represented the urban working class. Soon the two bodies found themselves competing for favor with members of the ruling Communist party, and rather than continue as rivals they merged in 1925 to form the Ukraine's most important literary organization, VAPLITE (Free Academy of Proletarian Literature). The group included among its members several of the Soviet Ukraine's leading writers, including symbolist poet Paul Tychina and short-story writer Nikolai Khvylovy.

The initial freedom which encouraged this literary renaissance began to disappear in the middle and late 1920s. The beginning of the end was marked by a series of polemical tracts authored by Khvylovy which advocated the end of any Ukrainian dependence on Russian culture and proposed a Ukrainian literary movement that drew exclusively from native sources or from European romanticism. To Bolshevik officials in Moscow—carrying the ideological baggage of Lenin's ambiguous policy on the nationalities and watchful as one of the architects of that policy, Stalin, built his power base as Lenin's successor—Khvylovy's polemics smacked of a call for cultural autonomy, a position which, as we have seen, the Bolsheviks had already denounced. Through 1927 and 1928, Stalin and various party officials answering to Moscow responded to Khvylovy's challenge by systematically undermining the institutions which promoted Ukrainian cultural autonomy. The party orchestrated the demise of VAPLITE and condemned the work of the Kharkov writers as intolerable nationalism. Ukrainian Communist party officials who defended VAPLITE found themselves ousted from power, and the party sponsored a rival literary organization. The crackdown culminated in a campaign of public ridicule directed at Khvylovy which succeeded in removing him from public favor and eventually led to his suicide. Similar manifestations of cultural autonomy were suppressed as the Ukrainian literary renaissance of the 1920s fell victim to the early phases of Stalinist cultural oppression.

Dovzhenko's three-year association with the Kharkovites (1923-1926) coincided with their period of greatest freedom and creativity. Although in later years Stalinist officials and critics would point to Dovzhenko's Kharkov associations when attempting to discredit his films for excessive nationalism, Dovzhenko left Karkov just before the 1927 crackdown and escaped, for the time being, the effects of the anti-VAPLITE campaign. If anything, the Kharkov years proved to be among the most personally rewarding of Dovzhenko's life. He joined Hart shortly after arriving in Kharkov, finding considerable intellectual communion among the group's peasants-turned-writers. He stayed on to become one of the founding members of VAPLITE. While practicing painting in his spare time, he earned his living as a political cartoonist for the newspaper *Visti* (News), the Ukrainian equivalent of *Izvestia*. He regularly worked in the newspaper's editorial office and took his subjects from the stream of telegrams and news bulletins which poured into the paper's headquarters. This experience finally provided him the opportunity to place his talents as an artist in the service of the Soviet system. He put his skillful pen and brush to work on contemporary subjects gleaned from the daily news. He aimed satire at numerous designated enemies of the Soviet regime: Petliura and the Poles, old civil war foes, became the targets of his cartoons, as did foreign statesmen and capitalists hostile to the Soviet system, and he directed ridicule at the domestic practices and institutions he found pernicious, such as the church.[13]

The principal legacy of Dovzhenko's experience as a cartoonist was a heightened consciousness of the possibilities of topical art as he took subjects from current affairs. This peasant from the Desna Valley, who had imbibed age-old legend, had only slowly and with great difficulty acquired political awareness. If his initial artistic source was a peasant heritage locked in the past, the exigencies of cartoon satire required him to immerse himself in modern political affairs. His cartoon work was rife with references to contemporary political figures and topical issues, and such specific references would continue in his films, where they would occasionally commingle with antiquated sources culled from peasant legend. (figs. 1 and 2)

A second legacy of the Karkov years was Dovzhenko's commitment to the position that the Soviet Union could tolerate vestiges of the past in its revolutionary policies. His Kharkov associates held the conviction that received national values could coexist with loyalty to the Soviet revolution. This was the credo of the Kharkov literati, and Dovzhenko would retain that VAPLITE doctrine long after the original organization had succumbed to the forces of cultural oppression.

Dovzhenko's original interest in cinema developed in Kharkov as a result of the encouragement of VAPLITE associates, some of whom had worked in the Ukrainian film industry. Conversations with fellow VAPLITE artists about the possible social utility of cinema began to make him aware that cinema was an art possessed of special power to reach and persuade the masses. He eventually reached the conviction that drawing and painting were becoming obsolete, that they were no longer able to influence popular opinion.

Dovzhenko's sleepless night in 1926 and the resulting move to the Odessa studio represented not an isolated whim but the logical culmination of his previous experience. He had escaped the provincialism of peasant life through education, retaining nevertheless a profound respect for his own peasant heritage. Then by entering the fray of the revolution, he formed a commitment to a socialist future for the Ukraine. His dual commitment was complicated by traditional Ukrainian ambivalence over links with Moscow and by the ambiguous official policy toward cultural autonomy for the Soviet national republics that derived from Lenin's early maneuvers. Finally, the doctrine of the Kharkov literary movement helped Dovzhenko define his dual social identity as nostalgic peasant and modern political partisan, as upholder of tradition and celebrant of revolutionary change. His cinematic project would be to propose that the Soviet system could profit from both impulses.

Dovzhenko entered the cinema at a propitious moment. Thanks to innovative government guidance, the previously moribund Soviet film industry was evolving into a major force, and the Ukrainian studio Dovzhenko entered was in the midst of rapid, major expansion.

Lenin's oft-quoted dictum that the cinema represented the most important of the Soviet arts derived from his conviction that the cinema held the greatest potential for mass persuasion and could serve as an ideological tool in the USSR's formidable modernization agenda.[14] Lenin set only general ideological guidelines for film, leaving the day-to-day administration of the film industry to the Commissariat of Education and to its capable chief, Anatoli Lunacharsky. One mandate did come from Lenin, however, and was defined by the Russian word *partiinost'*. Roughly translated as "party loyalty" or "party spirit," the term derived from Lenin's prerevolutionary writings and remained a fundamental ideological tenet in the Soviet system of one-party government, a system in which a party elite supplanted a dominant class as the source of social ideology. It expressed Lenin's conviction that the masses—often the victims of ignorance, illiteracy, and the deceptions of capitalist ideology—could not be trusted to recognize their own best

Figure 1. In a 1925 cartoon on Germany, Dovzhenko seizes on the inequities of the Weimar Republic. The influences of Georg Grosz and Heinrich Zille are evident in the drawing.

Figure 2. Dovzhenko satirizes the hypocrisy of capitalist diplomacy by linking the arms merchants with the statesmen. The original caption for this 1924 cartoon read: "Thus the bourgeoisie attempts to make total peace in one stroke."

interests; only a politically sophisticated elite group, a ruling party, could see through ephemeral conditions to recognize larger historical trends and make policy decisions that would move the conservative, disorganized masses in the correct direction. Lenin went on to advocate that writers and artists preach *partiinost'*—faith in the wisdom of the ruling party—in their work, thereby avoiding "bourgeois-anarchist individualism" in art.[15] A mass art like cinema seemed an especially appropriate vehicle for *partiinost'*.

Within the confines of these general admonitions, Lenin tolerated considerable creative freedom for the arts, a tolerance sustained briefly by Lunacharsky and others in the Communist party after Lenin's death. In June 1925 the party approved a resolution on literature permitting, within prescribed boundaries, a large measure of creative liberty. This liberal policy carried over into the other arts, assuring that the brilliant experiments in early Soviet theater, painting, and sculpture would continue for the time being at least, and the measure augured well for the still-young Soviet cinema.[16]

Such relative tolerance complemented Lunacharsky's pragmatic management of the film industry through the early and middle 1920s.[17] If the Soviet cinema was to measure up to Lenin's initial assessment, Lunacharsky recognized that it would have to be organized into an efficient, manageable industry. In the wake of the civil war, the Russian film industry, like numerous other segments of the economy, had virtually ceased to exist. Loss of production equipment, destruction of theaters, and the flight of experienced personnel into exile nearly ground operations to a halt; only thirteen features were released between 1918 and 1921. Lunacharsky's effort to rehabilitate the industry began with the initiation of Lenin's general New Economic Policy (NEP). Begun in 1921 and lasting through the decade, NEP placed much of the Soviet economy under a semicapitalist system featuring a market economy with a measure of government oversight. Under this pragmatic general policy and through a series of daring entrepreneurial ventures, Lunacharsky and his colleagues led the industry through a period of sustained growth. To secure much-needed capital, for example, he arranged for the importation of hundreds of foreign films into the Soviet market. Revenues from the commercial exhibition of these imports were invested in facilities for new productions. Meanwhile Lunacharsky solicited foreign capital and helped arrange for Soviet government investments in the young industry. These and other measures resulted not only in a steady increase in productivity—from 13 features released in 1923 to a peak of 109 releases in 1928—but in a broadly based, competitive industry wherein several studios operated with at least some creative and administrative freedom.

This NEP expansion and tolerance of competition facilitated the development of several national cinema organizations in the USSR's constituent republics, a phenomenon reflecting the Soviet Union's cultural diversity. Georgia maintained an active studio in Tiflis, and Erevan contained an Armenian cinema company. These were followed in the middle twenties by several new national film organizations: Belgoskino appeared in Byelorussia, for example, and Uzbekgoskino commenced operations in Central Asia. These and other national cinemas enjoyed a rather ambiguous status. Established with government sanction to appeal to minority audiences, they concentrated on subjects taken from regional history and culture and were staffed by local administrators and artists. But Communist party officials in Moscow kept an eye on non-Russian studios. Authorities directed such studios to make films which were "nationalist in form but socialist in content"; that is, if the films borrowed from indigenous sources, they were still expected to answer to Moscow for their ideology. Filmmakers from the minority republics were admonished not to step over the boundary into the murky region known in official circles as "nationalist deviation."

The All-Ukrainian Photo-Cinema Administration (Vseukrainskoe foto-kinoupravlenie), popularly known by its acronym VUFKU, served the Ukrainian movie market and welcomed Alexander Dovzhenko into its production headquarters in Odessa in the summer of 1926.[18] VUFKU had once held a reputation as an institution of modest achievements and conservative impulses, concentrating on adaptations of literary works and other tried sources. But by the time of Dovzhenko's arrival the studio had begun a bold course of reorganization, expansion, and experimentation. Benefitting from Lunacharsky's efforts to expand film production in general and regional production in particular, VUFKU emerged as the most powerful and innovative of the national studios.

VUFKU's growth proceeded at the direction of its energetic new chief administrator, a Ukrainian named Paul Neches, who proved determined to establish a distinctly Ukrainian film tradition by finding and exploiting native talent. A novice to cinema himself, Neches welcomed new faces into the organization, among them Alexander Dovzhenko. The ex-cartoonist and VAPLITE refugee moved to Odessa inspired only by a vague notion that film seemed the art with greatest social potential. He had nothing else to speak of in the way of film credentials; nor was he even much of a film enthusiast, rarely attending movies in his spare time. His only previous association with the studio stemmed from the fact that he had drawn film posters for VUFKU and designed the studio's logo. Nevertheless, he wandered into Odessa determined not only to work in the movies but to become a director, and he appeared at the studio facility each morning to watch productions in progress and to learn by observation.

Dovzhenko profited from Neches's open-door policy. The studio head knew Dovzhenko's reputation as an artist and willingly took him into the organization, soon promoting him to film director. Neches then generously supported Dovzhenko's work. Within a year of Dovzhenko's arrival, Neches permitted the neophyte director to organize a permanent production unit and cast, a close-knit group whose members respected and worked comfortably with Dovzhenko. Central to the group was Dovzhenko's new bride, Julia Solntseva, a Russian actress who had achieved a significant reputation in films, appearing in the title role in *Aelita* (1924), and who served as Dovzhenko's assistant director on project after project. Dovzhenko also won the services of VUFKU's chief cinematographer, the skillful Daniel Demutsky. At Dovzhenko's urging, VUFKU hired from an itinerant theater company the young actor Simon Svashenko, who would play central roles in *Zvenigora*, *Arsenal*, and *Earth*. And while working on *Zvenigora*, Dovzhenko discovered a modest country stovemaker and amateur actor named Stepan Shkurat who would eventually star in *Earth*, *Ivan*, and *Aerograd*.

Besides the recruitment of this repertory company, Dovzhenko benefitted from other aspects of Neches's expansion policies. VUFKU dramatically increased its physical plant in 1926 and 1927, expanding its production facilities in Yalta and Odessa and creating a new studio complex in Kiev. Dovzhenko would make use of these new resources at various times during the production of his early films, and Neches would back the new director's ambitions with ample funding.

The size and relative autonomy of VUFKU would serve Dovzhenko well. But he also would discover drawbacks. The very fact that Neches succeeded in making VUFKU a powerful enterprise meant that the Kremlin would keep close watch on this largest of national film organizations. Since VUFKU films found their widest exhibition in the Ukraine, Moscow party officials seemed especially concerned lest overly "nationalistic" VUFKU productions find too much favor with Ukrainian audiences. One of the first hints of problems to come, and an apparent retreat from the 1925 Communist party resolution endorsing creative freedom, emerged from a government review of the film industry in 1927 and 1928. Condemnation of an alleged lack of ideological rigor in Soviet films followed, and the Communist party called for greater control over the national studios to forestall those organizations' presumed tendency toward "nationalist deviation." Henceforth VUFKU would receive special attention.[19]

Thus, Dovzhenko's association with VUFKU constituted a mixed blessing. He could work in the security of a large, strong organization among trusted associates. But, as we shall see, the specter of the anti-VAPLITE campaign, which Dovzhenko narrowly escaped in 1926, seemed to reappear in later party criticisms of VUFKU in general and of Dovzhenko in particular. His goal was to emerge as a major Soviet, not merely Ukrainian, filmmaker, but he would not attempt this at the expense of the Ukrainian heritage he valued. Moscow's ambiguous policies on nationalism and the shape of the film industry under NEP composed the setting in which Dovzhenko worked through the 1920s. It remained for Dovzhenko to carve out his own place within that setting, and this he did through the sustained excellence of his early films.

III

Early Efforts

DOVZHENKO TENDED in later years to dismiss the films he made before *Zvenigora* as juvenile efforts unworthy of serious consideration. Those few historians who have assigned them any consideration, serious or otherwise, have tended to wonder about the absence of the themes of peasant culture commonly identified with Dovzhenko's later work and to remark on the early films' curious resemblance to American and West European movies.[1] Indeed, in their genre formulas, Dovzhenko's early productions seem most indebted to non-Soviet sources: *Love's Berry* is a slapstick comedy which betrays a debt to the likes of Harold Lloyd, and *Diplomatic Pouch* features a narrative of international intrigue somewhat in the manner of detective and espionage thrillers coming out of America and Western Europe. In light of these observations, what claims can we make about the relationship of such work to contemporary Soviet culture?

A close look at the films reveals a telling phenomenon: While Dovzhenko may borrow from abroad, he adapts the material to problems of immediate concern to the USSR. *Love's Berry*, for all its resemblance to American slapstick comedy, directs its humor at Soviet social values of the 1920s, and *Diplomatic Pouch* applies formulas of foreign thrillers to the politically charged issue of the USSR's uneasy status as the single socialist state in a capitalist world. Not quite the anomalies they appear at first sight, both films specifically invoke topical issues, and both involve a variant of the encounter with the new and novel that I have posited as the central concern of Dovzhenko's work. In these films, that encounter takes place in the form of the modern standards of behavior confronted by the courting couple in *Love's Berry* and the new burdens of political responsibility assumed by the characters in *Diplomatic Pouch*.

The "foreign look" of the early works would seem to owe much to the circumstances and period in which they were produced. When

Dovzhenko joined the film industry in 1926, he entered a market dominated by American and West European movies. Lunacharsky's policy of
importing films to raise revenues for the fledgling Soviet industry was in
full swing in the middle 1920s, when more than three-quarters of the
films playing on Soviet screens came from abroad.[2] Despite the tough
competition for audience favor represented by the imports, many young
Soviet directors professed to admire and learn from them. Reacting
against the stale drawing-room dramas and literary adaptations of the
old tsarist cinema, Kuleshov, for example, praised American cinema for
"an intensity in the development of action" and for a demonstrated ability to excite audiences, and he proposed wedding American narrative
conventions to Soviet ideology in future productions, a tactic that several
directors, including Dovzhenko, seem to have followed.[3]

No particular cinephile, Dovzhenko came to VUFKU without benefit
of formal training in cinema or extensive knowledge of film's traditions.
He had, however, been exposed to some American movie comedies in
Kharkov, where he took particular interest in Keaton. He saw some af-
finity between such comedy and his own cartoon work, including the use
of broad caricature and ridicule directed at hypocrisy and pomposity. He
moved to Odessa assuming he would make his career as a writer and director of comedies.[4]

His very earliest projects, at least, seemed to bear this out. Hired initially by Neches as a writer, his first creative effort was a brief and hastily
written scenario for a comedy titled *Vasia the Reformer*. Assigned to a veteran VUFKU director named Faust Lopatinsky, the production served
as Dovzhenko's apprenticeship, and he received co-director credit on the
low-budget two-reeler, which was shot and edited over a period of a few
days.[5]

The film itself is lost, but surviving accounts suggest that *Vasia* was a
satire directed at certain forms of greed and chicanery which surfaced
during NEP.[6] Its episodic narrative concerns the series of adventures experienced by the title character as he attempts to correct other people's
shortcomings. He rescues a drunken man from drowning, for example,
only to have the drunk turn on him and attempt to beat him up. He escapes this onslaught by jumping into a passing car but discovers that it is
a government vehicle used illegally by a local bureaucrat for afternoon
pleasure trips. Vasia eventually finds himself in a church operated by a
charlatan priest; he exposes the fraud, and the congregation converts the
church into a movie theater, with the former priest serving as a projec-
tionist. Finally, Vasia discovers a burglar in his own house and turns him
in to the police.

From this synopsis we can derive at least a sense of the film's satire.

Like Dovzhenko's cartoons for *Visti*, which often concerned domestic social problems, this production seems to have been a series of set pieces, each harking up a particular form of social misconduct which troubled the Soviet Union—drunkenness, private exploitation of public resources, the continuing power of the church, and, of course, greed. The film can be classified as part of a popular Soviet film genre of the 1920s that we might call, for want of a standard genre label, the satire of "nepism." This genre derived from the curious status of NEP as a transitional period between capitalism and state socialism. With NEP's mixed system came the recognition that the vestiges of self-aggrandizement which the Soviets had long associated with capitalism would remain in the culture and that individuals would practice profiteering and exploitation under the system's market economy. "Nepism" came to refer to the various forms of social irresponsibility expected but only begrudgingly tolerated under NEP. The "nepman" became the stock character of works which satirized NEP exploitation.

Initially applied to greedy entrepreneurs, the term *nepman* eventually encompassed a variety of philistines, opportunists, and shirkers more concerned with their immediate well-being than with overriding national concerns. Ultimately the genre bespoke the basic contradictions of NEP: that the Soviet Union had reverted to a largely capitalist system as a means of achieving socialism, that the government had to encourage private entrepreneurship as a way of reaching state control of the means of production, and that a competitive, private economy would serve the collective ideal. The government could not easily resolve such paradoxes in its political economy, but it could encourage ideological formations which criticized NEP's parasites; thus, the satire of nepism flourished in several media, including cartoons, posters, fiction, and, of course, film. The period saw several popular movies by such figures as Boris Barnet and Iakov Protazanov which featured characters exploiting the relative government leniency under NEP in get-rich-quick schemes. In such comedies, the self-centered bureaucrat, the duplicitous priest, the worker more interested in a drink and a good time than in his production quota, and the conniving trader and profiteer became familiar types to audiences of the 1920s.[7] The characters were to be found in Dovzhenko's cartoon work, and they populate the dramatis personae of *Vasia the Reformer*.

The film's narrative contains at least one pointed reference of specific interest. When the church is converted into a movie theater in the film, Dovzhenko acknowledges a plan promoted by the highest government officials to alter certain social habits which survived under NEP. Soviet rulers hoped that movie going would serve particular social, not merely ideological, functions by advocating that the movie theater supplant two institutions which Soviet officials decried: the church and the tavern.[8] In one of his Kharkov cartoons, Dovzhenko equates alcohol and religion as related narcotic forms, one physical and the other spiritual; and it is worth noting that in his first film project, he proposes cinema as the healthy alternative. Nothing much more specific can or need be said about this minor production, of which no prints and few references survive, except that it seems to represent the film equivalent of the kind of caricatures Dovzhenko practiced as a cartoonist, its episodic narrative like a series of discrete panels rather than a logical chain of events, with each panel containing a caricature of a recognizable bogeyman of NEP.

Dovzhenko took up NEP-related matters again in *Love's Berry*, the first film he wrote and directed alone. This modest, two-reel comedy, produced in just eleven days, treats sexual mores and notions of family responsibility, matters which were undergoing change in the Soviet Union in the 1920s. The film's narrative involves the repercussions of the love affair between the young man Zhan Kolbasiuk and his girl friend Lisa, centering on Lisa's schemes to make Zhan marry her. The film opens with Lisa and Zhan together on a park bench where Lisa holds a baby and behaves in such a way as to persuade Zhan that it is their illegitimate offspring, the "little berry of love" so sweetly euphemized in the film's title. When she leaves Zhan alone with the child and his own conscience, Zhan settles on a course of action—not to marry, but to rid himself of the troublesome infant. He sets out on a series of adventures trying to dispose of the baby, only to have it reappear under ever more embarrassing circumstances. He finally forces it on someone else. But his strategy backfires when Lisa pleads a phony case of child abandonment at a people's court, and Zhan is summoned before the judge and ordered to bring the baby along. Zhan then has to race around the city to recover the now-missing infant. He finally succeeds and honors the subpoena. After a stern lecture on parental responsibility from the judge, Zhan is coerced to the Hall of Marriages and reconciled to parenthood. Only after Zhan and Lisa settle into a domestic routine does Lisa mention that the child is not theirs but her aunt's.

The irreverent views of sexual relations, courting rituals, and marriage manifested in *Love's Berry* owed much to the culture's first tendencies toward frank discussion of the sexual realm. The early twentieth century saw the initial concerted efforts of Russian writers and artists to address sexuality, a trend which came in reaction to the traditional moralism and asceticism of the culture. This novel candor about sex developed further in the revolutionary period and culminated in the 1920s, and it owed something to Bolshevik measures to liberalize sexual relations. Marriage and divorce became simple secular activities after the 1917 revolution, and abortions became widely available to women. These and other reforms of the new regime removed some of the legal complications long associated with sexual activity. Such libertarian reforms were not easily reconciled to the strict moral standards long impressed upon the society by the Orthodox church. And it was not long before the leading Bolsheviks themselves began to worry lest their reforms result in decadence and hedonism. Lenin professed to hold conventional moral standards and publicly denounced promiscuity, and officials in a 1925 Communist party commission for health advised young men and women that "if you want to solve the sexual problem, be a public worker and a Party member, not a stallion or a brood mare," as if sexual longings could be sublimated through political activity. On the other hand, the Bolshevik party boasted articulate advocates of free love, most notably Alexandra Kollontai, who called for a "free union of men and women who are lovers and comrades." The ambivalence of the Communist party on sexual matters indicates something of the problem it faced in trying to manage a social revolution along with a political one. The Bolsheviks' "revolution from above" would have to descend a very long way indeed to alter the conservative population's most intimate values, and the key revolutionaries were anything but unanimous on the question of whether they wanted it to descend that far.[9]

The comedy of *Love's Berry* exists at the site of ideological intersection between the desire for new sexual sophistication and the society's history of sexual repression. The film's protagonist seems to embody this conflict. Zhan is an affected dandy, wishing to impress the world with his sophistication, and at the same time a naif, forever at the mercy of his own inhibitions; he is capable of carrying on a sexual affair with Lisa yet quick to give in to the moralistic judgments of others. Even his name reflects the split: "Zhan" seems to be an effort to affect in Russian the French "Jean" and invokes the notorious Francophilia that afflicted "sophisticated" Russians; but Zhan's surname, "Kolbasiuk," derives from the Russian word for sausage, connoting something of his backwardness and gullibility.

In his attire and behavior, Zhan cultivates the image of a dandy. He is a barber by trade, a line of work which already associates him with a concern for personal appearance, and he remains obsessed with the impression he might be making on others. Always the natty dresser, he sports a dapper suit, a straw boater, and a flower in his lapel, and his agile handling of his ever-present cane adds a jaunty touch. He strives through dress and manner to project an elevated social status that his trade does not automatically confer on him. Somewhat in the tradition of Harold Lloyd, a figure quite popular with Soviet audiences, Zhan manifests a fastidiousness and tendency toward social climbing. Yet few heroes are slower studies than Kolbasiuk. When Lisa produces a baby *ex nihilo*, for example, it nevers occurs to Zhan to inquire about the circumstances of her pregnancy. The best he can do by way of a paternity examination is to test the offspring's features against his own. In a witty bit of screen business, he holds up a mirror and desperately tries to find any physical resemblance between himself and the baby, and he accepts the infant as his own despite the decidedly unscientific nature of the examination. Only after the wedding does he bother to ask whether the baby is male or female, and only then does he recognize the deception. Such behavior belies Zhan's cultivated image of sophistication and draws attention to his shallowness. His notion of parental responsibility extends only to finding more worthy caretakers for the child, and his only imaginative moments come when he hatches schemes to foist the child on someone else, as when he attempts to convince a policeman that he merely happened on an abandoned child or, more craftily, when he slips the infant in among rows of baby dolls in a toy shop.

Zhan's shallowness finds its complement in Lisa's cunning. She exploits those around her in a premeditated scheme that plays on their shortcomings. She seizes on Zhan's obtuseness when she passes off the baby as their offspring and on the judge's sanctimony when she presents herself to him as a woman seduced and abandoned. She plays her roles well and alters them to fit the occasion. Even her attire helps us mark her duplicity. In the film's opening scene she acts the role of the naive waif burdened with an illegitimate child; there she appears in a frilly white costume that evokes the image of the innocent. Later, when her elaborate machinations become evident to the audience, we find her in a smart 1920s "flapper" outfit, complete with the small round hat then so popular with fashionable European women.

The central characters are designed to embody familiar traits of nepism. Zhan and Lisa represent, not the mercenary nature of nepism, but its self-serving, socially aggressive manifestation. They betray no overriding sense of social responsibility but only a concern with personal gratification. Appropriately, the story is set in Yalta, the highly commercialized resort city. A far cry from the revolutionary energy one often sees in Soviet films of the period, having nothing to do with factories, production, and proletarian behavior, the Yalta of *Love's Berry* is a sunny, leisurely locale which seems to be composed entirely of public parks and gardens where passing figures amuse themselves in endless, rather aimless strolls in the sun. In the entire film we see only two figures engaged in work: a clerk in a toy shop and Zhan in his barbershop. Significantly, both are soft, white-collar jobs that point to the consumer-oriented nature of NEP. To a degree, the film reveals its status as an NEP document in its absences—in the exclusion of productive labors in favor of service trades, of revolutionary work in favor of leisure diversions. The film projects an image of society engaged in the pursuit of gratification, as if the consumer accommodations of NEP served the selfish ends of the likes of Zhan and Lisa.

And in the NEP phase of the Soviet economy, which emphasized consumer demand rather than long-term industrial development, it seems significant that even the baby becomes a piece of merchandise. The infant is never given a distinct identity. It is distinguished neither by name nor by gender, and to the other characters in the film, the infant is never more than an object. It can be exploited in Lisa's scheme, passed off as a doll, and even sold over the counter in a business transaction, but it cannot be loved by any of the characters: that would not serve their plans. In the opening scene, Zhan offers Lisa a bouquet of flowers. She declines the gift but chooses instead to present Zhan with her own package, the baby. The gesture, in effect, reduces the child to an item of exchange, a token, like flowers, exchanged in the casual courting rituals of men and women. But this token does not cement their love; rather, it makes apparent their mutual shortcomings: Zhan's obtuseness and Lisa's mendacity.

The baby's status as commodity becomes all the more apparent when Zhan disposes of it in the toy shop. The infant promptly becomes the equivalent of a doll, an object that can command a price in the NEP marketplace. Zhan slips the baby onto a shelf of dolls and makes his escape. When the store clerk discovers that the doll is alive, the revelation summons up no Gepetto-like affection. In an example of comic nepism, the clerk decides to dispose of the troublesome baby and to turn a profit in the process. When a customer enters the store and requests a "lifelike" doll, one that will even cry when squeezed, the clerk finds himself in a position to exceed the customer's expectations. The clerk wraps up and sells a "doll" that will do that and more. The transaction spoofs the modern craving for manufactured items which produce the illusion of life. Modern dolls can perform many wonders—they can laugh, cry, and squeak—but the one advantage they enjoy over the real thing is that one can control when and where such activities will take place. Real babies are far less predictable, and so it is with this baby, as it asserts itself by a most spontaneous act, urination. The infant, in effect, reminds others of its humanity by wetting in their presence or on them directly. It spoils Zhan's all-too-dapper attire in the opening scene, and later, when the customer leaves the toy shop with his "lifelike doll" and repairs to Zhan's barbershop for a shave, the baby urinates on the floor, thus alerting the customer to the deception and Zhan to his enduring misfortune vis-à-vis the baby. This act amounts to more than a scatological gag in a broad farce. Dovzhenko had previously depicted the act of urination in one of his Kharkov cartoons, and the device would reappear in the tractor sequence of his *Earth*. In both instances he celebrates urination as a healthy act signifying one's link with the processes of nature, and in this film as well, he treats it as a natural phenomenon in opposition to the forms of hypocrisy found elsewhere in the film.

Such hypocrisy seems to find a measure of sanction from the film's representatives of state authority. The film ignores the government's efforts, tentative though they may have been, to liberalize sexual relations and instead represents an officialdom predisposed to uphold conventional morality and to force Zhan to "do the right thing." When Zhan first learns that he is stuck with the baby, for example, his initial response is to solicit police authority. He goes directly to a constable and recites a fabricated story about coming upon a foundling, but the policeman's skepticism and his air of moral sternness force Zhan to retreat, baby in hand, to safer territory. Lisa is more successful with representatives of state authority because she exploits their sanctimony to her ends. She appears in a people's court to file the equivalent of a paternity suit against Zhan. Her well-rehearsed story about seduction and abandonment persuades the magistrate, who promptly issues a warrant for Zhan to appear with the baby. To satirize the aura of power assumed by the magistrate, the bailiff he summons appears before the bench *ex nihilo:* stop-action photography in the manner of Méliès makes the bailiff pop up magically and disappear just as suddenly on cue. An ironic title later in the film also chides the officious nature of the legal apparatus: "Oh, wise Judge Solomon, apply your lynch law."

The judge's authority is sufficient to force Zhan and Lisa to the Hall of Marriages in the Soviet equivalent of a shotgun wedding. Marriage in the Soviet Union was supposed to be a secular activity, involving a simple administrative procedure and holding legal but not religious significance. But the thinly veiled piety which motivates so many actions in the film surfaces in comic form in the wedding scene as well. When Lisa registers for marriage, she surreptitiously makes a small sign of the cross as

Figure 3. *Love's Berry*

if to solicit from a secret source some special form of forgiveness for her
various deceits. Zhan also secretly draws a cross on the floor with the tip
of his cane. (fig. 3) The repeated gesture carries at least two implications: in a supposedly secular society, vestiges of religious sentiment remain along with other "antiquated" moral conventions; at the same
time, the central characters need, but perhaps do not deserve, indul-
gence for the series of sins that led up to their marriage. Hardly a sexually frank, open couple, they prove unwilling to admit even their own
doubts to each other. This modern couple, who ostentatiously sport the
latest fashion in clothes as well as morality, cannot escape the residual
sanctimony of their cultural history. That contradiction characterized
much of Soviet society as it uncertainly set about altering time-honored
standards of behavior.

Foreign mystery and detective films so impressed Soviet audiences in the
1920s that they earned a Russified genre name, the *detektiv*, a corruption
of the word *detective*. They included such popular imports as Feuillade's
Fantomas and Lang's *Dr. Mabuse the Gambler*. Soviet filmmakers soon developed their own offshoot genre, the "red detective" *(krasnyi detektiv)*, a
variant which maintained the mystery and thriller qualities of the original but which included stories of political consequence to the Soviet system. The red detective cycle typically involved tales of foreign spies,
White Guardists, or counterrevolutionaries attempting to thwart Soviet

development through intrigue and sabotage. Such popular red detectives as *Death Ray* (Kuleshov, 1925) and *Miss Mend* (Otsep, 1926) incorporated the stock devices of stolen secrets, futuristic weapons, and elaborate machinations and added a strong dose of political warning as Soviet heroes fought off foreign and domestic threats to the Soviet system.[10]

Dovzhenko's *Diplomatic Pouch* emerged from this cycle. After completing *Love's Berry,* Dovzhenko had planned to make another comedy, but instead he received an assignment from VUFKU to make this timely and openly political film. *Diplomatic Pouch* took its source from an international incident which shocked the USSR, the murder abroad of a Soviet diplomatic courier. White Guard sympathizers assassinated Theodore Nette in February 1926 as part of an effort to steal the government papers he carried in his diplomatic pouch. Nette promptly achieved martyrdom in the Soviet Union, where he was honored in various public media, including, not least, Mayakovsky's *Izvestia* poem "To Comrade Nette: Man and Ship." Dovzhenko had made friends with Nette during his stint in the foreign service and first learned of the murder while working in the *Visti* newspaper office in Kharkov. Dovzhenko was especially impressed that Nette, a Lett by birth, would sacrifice his life on behalf of the USSR, and considered this determination a tribute to the international spirit of Soviet-style socialism. Although not happy with the scenario VUFKU presented him—he considered it somewhat contrived—Dovzhenko was eager to honor Nette and the internationalism Nette seemed to embody, and he promptly commenced production.[11]

Though the production was occasioned by the Nette affair, the finished film uses the incident as a sign of the European proletariat's solidarity with the USSR. Thus broadened, the film links international socialism with the well-being of the Soviet Union, as a plot synopsis should suggest. The film opens in England, where two Soviet couriers depart from their delegation in possession of a sealed diplomatic pouch. Inspector White of the British secret police connives to intercept them and steal the pouch and its contents. White and his assistant attack the two couriers on a British train, killing one and seriously wounding the other, who nevertheless escapes with the pouch. A British railworker finds him and takes him home to treat his wounds. Just before the Soviet dies, he discovers that the railworker and his family are communists, who prove willing to see that the pouch is sent on to the USSR. The worker forwards the pouch to his son Harry, who happens to be a seaman on the Portsmouth-to-Leningrad run. Harry and the other British sailors, all of whom are communist sympathizers, collude to carry out the mission. Meanwhile, Inspector White traces the papers to Harry's ship, boards it, and with the help of his mistress, an exotic dancer named Ellen, tries to steal the pouch from the sailors, but the seamen resist his efforts. In the film's climax, as Ellen dances for the first-class passengers, the sailors throw White and his police assistant to their deaths in the sea. The ship steams ahead to Leningrad, the pouch safely in the possession of the militant sailors.

The film's linking of the British working class with the Soviet diplomatic service takes its inspiration from the USSR's policies vis-à-vis the non-Soviet Left, policies that derived from the USSR's uncertain status in the international community. The lone socialist nation in a largely hostile capitalist world, the Soviet Union was denied recognition in its early years by much of the diplomatic establishment. If the USSR was to establish foreign links, those ties would have to be with the international Left, with the various radical groups functioning, however uncertainly, in the very nations that had refused recognition to the USSR. The story of the Soviet Union's complicated, often contradictory dealings with foreign governments and with foreign radical groups, not just the Nette affair, provides the backdrop of *Diplomatic Pouch*. [12]

In the period immediately after the October revolution, leading Bolsheviks hoped that their revolution would set off a chain reaction in Western Europe and feared that their survival depended on the spread of socialism. But Soviet leaders also expected foreign communist organizations to put support of the Soviet Union ahead of activities designed to facilitate revolution. The first Comintern Congress, dominated like all subsequent congresses by the Russian delegation, called for foreign Communist parties to support the cause of the USSR's survival against threats of counterrevolution, even if that meant mitigating their own revolutionary activities. Subsequently, Lenin's "Twenty-One Conditions" had the net effect of requiring foreign Communist parties to follow the Bolshevik model, and many foreign parties obliged by subordinating the interests of their own proletariat to the sovereignty of the USSR. And while continuing to pay lip service to the ideal of world revolution, Soviet leaders recognized by the middle 1920s that no uprisings were in the offing and began to seek accommodations with major capitalist states, establishing trade and diplomatic relations. Stalin's policy of "socialism in one country," elevated to doctrine in 1926, took this trend to its culmination. This left the various foreign revolutionary groups to live out what Isaac Deutscher has termed a "pathetic contradiction in terms": the Communist International, the titular agent of world revolution, functioned as a consignee of Moscow, which in turn adhered to a policy of "socialism in one country."[13] Stalin counted on foreign revolutionaries to support the Kremlin while he politely did business with the capitalist governments that were supposedly the mortal enemies of those same revolutionaries.

Diplomatic Pouch's transposition of the Nette incident to Britain makes pointed reference to contemporary developments in Soviet-British relations. The contradictory policy of the USSR toward foreign radicalism obtained in the USSR's exploitation of the British Left. The USSR established links with the British trade union movement under the banner of the "United Front," while simultaneously trying to improve relations with the British government. Russian overtures to England began in the early 1920s, and when Labour came to power in 1924, the new cabinet broke the diplomatic ice by recognizing the USSR. Relations worsened when the Tories returned to the helm, and in a bitter parliamentary campaign, a letter allegedly written by Soviet official Grigori Zinoviev and urging British workers to commit acts of subversion became an issue which additionally strained official relations. Moreover, a general trade union strike received the Soviet government's public endorsement, adding to fears of Soviet interference in England's internal affairs. Relations hit bottom in late 1926 and 1927, when the possibility of war with the USSR was broached in British government circles.

Thus the Nette affair, the USSR's messy efforts at diplomacy with England, and the tortured definition of internationalism which accompanied "socialism in one country" intersected in 1926 during the production of *Diplomatic Pouch* and determined its topical references. This red detective film, like others in the genre, grafted current political problems onto the inherited formula of the thriller, in this case playing on Soviet-British tensions and on the Kremlin's assumption that the foreign proletariat would do its bidding. *Diplomatic Pouch* also addresses lingering fears of the White Guard, even as it invokes British hostility. The film makes Inspector White the agent of anti-Soviet intrigue, and although he is a British official, his name harks up the White Guardists who were the culprits in the actual Nette affair.

White's role in the film is crucial and deserves considerable attention. Although he is merely a middle-echelon police official, various incidents in the narrative represent him as the embodiment of unfettered authority, capable of ruling by unilateral decree. In fact, the film shows us no example of British officialdom except as embodied in White. His power extends beyond that of normal police activity as if to encompass every form of British government authority. Not only does he lead a police contingent—one, incidentally, that does not hesitate to kill, let alone vio-

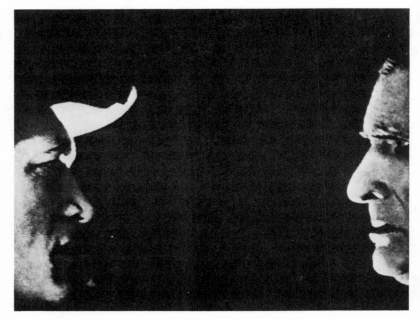

Figure 4. *Diplomatic Pouch*

late the sanctity of the diplomatic pouch—but he also assumes the power
to issue orders to British port authorities to help him catch up with the
ship carrying the pouch, and he supplants the ship's captain as master of
the ship, assuming the authority to issue a range of orders. The film, in
effect, dismisses the governing institutions of Britain and creates a fictional microcosm of a society ruled by the will of a single tyrannical individual.

White's aggression becomes his defining characteristic. While pursu-
ing the Soviet courier, White invades the home of the railworker without
invitation or permission. In a relentlessly grim series of shots, a rain-
soaked White looms over the dead body of the courier and drips water
on the corpse. Just before White's entry, the railworker's wife had gingerly folded the dead courier's hands and drawn the shades to preserve a
measure of dignity on the occasion of a man's death. White's sudden
and grotesque incursion spoils the serenity of the scene and its sense of
sanctuary, and he seems to bring the very harshness of the thunderstorm
outside into the quiet home—literally so, since he tracks in the storm's
rain and mud.

In the ensuing scene, White seeks to coerce and intimidate the railworker and his family in the hope that they will reveal the whereabouts of the pouch. In a stunning shot which evokes the sense of a test of wills between White and the railworker, Dovzhenko frames the two characters in profile as they stare intently at one another. (fig. 4) The shot balances White's intensity with the worker's determination not to divulge the information. Gradually White presses forward until his profile takes up the entire frame and the worker is forced out of the shot. The moment defines the social opposition at the center of the film's drama—the British representative of power at odds with the British working class, the former assuming authority over the latter while the latter resorts to subversive activity to establish independence.

If the moment establishes the railworker as White's immediate foil, it also anticipates the formation of a coalition to thwart the power structure at White's command. The authority embodied in White is challenged by a spontaneous proletarian movement. The worker's family spearheads the alternative organization, as the family members form a cohesive unit to oppose White. Each member assumes given responsibilities in complementary stages of activity: the railworker finds the dying Bolshevik and takes him home to receive care; the wife looks after his wounds; the younger son sneaks the pouch to older brother Harry at the port; and Harry smuggles it aboard ship. The ship's sailors then take over responsibility for the pouch with a similar coordination as if they constituted an extension of the railworker's family, banding together as the family had done to see that the documents proceed to Leningrad. The crew members act with a precision reminiscent of the family, passing the pouch from one sailor to another in a splendidly choreographed routine to keep it from White and his assistant. When White at one point tries to pursue the ship in a launch, the sailors surreptitiously disobey their captain's orders by pouring on more steam to outrun the smaller craft. During the sequence, a black sailor in the seamen's quarters dances a spirited hornpipe to the delight of his comrades. Dovzhenko crosscuts between closeups of the sailor's dancing legs and the churning pistons of the ship's engines. The parallel suggests that the exuberant energy of the sailors somehow translates directly into the ship's engines and bypasses the ship's traditional command hierarchy, as if the popular will of a proletarian group such as the sailors could supplant the kind of power structure White commands.

The ambitions of the two groups, the sailors and White's cohort, distinguish them as well. The crewmen reveal selfless motives as they convey the documents to the USSR, while White and his associates answer to base instincts. White's police assistant acts out of personal ambition, hoping to recover the pouch as a means of winning promotion. White's mistress, Ellen, aids White because of the personal power he holds over her. These motives become manifest during one sequence on the ship. White makes love to Ellen in a cabin as a means of persuading her to work on his behalf to recover the pouch. During this lovemaking, Dovzhenko cuts away to White's assistant standing on deck outside the cabin where he has been spying on the two. The assistant stands perfectly still and erect; then in a series of dissolves, he appears in a succession of different, elaborate military uniforms. The assistant's body becomes more stiff and the expression of ecstasy on his face more intense as the shots progress, suggesting that he experiences something resembling an orgasmic power fantasy. This sexual connotation is reinforced by Dovzhenko's continued crosscutting to White and Ellen in their tryst, a tactic which links the impulses of White's two servants and casts their motives in sexual terms. Ellen's sexual desires, realized in her affair with White, find their equivalent in the police assistant's quasi-erotic fantasies of power.

The sailors, by contrast, seem immune to such drives. They never answer to sexual instincts, although they live with erotic temptation all around them. In one scene, for example, Ellen tries to seduce a crew member in order to find the pouch. As she paws him, pretending to admire his physique, her hands search his body for the papers, but he resists her aggressive advances. At another point, several crew members gather at the Wet Deck Bar, a classic representation of a waterfront dive where nothing is forbidden. But the sailors use the location only as a cover, refusing to indulge in the wide selection of vices available to them on demand. Instead, they retreat to the back room for a strategy session and formulate their plan to guard the pouch. The sequence makes clear that the men choose political commitment over gratification and, like the proletarians of Eisenstein's *October,* reject the decadence of an established order, directing, even perhaps sublimating, their energy to political action.

This commitment manifests itself again in the film's climax, when the sailors conspire to kill White and his police assistant. As the sailors close in on White, Ellen entertains the first-class passengers with an erotic dance. Dovzhenko crosscuts between the dance and the sailors' grim mission, and the sequence harks back to the scene at the Wet Deck Bar. The grotesque, craven spectators among the first-class contingent who ogle Ellen seem to be a bourgeois equivalent of the assorted hedonists whom we had previously observed in the Wet Deck Bar, and the same panoply of sins, including drunkenness and licentiousness, is evidenced. At the Wet Deck the crew had formed a tight, separate circle to initiate their plan, and in this closing sequence they reestablish that circle away from the decadent entertainments of the ship's lounge to carry that plan through to its culmination—the murder of Inspector White. An ironic title which refers to Ellen's audience tells us that the "ship's society does not shun ART—especially that of naked women," pointing to the prurience of the first-class passengers. But the film issues no such condemnation of the sailors' methodical execution of White and his assistant in the same sequence. In fact, the instant the sailors throw White and his assistant overboard to their deaths, Dovzhenko cuts to shots of the first-class audience clapping. As a result of this abrupt transition, Ellen's spectators actually seem to applaud the deaths of the two men. In this one stroke, Dovzhenko links the deaths to the first-class passengers, as if the deaths were the logical extension of the passengers' vices, and he removes the onus from the sailors who actually carried out the executions, leaving us with the impression that, for the crew members, the killings were nothing more than acts necessitated and justified by their political commitment.

Dovzhenko has been at pains to remove any form of personal gratification, sexual or otherwise, as the motive behind that commitment. But the question remains, What finally motivates the thorough involvement of the British sailors and the British railworker's family in subversive activity? They remain perfectly willing to sacrifice their safety and well-being in a deadly intrigue on behalf of a foreign state. This conduct seems notably selfless—too much so, perhaps. Therein lies the film's most telling appraisal of foreign radicalism: we are asked to believe that British proletarians act solely out of a commitment to radical politics and, what is more, that commitment can only take the form of loyalty to the Soviet Union. For example, the dying Bolshevik courier discovers that he is surrounded by sympathetic proletarians when he sees a portrait of Lenin on the wall. "The documents are for him," the courier cryptically tells the railworker, who instantly understands that the somewhat ambiguous pronoun reference is to Lenin. In addition, the railworker promptly surmises that he must arrange to forward the documents to the USSR. This exchange, which seems to employ telepathy more than spoken language, implies that British radicals simply possess preexisting loyalty to the USSR and that they instinctively recognize their responsibility to support Soviet sovereignty and, if need be, to act as Soviet agents.

Political radicalism in the film is evidenced solely by a willingness to serve the USSR and is marked as much by what it omits as by what it includes. The film leaves out the possibility of a British communist movement as an autonomous entity serving the particular needs of the British working class. We do not see any evidence of a radical platform or political organization that speaks to the intrinsic interests of the British proletariat. The film barely hints at previous radical sentiment among the sailors when a search of the ship turns up leftist literature in the seamen's bunks. But this cryptic reference only signifies a somewhat inchoate rebelliousness on the part of the men. It requires the presence of the sacred pouch and the associated threat to Soviet sovereignty to transform that inclination into action, and once in action, the men never waiver or question their own motives.

Just as conspicuously absent is an explanation of the nature of the documents ensconced in the pouch. The documents bear more than a passing resemblance to a "MacGuffin," a favorite Hitchcock narrative device. In a Hitchcock thriller, a single mysterious item, the MacGuffin of the story, is usually sought after by competing factions—a roll of microfilm, for example, or the identity of the thirty-nine steps. But that item ultimately serves as nothing more than a mechanical device of narrative intrigue; its intrinsic value is left unexplained. Hitchcock claimed that "when you come right down to it, it doesn't matter what the spies are after."[14] The item's contents—the information on the microfilm or the true nature of the thirty-nine steps—matter not to the audience. The MacGuffin must be pursued for its own sake to drive the narrative forward.

The diplomatic pouch, the MacGuffin of this film, focuses the intrigue and defines the depth of loyalty of the British radicals who become the film's heroes, thus taking on an extra ideological dimension. While it is noteworthy that the audience never discovers the contents of the documents in the pouch, it is of greater ideological consequence that the radicals who handle the pouch never express any curiosity about its contents.[15] The pouch could conceal crucial military secrets or idle diplomatic correspondence; it matters not to the leftists, for whom it serves simply as a symbol of the USSR's sovereignty, and they treat it as an almost sacred object. Their loyalty to the Soviet Union is signified, in part, by their refusal to violate the immunity from inspection traditionally associated with the diplomatic pouch. In a larger sense, such unquestioning service to the USSR, marking the proletarians' status as virtual extensions of the Soviet diplomatic mission, represented the Soviet ideal of foreign radicalism, and it also betrayed the bind of Euro-

pean radicals, who were asked to put themselves at the service of a
sovereign state in order to define themselves as revolutionaries.

Dovzhenko's first efforts seem to have had little impact on the Soviet
film scene. *Love's Berry* attracted little attention. Received as a minor
farce, it was neither widely advertised, distributed, nor reviewed.[16] *Diplomatic Pouch* won somewhat more recognition, including exhibition and
reviews outside the Ukraine, but that proved to be a not unmixed reward. A Kiev critic praised the film guardedly: "Director Dovzhenko
uses everything in order to escape the cheap stamp of bare adventure.
And he succeeds in considerable measure."[17] But in an important Leningrad journal, *Diplomatic Pouch* was written off as an "antediluvian *detektiv,* thoroughly naive and illiterate."[18]

Perhaps mere coincidence dictated that Dovzhenko's film received a
gentle notice in the Ukraine and a harsh dismissal in Great Russia. But
it may not be too fanciful to attach some symbolic weight to this split decision. Dovzhenko's work had yet to win esteem outside the boundaries
of the Ukraine. He himself retained little regard for these first two experiments in which he coopted existing genre formulas from abroad for his
topical references. He still sought to find a subject and a combination of
ingredients through which he would achieve a wider audience and take
his place alongside the Moscow-based filmmakers who were exerting the
greatest influence on the USSR as a whole. He would do so one night in
Moscow when *Zvenigora* premiered before the Soviet cinema elite.

IV
Zvenigora

Eisenstein's famous account of *Zvenigora*'s Moscow premiere expresses something of the excitement and bewilderment experienced by many viewers on their first encounter with the film.

> Goodness gracious, what a sight!
> We saw sharp-keeled boats sailing out of double exposures.
> The rump of a black stallion being painted white.
> A horrible monk with a lantern being either disinterred
>   or buried—I am not sure which.[1]

Dovzhenko burst onto the Soviet artistic scene in dramatic fashion by astonishing the artists and dignitaries gathered at the prestigious Hermitage Theater. *Zvenigora*—with its camera trickery, its frequent narrative ellipses, its fantasy sections, and its many invocations of Ukrainian cultural arcana—baffled its distinguished Moscow audience. Dovzhenko made his mark, and to a degree, established his reputation, by presenting the most audacious work of his career.

Although *Zvenigora* was Dovzhenko's fourth film project, it has long been treated as his real film debut, his first production to deal with distinctly Ukrainian material and the work that marked the principal direction of his subsequent career. To Eisenstein it signified "the birth of an artist." Indeed, it evidences something of the audacity and energy of such celebrated inaugural works as *Strike, Un Chien Andalou,* and *Citizen Kane,* and it marks a leap from the somewhat conservative borrowings from foreign genre formulas that we find in Dovzhenko's earlier films.

Few films are as ambitious as *Zvenigora*. It ranges over centuries, combining material from ancient folklore with modern events into one sweeping narrative and presenting, in Dovzhenko's words, "in 2,000 meters of film a whole millennium."[2] In an effort to characterize the film's scope, critics have resorted to comparisons with medieval frescoes

46

and tapestries.[3] And anecdotes abound about the problems Soviet audiences experienced simply following the narrative: one story has it that VUFKU officials who had generously supported the film's expensive production could only sit silent and confused when they first screened the finished product. To no one's great surprise, the film was poorly received by general audiences when it went into commercial distribution.[4]

Certainly *Zvenigora*'s famed stylistic bravura accounts in part for the problems it poses for audiences. Our main concern, however, is with the narrative and its complex of references. Of special interest to us is how the referents range over centuries of Ukrainian history. As we shall see, the breadth of the narrative owed much to Dovzhenko's myriad influences. Various sources from different cultural realms fed into the film as it went through an elaborate process of revision. An examination of the project's sources, its stages of development, and its finished form helps to account for *Zvenigora*'s scope and to show how Dovzhenko attempts through inclusiveness to suggest links between the modern, revolutionary Ukraine and its distant past.

A preliminary synopsis of *Zvenigora* will provide a sense of the narrative's breadth. In some uncertain period of the Ukraine's past, the ageless Grandfather takes a band of Cossacks to the "treasure mountain" Zvenigora. They rout a group of Polish bandits at the mountain but are frustrated in their search for treasure by a magic monk who haunts the terrain. Grandfather reappears in the twentieth century with two grandsons, idle Pavlo and industrious Timosh. While Timosh fights in World War I, Pavlo and Grandfather search for the treasure still reputedly buried in Zvenigora. Timosh joins the Bolsheviks during the revolutionary upheaval, but Grandfather and Pavlo isolate themselves from modern events. Grandfather relates the ancient legend of Roksana to Pavlo: how Princess Roksana and her people were subjugated by invaders who demanded tribute; how the invader chief used magic to curse her; and how the gold of tribute remained buried in Zvenigora. Pavlo joins the White Guard after hearing the tale and fights Timosh's Red Army troops. After the war Pavlo raises money in Western Europe to finance another treasure hunt at the mountain while Timosh helps the Bolsheviks build a modern Ukraine. As Timosh rides a Soviet train past Zvenigora, Pavlo urges Grandfather to sabotage the tracks, but the old man does not do so. Pavlo commits suicide, and Grandfather is taken aboard the train and introduced to the new life of the Soviets.

As this summary suggests, the narrative of *Zvenigora* involves comparisons among different stages of Ukrainian history. The four-part structure—the prologue with Grandfather and the Cossacks, the section dealing with World War I and the revolution, the dramatization of the Roksana legend, and the section on the civil war and early Soviet period —permits Dovzhenko to develop parallels and contrasts between the modern Ukraine and the Ukraine of the past. Dovzhenko deals with contemporary political concerns in the modern sections, such as the efforts to solidify Soviet authority against native Ukrainian resistance and the industrialization of the Ukraine under the Soviet system. The material invoked in the ancient sections, tinged as it is with myth, contains a political strain as well, as when the prologue invokes the Haydamakas, seventeenth- and eighteenth-century Cossack bands who were a major political power in the Ukraine and who protected the land from Polish invaders. The ancient sections are the sort of mix of history and fantasy common in a peasant population's recollection of its own past, and provide Dovzhenko the opportunity to equate the Ukraine's folk culture with its modern revolution.

Dovzhenko's strategy reflects the fact that Slavic folktales have historically adapted to social change, having been revised and updated to encompass modern events. As an oral medium, folklore is more flexible than written literature, capable of being altered slightly at each narration to correspond to the concerns of the audience of the moment. For example, peasant uprisings against authority provided resources for countless tales during the period of serfdom, catering to a latent rebelliousness among the peasants. The seventeenth-century uprising led by Stepan Razin against landlords generated stories which contained numerous historical details—including exact dates, places, and names—mixed freely with utter fantasy, as when the hero Stepan proves invulnerable to bullets. In the wake of the massive Pugachev peasant rebellion of the eighteenth century, the established legend of Stepan fused with the more recent historical event; the overall narrative formula remained intact while particular incidents and characters changed, including the substitution of Pugachev for Stepan. The protean revolutionary strain of such peasant folklore continued into the twentieth century when the Bolshevik revolution provided a new supply of incidents that could be plugged into the older tales. One familiar narrative formula inherited from the past involved the splitting of brothers into opposing armies, a convention employed by Gogol, among others, in *Taras Bulba;* it often culminated with a fatal confrontation between the brothers. The formula survived into the modern period and involved one brother fighting with Red Army and the other with the White Guard.[5]

In this tried formula we find the source of *Zvenigora* as Dovzhenko adapted a familiar tale not only to a new age but to a new medium. Not surprisingly, this hybrid conception originated during Dovzhenko's Kharkov days and reveals the VAPLITE legacy. While still in Kharkov, Dovzhenko considered writing a novel which leaped back and forth over time and which contained scenes wherein ancient Cossack bands encountered troops of the modern Ukrainian revolution. He left Kharkov before developing the project, but other members of the Kharkov circle fashioned a narrative along similar lines. VAPLITE writers Iurko Tiutiunnyk and Mike Johansen collaborated on a story with the convention of a confrontation between brothers and added several ingredients from the assortment of Ukrainian legends dealing with buried treasure. This evolved into a film treatment which they submitted to Dovzhenko after he had established himself at VUFKU. In their treatment, an old man in a remote village holds the secret of a lost treasure, and while on the verge of death, he relates the information to his two young grandsons. The grandsons grow to maturity and separate during the revolutionary period, joining opposing armies. They finally encounter each other at the treasure site, but tragedy is averted when the Bolshevik captures his brother and converts him to communism. The two men recover the treasure and donate it to the new Soviet regime.[6]

This conception clearly reveals a debt to the VAPLITE strategy of grafting traditional material onto modern projects, and this initial treatment provided Dovzhenko with the eventual film's principal characters if not their ultimate functions in the dramatic conflict. Dovzhenko began revising this treatment in 1927 and fashioned a scenario which considerably broadened the original scope, adding elements from his aborted novel, including the conflation of events from different historical epochs. He would later claim that his revisions eliminated the "devilry and nationalism" of the Tiutiunnyk-Johansen version,[7] a remark that betrayed the somewhat ambiguous political position he occupied during the making of *Zvenigora*. In drawing on his national inheritance for the first time, Dovzhenko had to proceed carefully in 1927; for this was the very moment of the Communist party crackdown on VAPLITE for "nationalistic" tendencies. Moreover, 1927 marked the beginning of the serious party scrutiny of Ukrainian cinema, which was occasioned by the party's overall investigation of the film industry. Although Dovzhenko, as we have seen, profited from VUFKU's expansion and from its willingness to support ambitious projects like *Zvenigora*, such opportunities now carried with them the burden of greater official watchfulness. The party's review of cinema led to a policy statement mandating greater emphasis on *partiinost'*, and it put national studios like VUFKU on notice that Moscow would be wary of "excess nationalism."[8]

Not coincidentally, the first of many problems Dovzhenko would have with the party apparatus occurred in 1927 and helped determine his *Zvenigora* project. After finishing *Diplomatic Pouch,* he had proposed a film to be called *Insurrection of the Dead* which would deal with the fate of some White Guard troops and would treat them sympathetically as victims of their officers' manipulations. The project was abruptly halted when VUFKU received a message from Communist party representatives stating bluntly: "You cannot offer pity to the White Guard."[9]

Dovzhenko then turned to *Zvenigora* as a timely project, treating the Bolshevik revolution on the occasion of its tenth anniversary. In fact, a spate of films on the revolution—*October, End of St. Petersburg,* and *The Fall of the Romanov Dynasty,* to name some of the better-known—emerged after the party's intervention in cinema, in part a result of an official directive to the studios to make films marking the regime's first decade. *Zvenigora* was to be Dovzhenko's initial contribution to the nation's "jubilee year," as it was popularly known, and Dovzhenko consciously sought to include an appropriate measure of *partiinost'* along with his tribute to the Ukraine's folk heritage. He insisted of *Zvenigora,* "It is my party membership card."[10]

Yet the project would be no simple exercise in party doctrine, containing as it did elements that were beginning to be held in official disfavor. Indeed, as this complicated background should suggest, the production drew on a myriad of dissimilar sources—artistic, political, folkloristic, and personal—and emerged as Dovzhenko's most eclectic work, one that gave credence to his claim that from "a great quantity of material which would suffice for five or six pictures, I make one single film linked together by unusually strong tensions."[11] To trace those linkages and understand their ideological implications, we need to examine in detail the substantial revisions Dovzhenko made in the original Tiutiunnyk-Johansen treatment in fashioning his own scenario. Subsequently we will turn to the even more heavily revised finished film.

The full scenario that Dovzhenko fashioned out of the Tiutiunnyk-Johansen story considerably broadens the initial conception.[12] The scenario lays out the basic four-part scheme that would remain in the finished film. As in the finished film, the scenario alternates between sections from the present and from the past, and the events depicted sometimes complement and sometimes contrast with each other.

Grandfather has only one grandson in the scenario, Timosh; and much of the scenario focuses on Timosh's gradual transformation from a passive follower of Grandfather's antiquated ways to a committed, modern advocate of a new Ukraine. In the process, he rejects Grandfather's old superstitions and obsession with the legendary treasure of Zvenigora in favor of a revolutionary consciousness and a sense of social responsibility. Rather than retreating to a hole in the side of a mountain desperately looking for gold, Timosh eventually invests his energy in constructing a modern Ukraine.

Early in the scenario, however, he appears as a frivolous, provincial peasant lad, content with the quiet life of the country and passing his time by blowing soap bubbles (p. 65). The boy seems vaguely interested in Grandfather's insistence that a treasure lies buried in Zvenigora, and he becomes Grandfather's cooperative but otherwise innocuous assistant in the treasure hunt.

In the scenario, unlike the film, Grandfather actually does discover a treasure cache. But Grandfather and Timosh are forbidden to continue digging in the mountain by order of the presiding Ukrainian army general, because the army is supervising the construction of a railroad bridge there (pp. 68-69). These frustrations, along with the arrival of the revolution, prove so disheartening for Grandfather that he retreats into the past for solace. He recounts for Timosh his favorite legend, that of Roksana and her people under the rule of the invaders. The tale is no doubt an embellishment of the ninth- and tenth-century invasion by Scandinavian tribes who moved down the navigable rivers of Russia in their long ships and who were less interested in subjugating Slavic peoples than in establishing a trade route from the Baltic to the Caspian and Black Seas. But in the process they gained control over the Slavic tribes in the area, established the Kievan empire, and forced local inhabitants to pay tribute.[13]

In Grandfather's story, they arrive in Viking-like dragon ships pulled down the river by oxen. In keeping with the tradition of mixing the fantastic and the factual in such legends, the invaders are at once identified with cold, mercenary motives and with the supernatural. They immediately indicate that they seek tribute from Roksana's people, and their combination accountant and tribute-taker, the *virnik,* figures prominently in this section (p. 74). On the other hand, the invaders are associated with awesome supernatural power. Roksana initially mistakes the ship for a dragon when the vessel's bow looms up over her.

> The face of the girl with the wide-open eyes.
> Inspired she says, "Show me the night."
> Close-up.
> The dragon devours the sun.
> Close-up.
> The girl speaks.
> The people are in silent horror. (P. 73)

The tale constitutes a self-contained narrative as it depicts the subjugation of Roksana's people, the uprising against the invaders, and the invader chief's curse on the area. But it contains a number of ingredients that resonate throughout the script. For instance, at the beginning of the tale Roksana dreams she sees the head of a dragon. This dream not only anticipates the arrival of the invaders in the dragon ship but also echoes Grandfather's troubled dream about the head of a monk in the second section of the script (pp. 65, 74). That obsession with the supernatural remains with Grandfather. At the end of the script, encountering a Bolshevik train, he convinces himself that it is a monstrous serpent (p. 85). The conclusion of the legend contains an account of the origins of the Zvenigora treasure and landscape. After Roksana's people fail to expel the invaders, the chief issues a curse on Roksana and her people. His ship, laden with treasure, sinks into the ground to form the mountain. Then Roksana falls dead, and her features transform themselves into the landscape.

> The girl moves backward and falls over the goblet.
> The girl lies on the ground. From the goblet flows water.
> The face of the girl. In a close-up her hair becomes reeds;
>   her dark eyes become the close-up of a cave.
> The reeds are below the mountain and above them are dark caves.
> Beside the mouth of the goblet from which the water runs the
>   lake is seen. (Pp.77-78)

These images linger with Grandfather. When he sees a waterfall later in the scenario, he envisions Roksana's fallen goblet, as if the presence of the waterfall validated his faith in the legend (p. 83).

The diabolical monk who guards the treasure in the opening of the script also reappears in the other sections. In the second section he is reincarnated in the Ukrainian general who forbids Grandfather to dig, and he reappears as the chief of the invaders and as the "vagrant monk" in the final section. Dovzhenko suggests in this protean figure that reactionary forces endure over epochs, that they merely reappear in different guises, representing related counterrevolutionary forces, whether in the form of the military or of the church. The vagrant monk ultimately manages to exploit Grandfather's superstition. In the final scene he manipulates the old man into trying to destroy the Bolshevik train (pp. 83-84). Grandfather is led to believe that he should keep the treasure from being defiled by the train. Thus, the legend and Grandfather's belief in superstition drive him to irrationality so that he commits a desperate act.

If the scenario condemns such superstition, it also holds out the possibility of progress through modern rationalism. Timosh's response to the Roksana legend is precisely the opposite of Grandfather's, and it helps direct the young man toward a practical course. Timosh successfully relates the legend to the modern world and thus views the legend in its proper perspective. When he finds events in his own experience that parallel episodes of the legend, he realizes that Roksana's story is an allegory on the integrity of the Ukraine and on the need for vigilance against oppressive forces.

Roksana, for example, has a modern counterpart in the form of a peasant girl, Oksana. They have much in common besides similar names. At one point in the legend Roksana tries to fight the invaders by assassinating their chief. She throws a dagger that strikes the chief without harming him. Shortly after hearing the tale, Timosh encounters a modern remake of the episode. The peasant girl Oksana is attacked by the vagrant monk and in desperation throws a knife at him, striking him in the shoulder. Timosh equates the girl with the legend, and he recognizes that the monk represents the same forces of political oppression as the invader chief. Timosh and Oksana soon fall in love and participate in the building of a revolutionary, industrialized Ukraine, and their resolve is strengthened by the insight they draw from the Roksana legend.

> Timosh tenderly takes Oksana's arm.
> The silhouettes of Oksana and Timoshka; her arm lies across his
>   shoulder; they look at the bridge.
> Timoshka points to the bridge: "A different treasure, the
>   greatest treasure of all is our earth."
> Embracing, they walk toward the bridge.
> Timoshka stops the girl and looks into her eyes: "I will
>   obtain with you this treasure, Roksana."
> Oksana smiles: "Timoshka, darling, my name is . . ."
> Timoshka tenderly closes her lips with his hand. (P. 81)

Timosh recognizes the Roksana legend as a precedent for revolution, with modern bridges rather than legendary treasure troves representing the wealth of the new Ukraine. He studies at school to acquire the necessary skills to contribute to the modern system, which combines politics and industry. In his mathematics class, for example, Timosh works out several series of ciphers on the blackboard, and they culminate in his writing (in red), "25 October 1917," the date of the Bolshevik revolution (p. 80). Science, education, and revolutionary ideology blend together in the new order.

The initial relationship between Timosh and Grandfather is reversed by the end of the scenario. Timosh develops into a mature, determined man, while Grandfather ends up an ineffectual, even pitiful figure. Their diametrically opposite evolutions produce a final confrontation. Timosh and Oksana ride on the Bolshevik train which Grandfather tries to destroy. The train represents progress, and it carries the true treasure of the Ukrainian soil, coal that will serve heavy industry (p. 84). These modernists need not concern themselves with legends of treasure buried in Zvenigora. They hold a practical, utilitarian ethic.

Grandfather's continuing superstitions bring his downfall. He becomes convinced that the train is a great serpent, and he runs toward it trying to subdue it with a series of curses. But his rituals prove ineffective against the steel and raw power of the very real locomotive, and he is run over and killed. Such, the climax suggests, is the fate of those who choose to defy the irresistible power and progress of history, represented by the hurtling train. Anachronisms like Grandfather must be sacrificed to the new Ukraine. When Timosh sees that his own grandfather is the victim, he does not express any regret or offer any lament. He merely rejoins his comrades so that the train can continue its journey into the future (pp. 85–86).

Thus, Dovzhenko's scenario advances a relatively clear lesson about tradition and modernity based on a series of comparisons between the past and the present. The scenario's somewhat elementary old-new dichotomy is personified in the central characters and their generational split, with Grandfather retaining past legends and superstitions and Timosh recognizing them as societal allegories which have only symbolic consequence in the modern world. In fashioning the finished film, Dovzhenko maintained the balance between the two alternative positions while seeking the means of a reconciliation.

The most significant change Dovzhenko made in the finished film was in the organization of the principal characters. He reverted to the triangular arrangement suggested in the Tiutiunnyk-Johansen version. To refine his scenario's crude division between Grandfather and Timosh, Dovzhenko introduced the second grandson Pavlo and aligned him with counterrevolution. This, in turn, allowed Dovzhenko to free the grandfather from the burden of representing a purely reactionary impulse and permitted him to assign a more complex function to the character.

The grandfather plays a far more extensive role in the film than in the scenario, serving frequently to link the past and the present. He appears in all four sections of the film, providing an important measure of continuity from one section to the next. He even plays a part as a character in

Figure 5. *Zvenigora*

the Roksana legend, though he himself recounts the tale. Grandfather must survive through the ages to embody the enduring traditions of the Ukraine. He is called in an intertitle "the centuries-old guardian" of the treasure, and in this capacity he serves as guardian of the legends of the Ukraine as well. In the last shot of the opening section, for example, Grandfather begins to mount his horse, but he suddenly becomes frozen. He stays locked in one position in a still frame as the centuries pass, a sign of his timelessness. Appropriately, in the modern sections, he preserves the past through the tales he retains and recounts. He objects, for example, to the upheaval of the World War and revolution. He retreats to an eternal sanctuary from change, the peak of Zvenigora, and disheartened by the turmoil around him, he says to Pavlo: "In rebellion nation rose against nation, country against country, brother against brother. Sit down, my only consolation and hope." His action suggests that by understanding the immortal secret of Zvenigora one can conquer the ephemeral, in this case the political upheavals of the twentieth century. He endeavors to survive the uncertainty of modern politics by holding on to a legend that exists outside of time. When Grandfather recounts the Roksana tale, he sits atop Zvenigora like an oracle on a mountaintop. In the film, the character seems less a counterrevolutionary threat than a monument to cultural continuity. (fig. 5)

The insidious side of national tradition is personified in the film by the second grandson, Pavlo. He, rather than Grandfather, functions as the foil to Timosh, and the distinction between the two grandsons is made as soon as they are introduced. Timosh is practical and industrious; we first see him repairing shoes. Pavlo, by contrast, appears frivolous and irresponsible and is introduced in the act of blowing soap bubbles. Contrasts between the two young men run throughout the film. During the sequence set in the World War, for example, Dovzhenko cuts from Pavlo, huddled fetal-like in the "treasure" hole, to Timosh at the front, defiantly emerging from a trench to forge a separate peace with the Germans. Later Timosh expresses only vague amusement at Grandfather's tales, but Pavlo takes them to heart and becomes a ruthless reactionary as a result of hearing the tale of Roksana. Fired by a perverse romanticism, Pavlo presumes to uphold the heritage of the Ukraine, but he seeks to do so by joining the White Guard, as if counterrevolution were synonymous with tradition. After the civil war he makes a mockery of Ukrainian national customs during his exile in Prague and Paris. He walks down the street ostentatiously garbed in Cossack dress (fig. 6) and he exploits his status as a Ukrainian exile in his speech-and-suicide stage show. By the end of the film he appears as a thoroughly sinister force of reaction, and he cynically manipulates his own grandfather in his effort to destroy the Bolshevik train and recover the treasure. Pavlo has supplanted the monk of the script as the personification of evil, exploitative power. The film, in fact, directly links Pavlo with the monk who guards Zvenigora. In an early scene Grandfather dreams that the monk hovers over him and spits down on him. Through a dissolve, however, it is revealed that Grandfather's nightmare about the monk actually results from Pavlo's soap bubbles, which float down and land on the old man's face. Not only does this scene equate Pavlo with the monk, but it also subtly foreshadows Pavlo's ability to exploit Grandfather's superstitions.

In contrast to Pavlo's "education" at Zvenigora—an experience which is, in fact, nothing more than an indoctrination in superstition— Timosh's education is through a rational, utilitarian training at the workers' high school. (fig. 7) Timosh puts himself firmly on the side of modernization. From the scene of Timosh at the school, Dovzhenko shows education spreading throughout the countryside. Villagers gather to hear speakers and teachers imported from cities. And the train on which Timosh rides at the end of the film seems to be an agit-train, that ingenious Bolshevik institution for taking education and ideology to the hinterlands.

As a counter to such rationalistic trends, the film invokes vestiges of

Figure 6. *Zvenigora*

Figure 7. *Zvenigora*

superstition, something that is suggested in the title of the film itself. *Zvenigora* has two roots. *Gora* refers to the mountain. The prefix *zveni* derives from the Russian word *zvenet'* (Ukrainian *dzvenity*) meaning "to ring, jingle, or tinkle." Thus, the prefix evokes the gold coins supposedly buried in the mountain by harking up the metallic sounds one might associate with such treasure, and the title contains a sense of the supernatural in the suggestion that the mountain emits mysterious sounds. To reinforce this suggestion, the alternative Russian title of the film is *Zakoldovannoe mesto*—"bewitched place." Various forms of superstition appear in the film. The monk in the opening scene represents a diabolical cross between magic and religion. Belief in the supernatural produces comic effects in the modern sections. Oksana is frightened away from Zvenigora when Grandfather emerges from his hole because she assumes she has seen the appearance of the devil. The Ukrainian general proclaims that he will perform a miracle by quelling his soldiers' rebellion. Another general surveys the bridge and states, "My hands create miracles"—at which point the entire structure tumbles to the ground; little did the general know that the only miracle consisted of the fact that revolutionary saboteurs had gotten to the bridge before him.

Yet Dovzhenko distinguishes between such blind superstition and the elements of the supernatural common to folklore. The slow motion at the beginning of the first part as well as the slow motion and double exposure of the Roksana story lend both sections a quality of fantasy. The Cossacks in the opening may prove comic bunglers in their efforts to recover the treasure, but like the gallant Cossacks of legend, they show incredible powers in ridding the land of Polish parasites. In a passage borrowed intact from a Shevchenko poem,[14] the Cossacks sing songs about eliminating the perennial villains, and they then proceed, with their eyes closed, to pick off the Poles at will. This prowess finds its echo in Grandfather's strength in the Roksana legend, when he knocks down invaders like dominoes.

Such military success, however, is reserved for the legends. The modern sections contain no such battle glories, and the success of the revolution owes nothing to military power. Dovzhenko never shows a victorious revolutionary army. War only disrupts the natural flow of life. Dovzhenko prefaces the outbreak of the World War, for example, with a pastoral passage, showing people, animals, and the land in fundamental harmony. The people and the animals both feed off the natural fecundity of the land. Men working in the field rhythmically cut grain with their scythes. Dovzhenko intercuts these shots with women thrashing clothes at the riverbank to the same rhythm as that of the scythes, thus linking the social and natural realms. But the World War interrupts this scene. The steady swinging of the bell's clapper replaces the scythes in a graphic match. This warning bell announces the arrival of war and the termination of this harmonious, productive existence. In a dissolve, stacks of rifles replace haystacks to signify that the war will interrupt productive labor. The revolution also disrupts the general social order. The blowing up of the bridge in the second section originates the beginning of violent revolution. Men leave their jobs in factories and mines and pour into the streets in a general upheaval. But Dovzhenko never shows a Bolshevik victory in the field. The only battle in the revolution has Timosh's Red troops routed by Pavlo's White forces, and the cost to civilian life and property is grievous.

Dovzhenko suggests that industrial strength rather than military power assures the Bolshevik triumph. The revolution succeeds in *Zvenigora* not through the destructive efforts of an armed force but through the productive capacity of the workers and peasants. In a lengthy sequence following the Red Army's military defeat, a Bolshevik warns his followers: "The revolution is in danger." He urges them to build the revolution through industry. Power in *Zvenigora* emanates not from the barrel of a gun but from the shaft of a coal mine. In a montage of associations, Dovzhenko shows the development of a healthy, modern Ukraine under the Bolshevik policy of modernization. First we see coal taken from the ground. This coal is then used to make steel. Modern machines and tractors are produced from the steel, and this machinery, in turn, is transported to the countryside to increase agricultural production. This leads to an abundant harvest. As a result of the harvest, healthy men and women participate in celebrations and athletic contests. The revolution in *Zvenigora* is built from the ground up, and it creates a dynamic society. In contrast to the false belief in superstition and miracles, the Bolsheviks create a genuine miracle of revolution by transforming the Ukraine's social and economic systems.

Grandfather's tragedy is that he fails to recognize the true treasure of the Ukraine: its natural resources and potential for development. In the script, Grandfather discovers the treasure, but in the film he searches in vain. At one point Dovzhenko cuts on a graphic match from miners hauling a load of coal from the mouth of a mine to Grandfather backing out of his hole with a worthless, rusty sword. The relic is small reward for Grandfather's prodigious labors. It contrasts with the vital work of the miners and exposes the misguided nature of Grandfather's search.

Ironically, the true secret of Zvenigora resides in the legend of Roksana all along, but Grandfather merely misinterprets his own tale.

He thinks riches are represented by the invaders' gold-laden ship, but they actually are embodied in Roksana. When she dies and her features are magically transformed into the terrain of the countryside, we realize that the feminine, fertile aspect of the land is the source of life and wealth. The opening title of the film had proclaimed that the treasures of the Ukrainian soil had been "sealed in secrecy and shrouded in legend." It would be for the progressive, rational forces represented by Timosh to penetrate the symbolic nature of the legend to locate the actual treasure of the Ukraine.

Grandfather's error does not prove fatal for him in the film, as in the script. Only when the legends give rise to cynical exploiters of tradition, like Pavlo, do they become lethal. Fittingly, Pavlo, not Grandfather, dies at the film's climax. Pavlo's earlier sham suicide foreshadows the suicidal path he has chosen—the path of reaction. The scenes of the bloodthirsty Paris audience contain a superimposition of the enormous face of a bourgeois figure hovering over the crowd. This image harks back to the apparition of the monk whose face appears in large superimpositions in the prologue and during Grandfather's dream. By thus invoking the supernatural monk, Dovzhenko suggests the lingering potential for harm in legends when they are exploited for counterrevolutionary ends by the likes of Pavlo.

When the Bolshevik train takes Grandfather aboard, however, the gesture signifies the new Ukraine's generous tolerance of the old. Dovzhenko insists that the traditions associated with Grandfather should not be completely abandoned. The old man who enters the film leading a broken-down *telega* in the time of the Cossacks leaves in the twentieth century on a powerful locomotive. Ultimately, Grandfather's function is to mediate between those extremes. The progressive Komsomols welcome Grandfather aboard with an old form of communion, tea from a samovar, suggesting that the modern Ukraine must remain in touch with its past. (fig. 8)

The film concludes with the locomotive speeding at the camera like the prow of the ship at the end of *Battleship Potemkin*. The train, like the ship, rushes headlong into the promise of the future. Significantly, the train runs past the mountain Zvenigora. The juxtaposition of an aggressive, modern train with a tradition-laden pastoral environment illustrates the dualism of so much of Dovzhenko's work. Dovzhenko could not, in the final analysis, allow the train to kill Grandfather, as he had in the scenario. He needed the character to help effect a reconciliation.

In a larger sense, Dovzhenko uses the character to hold together his broad narrative by having Grandfather personify the various cultural conflicts the film seeks to encompass. A character constructed of antino-

Figure 8. *Zvenigora*

mies, Grandfather defines at once backward superstition and legitimate respect for folk legend, peasant conservatism and peasant rebelliousness against oppression, a political liability and a valued historical legacy.

That Dovzhenko's original audience often found his film, with its intricate conception and ambitious realization, to be incomprehensible disturbed the director. He chafed at reports of spectator confusion and criticisms such as the one printed in *Pravda* which stated that *Zvenigora* lacked ideological clarity.[15] Having designated this film his party membership card, Dovzhenko was forced to answer his critics, including party spokesmen, with the taunt, "Look for the reason for incomprehensibility in yourself."[16]

There is evidence, however, that Dovzhenko learned from *Zvenigora*'s reception. He had sought in the film to treat the relation between tradition and modernity through inclusiveness by spreading his narrative over different epochs. In subsequent films he would take up similar themes but would insert them into narrower, narrative frameworks. As one Soviet writer noted, if *Zvenigora* can be considered a "horizontal section" of Ukrainian history, one that ranges across centuries, then *Arsenal* is a "vertical section" of the same terrain, with events compressed into a single year of the Ukrainian revolution.[17] The two designs represent different means of dealing with similar problems.

V

Arsenal

In January 1918 the Ukrainian civil war came to Kiev. The ancient city became a battleground as pro-Bolshevik partisans fought Rada troops. At the center of the six-day battle was the effort to capture Kiev's "Arsenal" munitions plant. Factory workers and Bolshevik sympathizers barricaded themselves within the fortresslike plant and defended it to the last man against superior Rada forces. Today the arsenal remains standing in Kiev, complete with battle scars on the outer walls, as a monument to the revolution.[1]

This Alamo-like incident approached the status of legend in Soviet accounts of the revolution and merited commemoration on the occasion of its tenth in anniversary. Dovzhenko's *Arsenal* emerged from the film industry's continuing series of anniversary films. "The assignment to make the film was entirely political, set by the Party," noted Dovzhenko.[2] If, as the *Pravda* review of *Zvenigora* suggests, Soviet officials were concerned about the ideological ambiguity of *Zvenigora*, they may have expected Dovzhenko to pay unequivocal tribute to the revolution in this storied episode of worker militancy and sacrifice.

Although *Arsenal* thus originated as a political assignment under the Communist party's ever more stringent guidelines for cinema, the finished film contains its own ambiguities and remains, in fact, one of the few Soviet political films which seems even to cast doubt on the morality of violent revolution. Dovzhenko examines the revolution and civil war in moral terms in *Arsenal*, and he fluctuates between celebration of the revolutionary spirit and reservations about the turmoil and human misery caused by revolutionary violence. How, then, does he represent these conflicting strains in the film, and how does he try to reconcile them?

Dovzhenko's original design for *Arsenal* was significantly different from that of the finished film. He initially planned for the arsenal siege to appear at the beginning. From that point he intended to dramatize the spreading of the revolution throughout the Ukraine. All was then to end triumphantly with the capture of Kiev by the Red Army.[3] This version recalls the direct, simple structure of *Battleship Potemkin,* in which the spirit of revolution emanates from a single ship to encompass an entire fleet.

The final version of *Arsenal* more accurately represents the vagaries of the actual civil war experience. Dovzhenko captures this chaotic milieu in the film through a fragmented narrative. Rather than developing scenes as autonomous dramatic units, he shifts frenetically among various lines of action. Whereas *Zvenigora* employs a broad, episodic narrative, *Arsenal* is tightly structured through a network of internal allusions and recurring images. Each moment of apparently didactic exhortation to revolutionary action is counterpointed by sotto voce misgivings about the human costs of revolution. The same resonating motifs and visual details that weld the narrative together also convey the moral complexity that Dovzhenko sees at the heart of the Soviet revolution itself. The rich texture of the film derives from this tension.

A plot synopsis of *Arsenal* only begins to convey its intricacies. During the last months of the World War, domestic life in the Ukraine is characterized by economic hardship which renders the people callous to the point of catatonia. At the front, the German army doggedly advances on the Ukrainian position, but the Ukrainians have deserted the field to return home. The Ukrainian deserters meet catastrophe when their train crashes. With the war's end, the Rada attempts to solidify its position in the Ukraine with a parade, a rally, and a political convention, but the workers at Kiev's "Arsenal" munitions factory strike to declare their opposition to the Rada and their allegiance to the Bolsheviks. The central character, Timosh, commands a Red Army detachment which helps defend the strike from Rada forces. Rada troops attack the arsenal, disrupting life in Kiev. Revolution spreads throughout the Ukrainian countryside, but the Rada captures the factory and systematically executes its defenders. Timosh, however, makes a last stand against the Rada soldiers and proves invincible.

In its broadest outline, the narrative of *Arsenal* divides into two unequal parts. The prologuelike first part, roughly the first quarter of the film, concerns the last phases of World War I and the wartime deprivation in the Ukraine. Part two, the main body of the film, comprises the material on the revolution and civil war. Thus, *Arsenal*'s two-part structure encompasses two conflicts: one, a war resulting from corrupt, imperialist policies, and the other, a proletarian uprising to unite Moscow and Kiev in a socialist system. The first part, with its depiction of ubiquitous hardship and senseless cruelty, forms a sordid touchstone against which the viewer may draw a moral judgment about the revolution that follows in part two. This simple structure would provide a conventional propagandist with an opportunity to contrast the two wars, to make the revolution appear all the more glorious in light of the ugliness of the World War. But Dovzhenko insists that the revolution is morally ambiguous. The allusions that run through the film consistently equate the World War with the revolution, casting moral doubt on the revolutionary effort. In many respects, part two becomes a recapitulation of part one: the revolutionary dream gives way to the same debasement and chaos which characterize the World War. The consequences of war—the sacrifice of innocents and the waste of human energy and productivity—pervade proletarian uprisings as well as imperialist conflicts.

The train wreck sequence is pivotal, providing the break between the two sections. The train carries Ukrainian deserters returning from the front—men who have abandoned the futile war with the Germans and, in so doing, have rejected the old order and its policies. While the train crash is an enormous catastrophe, it is also an essential purging. The shot of the aftermath of the crash, with the smoke and twisted rubble, is an image of utter destruction. The only course is a completely new beginning, and as is traditionally the case, renewal follows purgation. The central character, Timosh, seems literally to rise from the dead when he emerges from the wreckage, as if he were granted a new life to participate in the rebuilding.

In the next two scenes Dovzhenko develops this theme of regeneration only to undercut it. The end of the World War is marked by tableaus of veterans from various European nations returning to their homes and their wives. The wives all stand with infants in their arms. The classic madonnalike poses of the women and the presence of icons in the homes lend religious overtones to the section. But these traditional images of renewal give way to bitter irony in the fact that the women have given birth to illegitimate children in their husbands' absence. An entire European generation, the sequence suggests, is made up of the war's bastard children. The following scene shows Timosh returning to the Kiev munitions plant to resume his peacetime occupation. Timosh appears before the factory boss in a composition which recalls that of the returning husbands. And the boss's question—"Who are you?"—echoes the "Who-Qui-Wer" questions the husbands put to their unfaithful wives. In a sense, Timosh is both returning veteran and bastard child, returning from war, yet figuratively "born" out of war's aftermath. He seeks to start anew in a constructive life divorced from militarism, but his two roles, "demobilized soldier and arsenal worker," are both associated with warfare. His civilian craft is an extension of the soldier's art. In both scenes, the promise of uncorrupted renewal is betrayed. The contaminating remnants of the conflict linger on.

No class in *Arsenal* is without a measure of responsibility for the general degradation that accompanies combat. In the early sections detailing the hardships of civilian life during the World War, a peasant woman attempts to sow grain in an enormous field. She staggers under the weight of her grain sack and the even greater burden of the hopeless prospect of making anything grow in the war-ravaged terrain. The preceding title—"The mother had no sons"—is an ironic comment on the cause of her toil; Dovzhenko cuts to a shot of her crippled son, a legless veteran sitting on the floor of their home. He has been rendered the equivalent of an inanimate object, as useless as the military medal which shines on his chest. As the woman stumbles and falls exhausted in the field, Dovzhenko cuts to shots of Tsar Nicholas II making a trivial diary entry and a worker in the Kiev munitions factory in a pose mirroring that of the tsar. This juxtaposition ascribes to the callous, petty tsar responsibility for the woman's plight. But the worker who is equated with the tsar also seems implicated. He helps to execute the tsar's misguided policies by manufacturing the materials of war. The resultant fighting cripples the son, and the woman in turn must do a man's work in the field. The World War consists of an elaborate, vicious system of destruction which incorporates all classes in the Ukraine.

An equally pernicious and pervasive system forms in the second part of the film, growing out of the revolutionary hostilities. The Rada troops lay siege to the Red Army forces in the Kiev arsenal, and sporadic shooting between the two sides disrupts life in the city. Dovzhenko does not show the firing of rifles by the opposing factions; he focuses instead on the targets, the innocent civilians capriciously struck down by invisible bullets. A proletarian woman carrying food to the arsenal and a bourgeois man drinking water simultaneously fall prey to snipers: two acts designed to sustain life are suddenly terminated by random death in civil strife. A close-up of the dead woman stands as a parallel to the image of the woman who had fallen in the field in part one. One carried seed to grow food, the other food to preserve life. The waste of innocent life is as much a part of revolution as it is of an imperialist war.

The fighting also perverts the productive capacities of men. Part one contains a section on the manufacture of munitions for the World War at the Kiev factory. Close-ups of machines display abstract patterns of revolving gears and rhythmic engine parts. In numerous other Soviet films such a passage would represent a paean to the aesthetic beauty of the machine. But this sequence falls in the context of scenes depicting war's waste, and Dovzhenko deplores the irony of the efficient production which translates into misery and death. The munitions plant itself evokes a two-edged association. It is both productive, a working factory and a storage center providing the livelihoods for the workers in the film, and destructive, the source of the munitions which ravage the Ukraine. Ironically, the workers become victims of their own industriousness; they produce the ordnance which ultimately ruins their homeland.

Machines fare badly in part two as well: a train crashes, an armored car explodes, a machine gun misfires. As the battle for the factory reaches its climax, the entire Kievan economy breaks down: "There is no blacksmith. And where is the mechanic?" Images of the stilled gears of the machines follow these titles reminding us that the men killed in battle will never resume their trades. The machines have finally ground to a halt. They stand idle in the wake of the war's crippling effects.

War seems almost self-perpetuating in *Arsenal;* it grows and spreads beyond anyone's control. The German line in the World War advances on what the Germans believe to be the Ukrainian position, but it is only an empty trench; the Ukrainian troops have abandoned the absurd venture and begun their journey home. For the remaining German forces, the war continues even without the Ukrainian enemy. The faceless German line must press forward even though the justification for the campaign has evaporated. When one German soldier discovers the empty trench and asks, "Where is the enemy?" he questions the rationale for the entire undertaking. His question is answered when a German officer materializes and executes him for refusing to continue the senseless advance. The German officer supplants the Ukrainians as the enlisted man's enemy. The scene implies that class enemies cut across national identities and sets up the class conflict that ensues in part two of the film.

That conflict crystallizes in the second part when the bourgeois Rada seeks to suppress the workers' strike, and Kiev is rent into warring camps. Dovzhenko addresses the moral dilemma of a class war which fragments society. He cautions that the proletariat stands to lose far more than its chains; also at stake for the workers is their recognition of the common humanity of all classes. A worker at a political rally asks if it will "be all right to kill officers and bourgeois in the street if we find any?" The question concerns more than tactics. It confronts the fundamental moral issue of the revolution: Given that there are class enemies, does the proletariat possess the moral authority to eliminate them sys-

Figure 9. *Arsenal*

tematically? As the fighting in Kiev intensifies, the worker's question
echoes in increasingly bitter contexts. A scene in a makeshift hospital in
the arsenal finds a nurse writing a letter dictated by a dying proletarian.
The letter reiterates the question asking permission to kill officers and
bourgeois. When the nurse inquires to whom she should address the letter but discovers that the soldier has already died, she turns, faces directly into the camera, and speaks to the audience. (fig. 9) "I ask you—
all of you," she says, "is it all right to kill officers and bourgeois in the
street if I find any?" She speaks for the dead worker, and in calling on
the audience ("all of you"), she turns the moral problem posed by the
question outward. Shots of desperate hand-to-hand combat between
Rada and Red Army troops follow her question. One might be tempted
to assume that Dovzhenko answers the question with an emphatic yes. A
revolution, he seems to proclaim, requires ruthless measures. But
Dovzhenko remains apprehensive about any such merciless conclusion.
The shots of street fighting, with the bodies of the dead trampled under-
foot, suggest pure anarchy. The identities of the factions are blurred, the
killing indiscriminate. The chaos of the image acknowledges that the issue
of executing class enemies is posed in deceptively rational terms; the men
involved in the street fighting cannot isolate and exterminate class enemies
with any of the surgical precision implicit in the question. The rev-

Figure 10. *Arsenal*

olution, like the World War, becomes a self-perpetuating phenomenon engulfing all classes in the Ukraine.

War not only destroys; it cruelly deceives. During the German army's advance on the empty trench in part one, a German soldier becomes intoxicated by the laughing gas of his own contingent and sheds his gas mask in a fit of hideous laughter. Dovzhenko intercuts close-ups of the soldier's laughing face with shots of the grinning death mask of a German corpse. He literally laughs at death, the ultimate nihilistic act of a man who has yielded to the madness of armed conflict.

The celebration of the Rada troops after their triumph in part two harks back to this sequence. A victorious Rada soldier breaks into a spirited dance, and Dovzhenko cuts from the smoke of battle to a close-up of the soldier's grinning face. The smoke parallels the gas in the World War, and the grinning soldier resembles the laughing German. (figs. 10 and 11) This ecstasy is as perverse as the German soldier's grin. The Rada forces prove as intoxicated with the battle as the German soldier was with the gas; their victory is as false as the German's euphoria. Dovzhenko extends the analogy by cutting to the staring face of a dead worker, a repetition of the juxtaposition of the laughing German with the corpse. There can be no true joy or celebration in such contexts. Even the victors abandon their reason, and the corpse has the last word.

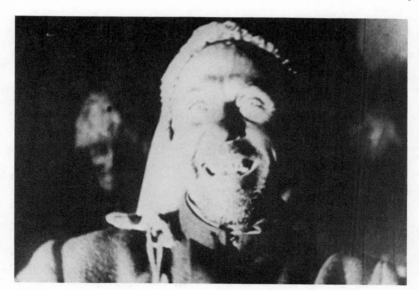

Figure 11. *Arsenal*

Technology is frequently the demon in *Arsenal,* not because it is inherently harmful, but because it magnifies the follies of men. Men misuse or lose control of the machine, and it in turn punishes them. The train exemplifies the paradox of the man-made instrument which defies human direction. The Ukrainian deserters initiate the disaster by insisting that the train proceed despite faulty brakes, but during the journey the train seems to take on a diabolical will of its own. It rushes headlong, bewildering its ineffectual, amateur engineers, and the soldiers leap desperately from the train just before it crashes. The train destroys not only its human cargo but also the station for which it was bound—a savage punishment for the initial poor judgment of the too impatient veterans.

Several sequences in part two elaborate this theme of the workers' relationship to technology, and allusions to the train ride abound. Dovzhenko constructs the sequence of the return and burial of the Bolshevik soldier as the antithesis of the train sequence. While the train represents technology gone berserk, the odyssey of the dying Bolshevik features men working in harmony with the land. The passage opens with the bodies of countless Red Army soldiers lying alongside a railroad track. The rows of bodies remind us of the men who had leaped to their deaths from the train. One man lying near the track senses he is near death, and he asks his comrades to carry him home for burial via a horse-drawn gun carriage. The horses meanwhile feed on grass growing between the railroad ties; technology gives way to these animals, emphasizing the difference between this journey and the train ride. Not only does the organic realm supplant the mechanical, but the sequence unfolds by reversing the direction of the train ride. The train had been returning from the front; the carriage moves into battle. The horses convey both a dying man and a machine gun. The Red Army soldiers who urge the horses forward have a double mission. They must take their comrade to burial, and then they must move on to relieve the beleaguered Bolshevik partisans in Kiev.

The men face no danger of mechanical failure in this sequence; rather than relying on unpredictable machines, they work in perfect harmony with nature. The horses sense the revolutionary élan and the excitement of their mission. In part one, a horse verbally chastises an old man for his pointless brutality. Now horses again speak, but this time they affirm the bond of revolution they feel with their masters. They recite a litany dedicated to the revolutionary ideal. "We feel it in the air," the horses proclaim, and the rapport between man and nature pervades the sequence. The carriage comes upon a woman who stands by a freshly dug grave. She seems a permanent, indelible part of the landscape, a stoic figure waiting specifically to take in the fallen soldier. In the collective spirit of the land, it matters not whether this is her son, and the association of the mother and the grave physically represents the life cycle. "There is no time for explanations," the soldiers tell her as they lay their comrade to rest. "Such is our revolutionary life." As the carriage moves off, Dovzhenko cuts to a close-up of the machine gun. With the first part of their mission completed, the men must take their second burden, the gun, into battle. The revolutionary course, the juxtaposition implies, has become the consuming mission of these men during their brief interim between the womb and the grave.

The carriage's destination is Kiev, where the furious street fighting contrasts with the serenity of the grave scene. The Rada's chief weapon is an armored car, a sinister mass of black iron which rolls through the streets of Kiev. Whereas the Bolsheviks in the previous scene are identified with the natural rhythms of the land, the Rada relies entirely on technology. As the armored car approaches a Bolshevik soldier who lies apparently dead across a set of trolley tracks, the man suddenly springs to life and ignites a bomb which blows up the machine. His feigning death on the tracks again alludes back to the men who died during the train sequence. This man "comes back to life" to destroy a piece of machinery which is even more odious than the train.

When the Bolshevik fighter is captured and brought before a bourgeois Rada official, he engages in a test of wills with his enemy. The
Rada official had been a speaker in the ceremony in St. Sofia Square
and a delegate to the subsequent convention, while the Bolshevik had
been a member of the central committee of the workers' cell at the munitions plant. Both men hold formal political positions in opposite camps,
but now they confront each other in a test which far exceeds the demands
of political office or ceremony. The purpose of the confrontation is the
execution of the Bolshevik, but the Rada official lacks the determination
to fire his pistol at the defenseless prisoner. When the Bolshevik takes the
gun from the bourgeois, he addresses the earlier question of killing officers and bourgeois. The Bolshevik is prepared to act ruthlessly. He
barely hesitates before firing the fatal shot, and in so doing seems to confirm the necessity of dispassionately shooting down enemies of the revolution. But again Dovzhenko reneges. Just as the Bolshevik fires the
gun, Dovzhenko cuts to a pile of smoking shell casings and equates the
effect of a single pistol discharge with the extreme consequences of a full
artillery barrage. Moreover, the image of the smoking shells recalls the
rubble of the train wreck, thus linking the effect of revolutionary violence with that earlier holocaust. An image of devastation continually
haunts Dovzhenko's revolutionary vision. (figs. 12 and 13)

Finally, Dovzhenko does not even promise that a harmonious socialist
society will emerge from the turmoil of revolution. For the workers, the
price of the struggle is so dear, the experience so painful, that they never
envision anything more optimistic than some abatement of the hostilities. During the last desperate hours of the siege, the Red Army soldiers
entertain no illusions of militancy or valor. The factory defenders lie on
the ramparts beside their weapons, weary and abject as a result of the
unending siege. One man asks, "I wonder what the weather is going to
be tomorrow?"

The question recalls the tsar's diary entry in part one in which Nicholas had complacently noted that the weather was fine. As far as the indifferent tsar was concerned, all was well with the world. The men at the
factory, however, consider the future—tomorrow's weather—and the
outlook is bleak. "Tomorrow," a comrade says, "I thought it would be
finished—but we went and stopped—stopped." They completely dismiss the future and remain resigned to defeat as the only relief from their
ordeal.

The collapse of the revolutionary effort, the defeat of the arsenal
strikers, culminates in the breakdown of all social relations. The strike's
only legacy is chaos. *Arsenal* apparently does not even promise that the

Figure 12. *Arsenal*

ideal of revolution will persist. Or does it? The film concludes with a
dramatic turn. Timosh makes a belligerent last stand, and when his machine gun jams, enemy troops overrun his position. Timosh brashly in-
vites them to shoot, but their bullets fail to harm him. Then in an
extraordinary denouement, the Rada soldiers literally disappear in the
face of his defiance. Timosh's sudden invulnerability stems from his development as a representative of revolutionary idealism. As the film progresses he achieves an increasingly acute revolutionary consciousness.
He eventually becomes a spokesman and leader for the Bolshevik forces,
and he takes on a strength of mission which renders him invincible. He
becomes less a soldier than the personification of an ideal ("There is
something here you cannot kill"). As such he is more awesome than the
armored car ("Is he wearing armor?" a foe asks) and a more effective
weapon than a machine gun. Despite the military debacle, the revolutionary ideal endures and inevitably triumphs. It is as infinite and eternal as the land. The question is not one of killing officers and bourgeois
but of developing revolutionary commitment that will render them ex-
tinct.

Yet this effort at an exhilarating finale strikes a somewhat false note,
no doubt because it comes in the wake of all the agony associated with
the revolutionary effort itself. This deus ex machina ending is intended

Figure 13. *Arsenal*

to resolve the moral dilemma inherent in revolutionary action. In *Zveni-gora* Dovzhenko looks to industrial development rather than military prowess to account for the revolution's success. But that course is ruled out in *Arsenal* by the film's meticulous documentation of the industrial chaos wrought by war. Instead *Arsenal* offers the option of sidestepping the bloody revolutionary violence in favor of a vaguely defined but supposedly invincible ideal.

Such is Dovzhenko's effort to reconcile the film's military topic to its pacifistic reservations. Significantly, Dovzhenko rallies folklore to his task. His Soviet audience would recognize the venerable source for the film's conclusion in a set of tales about peasant leader Oleks Dovbush, who led an eighteenth-century peasant rebellion and who, according to legend, possessed the power to repel bullets: "And then the whole army shot at him, but the bullets bounced off him as if off a cast-iron slab. They shot him in the mouth, and he swallowed the bullets as if they were cherry pits."[4] Characteristically, Dovzhenko looks to the past to resolve a modern dilemma. In this film in which horses not only talk but address the burden of revolution, we should not be surprised that Dovzhenko appeals to an enduring folk motif to help him address a problem of the modern political realm.

Arsenal's interrogation of the revolution's consequences may have undercut the production's original commemorative assignment, but of more immediate concern to party officials was the absence of reference to the Bolshevik leadership. Unlike Eisenstein's *October,* for example, *Arsenal* ignores the platforms and strategies of the party elite to concentrate on the sacrifices of private individuals, a tactic at variance with the *partiinost'* mandate. This brought public criticism from Communist party representatives, leading Dovzhenko to answer angrily, "I wanted to make a film about the revolution, not the palace revolution, but the revolution of peasants, workers, and intellectuals who made the revolution and then did not get anything."[5] Such open debate over such a seemingly minor omission revealed the potential for public criticism and conflict that Dovzhenko's growing stature gave him, especially in light of the increasing rigidity of the Stalinist political apparatus. Dovzhenko's next and most controversial film would provide the test.

VI
Earth

IN THE SPRING OF 1930 the city of Kharkov hosted a major cultural event. The principal figures of Soviet Ukrainian arts and letters—at least those who had survived the anti-VAPLITE campaign—gathered to honor Alexander Dovzhenko, an artist who had emerged from their own ranks, and to preview the film recently touted as the finest yet produced by the Ukrainian cinema, *Earth*. The assembled artists, poets, and journalists proved an enthusiastic audience, bursting into applause at the film's conclusion. This film, they rightly predicted, would become the work for which Dovzhenko would be best remembered.[1]

The congenial atmosphere was short-lived, however, as *Earth* became the subject of an intense controversy. Even in this sympathetic Kharkov audience, the film found a detractor, a journalist who pronounced the film ideologically "vicious," and that judgment foreshadowed harsher responses.[2] When *Earth* went into general distribution, Dovzhenko found himself in the midst of a national controversy as the political and artistic press subjected the film to unusual scrutiny. *Pravda* praised the film for its beauty and originality but condemned its political message as "false." An official preview before government representatives added to the controversy: Red Army spokesmen endorsed *Earth,* but a party official used the occasion to accuse Dovzhenko of squandering much-needed public funds on politically useless films.[3]

The most influential criticism came from Demian Bedny, a confidant of Stalin and the recognized "Kremlin poet," who published a stinging review in *Izvestia* in the form of a satirical poem which ridiculed Dovzhenko for taking an overly "philosophical" attitude toward political reality. Bedny offered the review's title, "Philosophers," as a term of derision.

75

On homebred
Cine-simplified philosophers,
On political dispassion
And on the movie *Earth* in particular.

.   .   .   .

I am now an active saboteur.
Not that I have enmity toward Soviet work
But simply to me this film is STRANGE![4]

Dovzhenko had fielded easily enough the charges directed at *Arsenal* and *Zvenigora,* the accusations of incomprehensibility and calls for greater commitment to *partiinost'*. Now for the first time in his career, his work generated controversy that assumed the character of national urgency. Certainly few Soviet films gave rise to as much domestic debate as *Earth*. Like Eisenstein's *Old and New* the film concerns rural collectivization in the Soviet Union. It appeared at a crucial moment in the implementation of that policy, and the sense of crisis that accompanied all-out collectivization accounts, in part, for the degree of official concern over this film. The passion of *Earth*'s original reception should encourage us to inquire about the film's relationship to its historical moment, something that Western scholars have generally refrained from doing, preferring instead to limit discussion to the film's style.[5]

As is his wont, Dovzhenko fashions a tale out of social conflict and then seeks a narrative strategy of resolution. *Earth* certainly draws from the record of social antagonism that marked collectivization: indeed, the central action of the narrative, Vasyl's murder, takes its historical source from the assassination by kulaks of a Soviet agent in Dovzhenko's home district.[6] In examining the tactic Dovzhenko employs to resolve the conflicts the film invokes, we will see that he creates a fictional "natural order" of life, death, and rebirth in the film's narrative and inserts collectivization into that cycle. Through juxtapositions that equate the processes of nature with human actions, the narrative of *Earth* seeks to "naturalize" collectivization, to represent it as predetermined and proper, deriving from an innate quality of nature rather than from the policies and practices of government.

The film's narrative is simplicity itself. It opens with the death of Grandfather Simon in an orchard. He is attended by family and friends, including his son Opanas, his grandson Vasyl, and his old friend Peter. Meanwhile local kulaks vow to resist efforts to collectivize the farms of the area. Opanas is one of the opponents of the policy, but Vasyl and the local Komsomols actively support the collective. Vasyl leads a delegation which brings the collective its first tractor. With the help of the tractor, the peasants have a successful harvest. While Vasyl dances the *hopak* to celebrate the harvest, he is murdered by the kulak Khoma. Inspired by his son's sacrifice, Opanas decides to support the collective and leads the funeral procession which helps unite the village in support of the new system.

To appreciate the problems addressed in this deceptively simple narrative, we must look briefly at the Soviet rural situation and the conflicts collectivization generated, conditions that Dovzhenko knew firsthand.[7] The roots of the issue lay in the nineteenth century and in the shortage of arable land to support the peasant population. With the emancipation of 1861 came the necessity to distribute land among landlords and ex-serfs, and this gave rise to the commune system, whereby groups of peasants shared blocks of land. This system proved somewhat inefficient, as it stifled individual peasant initiative, and in 1906 the tsarist regime commenced a gradual set of reforms in which communal land was split into individual holdings. For the first time in much of the empire, peasants were permitted to own land, bequeath it to heirs, and experience a measure of economic independence. But the redistribution proved a slow, arduous process and often only increased the power of the kulaks. When the Bolsheviks came to power in 1917, they had to contend with an abiding desire among much of the peasantry to maintain family farms. Through the NEP period, the government tolerated private farming and the right of peasants to sell harvests at whatever price the market would bear. Formation of cooperative farms was encouraged under NEP but remained voluntary.

When Stalin initiated rapid industrialization of the Soviet economy in 1929, he called for consolidation of private holdings into large collective farms and an end to "rural capitalism." Serious grain shortages in the late 1920s, stemming in part from peasant work slowdowns and kulak manipulations of the market, prompted the timing of forced collectivization, but as important was Stalin's general recognition that if his industrialization plans were to succeed, the government would have to take control of the rural economy, reorganize and integrate agricultural production, and put an end to kulak authority in the villages. Predicting that kulaks would encourage resistance to such a plan, Stalin issued an ominous proclamation: "We must smash the kulaks, eliminate them as a class."[8] Collectivization would be accompanied by "dekulakization," and previous tactics encouraging voluntary enlistment in collectives would give way to force.

Rural collectivization proved to be one of the bloody passages of Soviet history. Harsh government tactics only stiffened peasant determination to retain private holdings, and peasants fought back with sabotage, including destruction of crops and livestock. Kulaks resorted to acts of violence against Soviet officials, and government agents responded by increasing the brutality of their own tactics. The situation reached a crisis point in the spring of 1930, when Stalin had to step in and warn followers against "excesses" in the enforcement of collectivization. But as the process continued through the early and middle thirties, it was estimated that the famines, killings, and labor camp deaths which accompanied collectivization took a toll of human lives running into the millions.

Such violence especially characterized the situation in Dovzhenko's native Ukraine, the setting for *Earth.* The Soviet government was particularly determined to enforce collectivization in this rich agricultural region, but the plan met much popular resistance in the Ukraine because Ukrainian peasants had long worked under a system of individual holdings, even during the era of serfdom. With the emancipation, they retained their family plots and generally fared better than their Russian counterparts in the rural economy. Hence, Ukrainian peasants had a greater stake in the status quo and proved fiercely loyal to the tradition of private ownership, making Ukrainian collectivization especially difficult.[9]

Through it all, the government and the peasants adopted something approaching a war mentality. The government apparatus organized to enforce the policy consisted largely of Red Army veterans, who often employed tactics they had learned in the civil war, and combat motifs figured prominently in government rhetoric on the program. In the midst of the equivalent of a military mobilization, at a moment of upheaval that had Stalin worrying publicly about "excesses," Dovzhenko offered as his contribution to the new system his lyrical *Earth.*

Dovzhenko in *Earth* appeals to the pastoral traditions which were part of his background and which he calculated were closest to his intended audience, the Soviet peasants who would be most affected by collectivization. *Earth* represents the most restrained and least oblique of Dovzhenko's major silent films. The narrative lacks the many disjunctive devices of *Zvenigora* and *Arsenal,* and its very simplicity has ideological significance. In the earlier films Dovzhenko dealt with the chaos of the Ukrainian revolution, and he sought to project that condition through narratives marked by sharp discontinuity and through his professed tactic of compressing the material of several films into one. The concern of *Earth,* however, is with cohesion and continuity as Dovzhneko creates an image of a world in repose and suggests that social revolution can still sustain order, an order that comes from the stability of nature.

As indicated in the film's title, the natural terrain is the central concern, and in fact, the Ukrainian-Russian title, *Zemlia,* actually means soil, land, or ground. The soil—rich, stable, enduring—serves as the film's title character.

The film's rhetoric of naturalization suggests that the opponents of collectivization were somehow destined to pass out of existence as the seasons pass and that time and nature would heal social wounds. Dovzhenko represents social revolution as the equivalent of seasonal transition and endeavors thereby to provide a fictional reconciliation of the social conflicts that surfaced during the turmoil of collectivization. The specific strategies Dovzhenko employs to this end can be understood through a fuller discussion of the film's narrative.

The sense of tranquility that dominates the narrative of *Earth* is made manifest at the very beginning of the film. Consider the opening scene and the resignation with which old Simon faces death. Dovzhenko has remarked of the scene that the old man seems simply to fall "from life like an apple from a tree."[10] The scene's mood suggests that the old man, having lived a full life, now faces death with complete equanimity. His death evokes a sense of unity between man and nature. After a series of dissolves among shots of apples on trees, Dovzhenko dissolves to the figure of Simon on the ground. The numerous graphic matches on the round shape of the apples culminate with a shot of the soft, round head and face of Simon, suggesting that he is as natural and innate a part of the terrain as the apples.

The connection between the grandfather and the fruit reappears in a series of associations that pertain to both life and death. Before Simon dies, he eats from a fresh apple. The crisp, clean fruit connotes health and vitality, especially since the infant children at Simon's side also munch on fresh apples. Simon's apple is offered to him in almost ceremonial fashion, as if he were partaking of communion. The granddaughter is then shown holding her bowl of apples at her stomach in a pose that is later matched by Opanas's pregnant wife holding her bulging stomach, thus linking apples with fertility. Surrounding Simon on the ground, however, are fallen, overripe apples. (fig. 14) The fruit that lies on the ground, like the old man, is associated with death. These apples will never be eaten; they will decompose and enter back into the soil. But there they will replenish the ground and thus serve as a source of renewal. This opening scene is built around a series of associations of life, death, and regeneration, and these elements run throughout the film.

The notion that Simon, like the apples, returns to the earth to give rise

Figure 14. *Earth*

to new life recurs later in the scene at Simon's grave. There the superstitious Peter attempts to communicate with the dead Simon to learn whether his friend can fulfill the promise to tell him of the experience of death. He kneels above the grave and asks, "Where are you, Simon?" He then puts his ear to the ground in the hope of hearing a response. Meanwhile, young children hiding behind a nearby grave tease the old man by making noises which he mistakes for Simon's answer from the grave. In addition, when Peter places his ear on the ground, Dovzhenko cuts to shots of Opanas plowing with oxen nearby, implying that Peter also hears that activity.

While this scene gently chides Peter's superstition on one level, on another level it subtly argues that there does indeed exist a form of life after death through biological renewal. The juxtaposition of the shots of the children, the plowing, and Peter at the grave provides a possible answer to the old man's question, "Where are you Simon?" In a way, the sounds Peter hears *are* Simon's response. If Simon is anywhere, he is one with the soil, the very soil Opanas tills. Moreover, he is, in a sense, reincarnated in his grandchildren who play nearby. The infinite possibility of replenishment is the ultimate lesson of Simon's death. The answer to Peter's question lies, the scene suggests, less in a religious or mystical definition of life after death than in a natural process of renewal.

The bond between man and his environment takes several forms in the film, including anthropomorphism. Frequently the natural environment seems to become animate and to interact with humans. When the family members stand together looking down at Simon in the opening scene, one shot shows an enormous sunflower bent in a position similar to that of the family members, seemingly gazing down at the old man. When Vasyl is carried off in the funeral procession, the branches and leaves of the trees gently brush against his face, as if they were reaching out to touch him one last time before he is taken to his grave. During moments of great excitement, horses react with the same fervor as the peasants. When village lookouts first spot the new tractor arriving in the distance, the horses turn their heads and glance down the road in eyeline matches which resemble those of humans, and when the villagers scurry to join the ranks of Vasyl's funeral, horses also lope toward the procession.

The most lyrical sequence suggesting the harmony between humans and nature occurs in the nocturnal passage that follows the harvest. The harvest had involved a dynamic ecstasy of labor, and the night scene shows the quiet satisfaction of rest. Various couples sit together under the summer moon in motionless rapture. The soft focus of the imagery and the summer mists of the landscape give the section a sense of peace. Some of the men have their hands on women's breasts, and the older couples lie in their marriage beds. This element of sex and fertility also relates to the lush, fertile landscapes of the evening and to the promise of health and life after the successful harvest. Vasyl's hopak which concludes the scene, a dance traditionally associated with a successful harvest, seems the culmination of his satisfaction, stemming from his unity with the environment; even the dust he raises with his dance lingers in the air and graphically resembles the night mists shown earlier, further associating him with the natural setting.

Vasyl's death at the climax of this sequence seems tragic because it represents a disruption of this sense of order. Death per se is not defined as tragic in *Earth;* it remains part of the process of assuring rebirth, as we have seen in the scene of Simon's death. The grandfather's death is open and public; the entire family is present for his final moments, and they accept it with equanimity as something proper and natural. But Vasyl's death is abrupt, untimely, a crime in violation of what the narrative has represented as the proper sequence of events.

Yet even Vasyl's death has its purpose because, like the death of a god in spring fertility rites, Vasyl's martyrdom solidifies the peasants. In other Soviet films as well, martyrdom serves to confirm the resolve of the other members of the community. The deaths of the bull in *Old and New,* of the boy in *Bezhin Meadow,* and of the juvenile in Ekk's *Road to Life* inspire the followers. Vasyl's death leads to the "Song of New Life" sung by the young members of the collective in the final scenes. What is more, Vasyl's funeral is juxtaposed with several references to fertility: the young people of the procession carry bouquets and branches, and as the funeral is underway, Vasyl's mother goes through labor and gives birth. We sense from this that nature provides its own compensation for Vasyl's death.

This routine of life, death, and rebirth, Dovzhenko suggests, is as fundamental as the seasonal blooming and withering of foliage. The kulaks prove the villains of *Earth* precisely because they fail to recognize the inevitability of the order and attempt to disrupt it. The kulaks are associated with death—and not the death that promises renewal—but the death of sterility and obsolescence. The assassin Khoma's last name is Belokon, which translates roughly as "white horse," a traditional symbol of death. The kulaks, furthermore, engage in wanton destruction; Khoma's father would rather slaughter his horse than surrender it to the collective. Finally, when Khoma goes berserk with guilt near the end of the film, he dances an ugly parody of Vasyl's dance. Whereas Vasyl's hopak is a private, spontaneous celebration, Khoma's frenzied dance becomes a comic spectacle. Significantly, it is acted out in a graveyard, suggesting that Khoma and the kulaks are doomed to obsolescence. The idea carries over from the scene of the tractor's arrival. Dovzhenko cuts on a graphic match from three oxen to three kulaks, implying that if the tractor will remove the need for oxen the collective will do the same for the kulaks. The refusal of the collective to recognize the kulaks at the film's end assures the eventual demise of the class. Khoma is left to dance alone in the graveyard until he simply falls to the ground in exhaustion and frustration. Vasyl's death is compensated in the end when his mother gives birth to another child, but there are no signs of fertility among the kulak families.

One of the tragedies of the civil war represented in *Arsenal* is the turmoil that robs the land of its natural fecundity; and the misuse of technology proves a major factor in this. But in *Earth* people work in conjunction with technology to cultivate the land. The machines improve humans' ability to perform the traditional labor of tilling the earth. When machines break down in *Arsenal* they produce catastrophe; when the tractor stalls in *Earth* it provides only a brief dilemma and somewhat comic solution. The peasants repair it by urinating into the radiator, thereby blending the organic and mechanical realms. Machines, like humans, can work in harmony with nature in this film. At

Vasyl's funeral, a Soviet speaker tells the villagers that Vasyl's fame will circle the globe. As a manifestation of this phenomenon, the orator does not seize on a mystical, ghostly image, but on a mechanical one; he compares Vasyl's spirit to a Soviet airplane that conveniently flies over the village at that instant. More important, the introduction of the tractor to the collective produces a work routine in which men, women, and machines operate in perfect unison. In the harvest sequence, Dovzhenko cuts between the work of the machines and the labors of the peasants, and the peasants develop an ecstatic rhythm as they work in synchronization with the machines.

The harvest sequence occupies a central position in the narrative and in Dovzhenko's effort to rationalize collectivization, and it is as important for what it omits as for what it includes. The sequence shows the stages of the growing and harvesting of the grain and the baking of bread. It begins with the initial plowing of the land. The sequence then proceeds to the cutting of the stalks with reapers. The stalks are promptly bundled and tied by hand. Machines shuck and separate the grain. The grain is then sorted, and we finally see the dough made from the flour kneaded, shaped into loaves, and baked. The sequence presumes to show the production of bread from the first planting of the seeds to the baking of the loaves.

One detail, however, remains conspicuously absent from the sequence. In the whole series of plowing, sowing, harvesting, and processing, the growing season is completely omitted. The entire operation seems to take place in one sunny afternoon in a single, labor-intensive effort. The crop is planted and harvested in a continuous process in the film, without an interval of growth or cultivation. In a sense, the role of nature is omitted in this sequence. The labor of men, women, and machines seems to take care of the entire operation. Nature's role is not so much denied as supplanted by labor and technology, the culmination of Dovzhenko's effort to link social organizations to natural processes.

One social organization of central importance to the film is the family, and in the final scenes, the entire definition of the family is broadened. At Simon's death, in the first scene, he is attended by both his son and grandson; two generations are present to bid farewell to the patriarch. This sense of family cohesiveness dissolves when Vasyl splits with Opanas over the issue of whether to support the collective. Vasyl joins the other Komsomols in berating his own father when Opanas insists on maintaining a single farm. With this act, Vasyl shifts his primary loyalty from his family to the collective. After Vasyl's death, Opanas follows his son's path by appearing before the Komsomols, the same men who had previously criticized him, to ask that the young members of the collective bury Vasyl. Opanas has lost both a father and a son, but he realizes that such losses can be overcome through the communal spirit of the collective. The small family gathering at Simon's death, represented in a series of close-ups of individual faces, contrasts with the sea of faces seen in a single long shot at Vasyl's funeral. Collectivization is more than a matter of consolidating farm plots, introducing machinery, and improving harvests. It involves a reordering of social institutions and the substitution of the collective for the single family.

The revolutionary spirit in *Earth* does not involve violence. The true revolutionaries, Dovzhenko insists, are those who recognize the pervasiveness of the life cycle and who build a progressive system in conjunction with it. The rhetoric that runs through *Earth* is one of harmony: between man and nature, nature and technology, life and death.

In an attempt to naturalize the collectivization process, Dovzhenko presents an image of a countryside in harmony with itself. Naturalization is commonly understood to be an ideological tactic to defend the status quo, to make the existing social order seem to be the "natural order," one that can not or should not be changed. Dovzhenko, however, employs the tactic to make a large-scale change appear spontaneous, practical, and palatable to a population resistant to collectivization.

But the grim policy of "dekulakization" was at the center of Stalin's collectivization effort. Strident antikulak agitation proved to be the more effective rhetorical weapon in 1930, and the government exploited it fully. Party aggression and violent kulak resistance combined to provoke, as one historian has noted, "during the winter of 1930, an outburst of mass violence the like of which had not been experienced since the horrors of the Civil War."[11]

Dovzhenko's film was caught in its own historical contradiction. Conceived in a period of voluntary collectivization, it appeared during the harshest phases of dekulakization. At a time when the Soviet press called for an all-out assault on kulaks in articles which sounded more like military communiqués than agricultural reports, Dovzhenko came forth with his most understated work. The appeal to nature and to pastoral traditions—not bellicosity—is the fundamental persuasive device of Dovzhenko's rhetoric. In light of what we know about collectivization, it seems clear that the *apparat* had every justification to worry about *Earth*. Ironically, to recognize that fact is to praise the film.

VII

Ivan

THE TROUBLED RECEPTION of *Earth* affected Dovzhenko personally, driving him, as he later admitted, into a brief but nearly suicidal depression.[1] Serious as the matter may have seemed at the time, it turned out to be merely a foretaste of worse things to come; for the level of government interference in creative matters seemed to increase exponentially in the succeeding months and years. The 1925 resolution sanctioning artistic heterogeneity faded into memory, replaced by the forces of conformity. As the USSR moved into the 1930s, Stalin solidified his authority and began remaking Soviet culture in his own dull image. Lenin's comparatively modest *partiinost'* directive gave way to elaborate guidelines imposed on all the arts by a pervasive, stultifying bureaucracy. Artists found their productivity progressively curtailed as they subjected their projects to various censoring agencies and came to expect damning official commentaries. After *Earth*'s release in the spring of 1930, two and one-half years would pass before Dovzhenko completed his next feature film, *Ivan,* during which time he visited Western Europe to investigate new sound equipment. Compared with the hiatuses between subsequent productions, that interval would seem brief. In the last quarter-century of his life Dovzhenko would complete only three features and contribute to a few wartime documentaries, a pitiful record of inactivity in light of the six productions he had turned out in the few years after entering the industry.

Dovzhenko's career—indeed the entire social structure upon which he founded his work—had reached a turning point. During the 1930s Soviet society changed fundamentally and irrevocably. Stalin created an age and an "ism" that would forever bear his name as he led the USSR out of NEP and into a planned economy, out of the interval of cultural diversity and into the period of regimentation, out of the brief moment of creative experimentation and into the era of official artistic doctrine.

We must pause in our survey of Dovzhenko's career to take stock of the changes Stalin effected and to characterize the institutional scaffold he erected in the early 1930s to support his new system. This will serve not simply to describe the immediate circumstances in which Dovzhenko completed *Ivan* but also to mark out the ongoing creative restraints under which he and his colleagues in Soviet cinema would labor in the subsequent years and even decades, restraints that would shape the remaining Dovzhenko projects. Of particular consequence to us are the political and ideological systems which are associated with Stalinism and the reorganization of the film industry under those systems, all of which determined the mode of artistic production for Dovzhenko's later work.[2]

The USSR's concentrated effort at industrialization, which accompanied rural collectivization, commenced in the late 1920s and continued through the 1930s with the implementation of the Five-Year Plans. Stalin phased out the old NEP market system in favor of tight governmental control of every economic sector in an effort at managed development. The new system emphasized long-range growth and ambitious large-scale projects in heavy industry. Soviet planners concentrated on building the industrial foundation of a modern society by manufacturing producer rather than consumer goods, a strategy which created severe consumer shortages and required the population to live with various privations. The Soviet masses endured constant want and at least one severe famine, taking such consolation as they could from frequent government promises that the initial concentration on heavy industry would eventually lead to a thriving consumer economy, promises that were destined to remain unfulfilled. Production quotas, unrealistic projections, and relentless government pressure to produce more goods for less reward represented the lot of workers and peasants under the crash industrialization effort.[3]

Such a system required rigorous social discipline and control to force ever-greater sacrifices from the working population. To this end, the system was buttressed by a complicated ideological structure that served to rationalize the privations and controls, a structure cogently analyzed by Herbert Marcuse.[4] Soviet leaders, according to Marcuse, justified continuing restrictions on individual liberty by claiming that the long-term "historical reality" of socialist development would remain beyond the ken of the masses. Most members of society, as Lenin had taught, could recognize only the immediate, ephemeral, "apparent reality" of their situation. Only the party elite, steeped in the lessons of Marxism, could define essential long-term trends, and the party would have to manipulate and exploit the population in the name of distant, overriding social goals. It could thus rationalize oppression of the masses in the name of their ultimate liberation, a tenet that led to "the fundamental ambivalence in Soviet development; the means for liberation and humanization operate for preserving domination and submission."[5]

Industrialization and modernization represented the USSR's acknowledged long-range goals, and anything that contributed to them fell under the rubric of "historical truth" and could thus find justification. Any official deceptions or inflated claims—whether they be the byzantine explanations for the purge trials or merely inflated production figures—could be considered true if they advanced general goals. Outright lies which helped persuade the population of the "historical necessity" of government policies became the "truth" because, as Marcuse notes, "their 'truth' is in their effect."[6]

This paradoxical definition of truth informed Soviet artistic policy as well. Marcuse identifies what he calls "Soviet realism," a codified system of expression which determined the artistic doctrine we commonly identify as socialist realism. Soviet realism, according to Marcuse, was not simply a matter of aesthetics or politics; it represented the "general pattern of intellectual and practical behavior demanded by the structure of Soviet society." It consisted largely of artistic and literary works which projected absurdly optimistic images of Soviet society. The ubiquitous paintings and stories about happy, toiling factory workers and healthy, robust *kolkhozniks* may have been belied by the fact of famine and constant hardship, but "their falsity does not invalidate them, for to Soviet Marxism their verification is not in the given facts, but in 'tendencies' in a historical process in which the commanded political practice will *bring about* the desired facts."[7] The arts of Stalin's Russia may have spread a litany of lies, but they were posited on the "historical truth" of socialist construction.

Soviet realism easily adapted to the developmental ambitions of the early Five-Year Plans. Consistent with the emphasis on developmental goals, the artist began giving aesthetic form to the economic planner's glowing forecasts. Art's task became one of dealing with an idealized future as well as the observable present. The artist's public responsibility was not simply to represent what he found in the contemporary world ("apparent reality") but to project developmental trends and to posit whither history was tending ("historical reality"). If "reality" was the USSR's relentless economic progress, then "realistic" art had to acknowledge the work that remained to be done, and it had to give form to the promised utopian future.

In order to insure art's official status as vehicle of Soviet realism, the government revamped much of its artistic bureaucracy in the early and middle 1930s, creating a complicated set of censoring agencies, and the film industry was duly overhauled. Lunacharsky and his pragmatic policies were gone, his authority over cinema eventually passing to the stern *apparatchik* Boris Shumiatsky and, after Shumiatsky entered the ranks of the "nonpersons" during the purges, to the equally doctrinaire Ivan Bolshakov. This new administrative breed saw its primary task as one of enforcing artistic conformity, and accordingly, it redesigned the industry's administrative and creative hierarchy to assure strict control over all studios and over all individual projects.[8]

Shumiatsky's primary legacy was the censorship apparatus which he created to control new productions from initial treatment to final cut and which promised to permit greater Communist party input into the creative process than ever before. He organized scenario departments in every Soviet studio, departments heavily staffed by party members and serving primarily as censoring bodies. Every new project underwent painstaking review in a multistage process. The first step involved the submission of a story synopsis to the scenario department for its approval. If the synopsis won acceptance, the author received a commission to develop a full scenario. The completed scenario then went back to the department for scrutiny, at which time department members could, and usually did, demand extensive revisions. If the sometimes contradictory recommendations could be incorporated into the scenario, it would be duly amended and resubmitted for final approval. Only then could production begin, and even then the shooting could be halted at any time if additional changes were deemed necessary. Control was further centralized in the late 1930s, when a single central scenario department in Moscow supplanted the various studio-based units.[9]

The review ritual became so exacting that productions dragged on for months and sometimes years. Fewer projects satisfied the meddling bureaucrats, each of whom seemed to possess veto power, and industry productivity declined markedly. From ninety-four features released in 1930, production levels dropped annually, totalling just thirty-four in 1936. After a brief revival, the decline continued through the subsequent years, bottoming out in 1952, when only five features were released.[10]

This centralization of authority took a particular toll on the studios of the national republics. The old heterogeneous, competitive industry of the 1920s, which assured the national studios a reasonable degree of autonomy, gave way to a plan of industrywide consolidation beginning in 1930, as the various studios of the USSR were placed under the auspices of a single administrative entity, Soiuzkino. The individual studios gradually lost many of their distinguishing characteristics and began to resemble mere production centers for the new unionwide system. In addition, many native administrators were removed from control of the national studios and replaced by Great Russians. Dovzhenko's Kiev studio VUFKU was especially affected by the new guidelines. Renamed Ukrainfilm, the studio became the object of an administrative overhaul, and many of Dovzhenko's old Ukrainian colleagues were purged from the studio hierarchy.[11] In light of Moscow's efforts to compromise Ukrainian cultural autonomy, such maneuvers did not represent innocent administrative reshuffling, and the lesson could not have been lost on Dovzhenko. The major Muscovite directors such as Eisenstein, Pudovkin, and Kuleshov would have to alter their film styles to survive in the 1930s and 1940s, but the problem touched deeper roots in Dovzhenko's case. Stalinist authority over Ukrainian cinema involved far more than a question of cinematic technique. It was tied up with the entire history of the Kremlin's uneasy stewardship of Ukrainian culture, and Dovzhenko would feel the burden of that history as never before.

Dovzhenko's *Ivan* explicitly treats the changes effected under the first Five-Year Plan's rapid industrialization by centering on the Dneprostroi project, the building of a massive dam and hydroelectric complex on the Dnieper River in central Ukraine. Calculated to tame the barely navigable river, to irrigate parts of the surrounding terrain, and to provide electricity for subsequent industrial development, the Dneprostroi became one of the centerpieces of the first Five-Year Plan, and its construction represented the largest single outlay of labor and material hitherto undertaken by the Soviets.

Dovzhenko seized on the project to examine the effect of industrialization on Soviet workers. He constructs his narrative around a fictional case study of a single Dneprostroi construction worker, the Ivan of the title, who is swallowed up in the mass-labor system of Soviet-style industrialization. The film opens with a prologue about the Dnieper River in its natural state prior to the dam's construction. The narrative proper takes up with the construction project that will alter this pristine setting. A Soviet official visits a Ukrainian farm village to recruit volunteers to work at the construction site. Among the villagers who set out for the project are Ivan, a strapping young man, and a lazy peasant named Stepan Guba. Ensuing scenes reveal the daily routine at the project, where Ivan works hard driving rail spikes while Guba becomes a "slacker." One day a worker is killed in a construction accident, and his mother mourns his death. Later, Ivan strives to earn the honor of "shock worker," but he becomes frustrated and angry when he loses an organized "socialist competition," a race to drive the most rail spikes. He begins to feel insignificant when other workers are honored and when an

iconoclastic intellectual denounces Soviet industrial procedures for allegedly destroying worker individuality. The climax comes at a mass meeting of the workers. There, an urgent message informs the workers that a
section of the dam is endangered. After they rush out to meet the challenge, we are shown a lengthy military parade. The mass meeting recon-
venes, and the dead worker's mother speaks to the gathering, exhorting
the workers to their best efforts. In a brief epilogue, Ivan is shown entering a workers' school.

As this summary indicates, Dovzhenko fabricated a limited case study
of a single laborer to highlight the problems of adjustment to modern
working conditions inherent in Stalin's industrialization program. The
Ivan of the film is given the most common Soviet name to broaden the
implications of his situation and to establish him as a representative of
countless such laborers. Dovzhenko described his title character as an
"unheroic hero," one possessed of no special qualities.[12] He does not repel bullets nor sacrifice himself for a commune: he simply drives spikes
on a rail spur, nothing more.

The case study provided Dovzhenko the opportunity to explore the
troubling effects of Soviet industrialization on the individual worker.[13] In
the mass projects necessitated by rapid industrialization, workers suffered from psychological and spiritual deprivation. Marx had identified
the dehumanizing effects of mass production and the alienation of the
worker from the product of his labor as functions of capitalism, and Soviet leaders pointed to that failing in the capitalist West. But in initiating
their own industrialization effort, they employed production methods
modelled on those of the very capitalist nations they had denounced, giving rise to one of the numerous contradictions of Soviet development:
the crash industrialization mounted in the name of the Soviet proletariat
only added to workers' sense of oppression, and individual Soviet workers on large-scale projects like Dneprostroi ran as great a risk of alienation and brutalization as their American counterparts on a Detroit
assembly line.

Ivan's fictional case addresses a related problem of Stalin's all-out industrialization effort: much of the industrial labor force consisted of
transplanted peasants. To supply the labor for this burgeoning industrial
sector, legions of peasants—nearly twenty million by some estimates—
were removed from their homes, transported to manufacturing centers
in unfamiliar surroundings, and housed in austere factory towns or barracks. The hasty training they received for their new tasks proved inade-
quate to offset the deeply ingrained habits of generation after generation
of rural existence. Agricultural work consisted of a variety of tasks undertaken in association with trusted family members and village ac-

quaintances, not the dulling routine of a single repeated action performed among virtual strangers in an enormous, unfathomable industrial complex. Moreover, agricultural tradition called for intervals of intense activity—principally spring planting and fall harvesting—followed by long passages of repose, a far cry from the day-in-day-out rhythm of manufacturing. All of this aggravated the problems of adaption to new surroundings.

Worker morale further suffered from the restrictions on consumption which accompanied this heavy-industry phase of development. The labor force worked harder for less material reward than ever before. At Dneprostroi and other industrial centers, the government sought to compensate with nonmonetary rewards for high productivity, a tactic invoked in *Ivan*. Workers who exceeded quotas received certificates and medals in formal, highly publicized ceremonies modelled on military honors. The Soviet media gave birth to the "shock worker" *(udarnik)*, the man or woman who consistently surpassed quotas, and groups of workers formed "shock brigades," whole factory or construction units which performed exceptional work. Bosses organized "socialist competitions," workers pitted against each other at given industrial tasks. Workers at the bottom of the productivity scale, however, ran the risk of public humiliation, and the figure of the "slacker" *(progulshchik)* became one of the official bogeymen of the first Five-Year Plan. Such pressures only fragmented the Soviet proletariat, resulting in physical attacks on shock workers by their fellow laborers and compromising the collective ideal in a climate of competitiveness.

Besides serving as a test of the new production system, Dneprostroi represented a national symbol, an emblem of the USSR's transformation from an agricultural to an industrial economy. Under construction for the better part of five years, between 1927 and 1932, and employing up to 36,000 workers, the project was a source of national pride as much for its size as for its utility, as the Soviets turned Veblen around by practicing conspicuous production. Soviet leaders proudly pointed to the staggering mobilization of labor that went into Dneprostroi's construction while simultaneously trying to correct the signs of worker discontent—the drinking, fighting, and embarrassing rate of labor turnover—which surfaced there.

Dneprostroi's showcase status accounts for Dovzhenko's decision to make it the subject of his study of industrialization. He had originally proposed a film on the explorer Roald Amundsen as his next project after *Earth,* but Ukrainfilm's scenario department rejected the proposal, suggesting that he write something "about our present-day life in Ukraine."[14] He turned to Dneprostroi as a subject appropriate to the timely issue of industrialization and as a possible companion piece to *Earth,* which treated changes in the agricultural realm.

He undertook the project with all the enthusiasm of a proper shock worker: "With the film *Ivan* I hope to contribute a small piece to the realization of the great task, the task of illuminating in art the collective type of young person of the reconstruction period."[15] Yet the film's production and release generated a series of frustrations that left Dovzhenko personally and professionally scarred. He soon found it "difficult to work on *Ivan* because Bedny's *feuilleton* [against *Earth*] continued to weigh heavily" on his mind.[16] He fell behind schedule and could not complete the production in time for the dam's dedication as originally planned. He was denied the final cut, and studio editors shortened the film from Dovzhenko's planned length. He was also dissatisfied with the technical quality of the sound recording on this his first sound film. Soiuzkino officials considered the film such a political liability that they severely restricted its distribution, and it barely found an audience. The Soviet critical establishment treated it even more harshly than *Earth.* Soiuzkino's assistant director branded the film a "complete failure," and a Communist party spokesman accused Dovzhenko of fascism.[17]

This measure of vitriol suggests that Soviet officials saw something other than slavish praise for the Five-Year Plan in *Ivan,* something outside the accepted definition of Soviet realism. They may have recognized Dovzhenko's skeptical interrogation of the human consequences of Soviet-style industrialization, of the toll it took on individual dignity, and of the contradiction inherent in a developmental formula advanced in the name of the working class which, in fact, degraded the members of that class.

Dovzhenko assigns the film's title, not to the construction that occasioned the film, but to one of the project's thousands of individual workers, somewhat privileging the status of the individual. The film consistently plays off this single figure against the monumental operation which surrounds him. In its broadest outline, the narrative alternates between the working individual and the dam itself, a tactic that involves a comparison between labor and product. Much of the first half of the film concerns day-to-day construction activity, with sequences shifting from Ivan's limited responsibility of driving spikes in a rail spur to long shots showing the complex, integrated efforts of whole teams of workers on the dam. As Ivan's sense of personal insignificance develops, his restlessness gradually becomes the focus of the film's second half. The narrative gradually turns away from the dam to concentrate instead on Ivan's personal discontent, a shift which suggests that the product of Ivan's labor is both public and private, the dam and his anguish.

To underscore the absence of personal fulfillment inherent in such mass projects, the film never provides an end or climax to the work represented. This differs from the representation of labor in *Earth,* wherein Dovzhenko shows a single burst of energy during the scene of the planting and harvesting followed by a long passage of rest, a configuration calculated to evoke the pace of rural existence. But *Ivan* shows a new kind of work, one that progresses ceaselessly, day and night, pointing up the relentlessness of the new industrial campaign which inspired the film. On two occasions characters are shown in their off-hours in the evening gazing out barracks windows at the work which continues through the night; the scenes emphasize the new labor system's round-the-clock schedule, a schedule no longer governed by biological rhythms as in *Earth.* Moreover, none of the work in *Ivan* contains the sense of urgency or ecstasy associated with the concentrated effort in *Earth.* The men and women in *Ivan* do their jobs coolly and professionally, repeating the same manual tasks time and again in predictable fashion.

And while the work never stops, the dam never grows. In several sequences Dovzhenko intercuts shots of workers and machines performing their designated labors with long shots of the unfinished dam. But we do not see the dam progressively take shape in any of these passages, nor does the film provide any indication that the construction project nears completion. In a previous script, Dovzhenko had planned to show the finished dam in a scene in which Ivan and a fellow worker survey the completed project, proud of their achievement.[18] The absence of a finished product in the film proves significant, since the workers are provided no opportunity to take final satisfaction in a job well done. Nor does the film provide a clear sense of what a completed dam will mean to the Ukraine. Unlike Pare Lorentz's *The River,* for example, we are not shown how the dam will affect the landscape; we do not see signs of irrigation nor hear of a single kilowatt of electricity deriving from the massive investment of labor. Those absences throw the emphasis precisely back on the labor itself. The labor must be performed for its own sake, constituting its own reward. Dovzhenko stresses the *process* of socialist construction and represents that process as unending.

In closing off consideration of the effect that the finished dam might have on the society, Dovzhenko forces our attention on the social effects of the building process itself. In the first scene of the story proper, Dovzhenko suggests how the reordering of labor associated with the first Five-Year Plan would disrupt the continuity of village life. A Soviet recruiter addresses a village assembly and calls for volunteers to join the workers at Dneprostroi. He speaks of the need to replenish the proletariat with fresh recruits from the ranks of the peasantry in order to proceed with the tasks of the Five-Year Plan. In *Earth* the villagers had assembled to receive the benefits of modernization, a tractor that would make their lives easier. Here, by contrast, they must surrender part of their community and a part of their labor force on behalf of modernization. Families will be split, friendships interrupted. The social cohesiveness of village life will be sacrificed to the new industrial order.

The sequence concentrates on the impact of that sacrifice on the community. After the meeting the scene moves from the center of the village to its outskirts, and we see the group of volunteers starting down the road on their trek to the Dnieper. As this small contingent moves off, we see the rest of the village peasants lined up at the edge of town. Dovzhenko shows us only the end of the official farewell celebration, and he pauses over that to draw out the sense of loss. The moment is made all the more poignant because we register the stoic sadness of the remaining villagers in the wake of the organized celebration. The group of volunteers carries the song of their village as they march off on an uncertain adventure, but Dovzhenko lingers over the images of the silent, motionless villagers who will stay behind, reminding us that losses suffered by the peasantry will be as profound as the advances in heavy industry.

Dovzhenko also hints at damage to the rural economy. A single long shot at the end of the farewell sequence shows a haystack and the villagers' idle farm machines. This modern machinery, which we saw introduced into village life in *Earth,* now stands unused as a subtle reminder that the shift of labor from agriculture to heavy industry would eventually lessen village productivity. This moment takes on special significance when we note that the industrial progress Stalin effected in the 1930s entailed a ruthless exploitation of the peasant class. Fewer peasants were forced to produce enough to feed an expanded industrial force. The government raised harvest quotas but cut the payment to the villages, meaning that peasants lived on the edge of starvation, and some rural areas experienced a devastating famine in 1932.[19] Dovzhenko's image of idle machinery makes cryptic reference to this plight.

In subsequent scenes Dovzhenko addresses the transplanted peasants' difficult acclimation to their new circumstances. To this end, the narrative centers on Ivan's troubled adjustment, and certain scenes represent him as something of a social isolate. In the scene in which Ivan is introduced to other workers in their barracks, the sound of a train whistle draws him to the barracks window. In a series of long shots representing

Ivan's point of view, and constructed with an exact symmetry, we see the integrated efforts of various crews. The sequence begins with a scene of Ivan looking out the window. The next several shots define what his gaze takes in: a train pulling buckets of cement; the cement lowered by crane into the mold; the crane lifting back up; the train moving off for another load. The sequence then ends with a second shot of Ivan at the window. The symmetry of the sequence—Ivan/train/crane/mold/crane/train/Ivan—is only one device employed to represent the general coordination of the construction work. The musical score is similarly integrated; it incorporates a myriad of construction sounds into the orchestration. The train whistle and the sounds of the engine, drills, horns, and saws blend into the orchestrated score, all of which reinforce the suggestion of coordination among the various parts of the project. The meaning of this spectacle is clearly registered on Ivan. He comes away slightly awed by the size and complexity of the operation. The sequence marks the gap between the single figure seen in isolation at the window and the highly integrated production system that he observes, and it crystallizes the question of whether and how successfully he can enter that system.

The sequence finds its complement in a scene showing Ivan working on the rail line. He pauses momentarily to survey other activities. We see a woman put a load of cement onto a crane. The crane then lowers the basket of cement into a pit, where workers place it on a train car which promptly pulls away. We then return to Ivan who resumes work. Once again we are treated to a general survey of the labor, and again it is motivated by Ivan's response to the size and scope of the work around him. Clearly Dovzhenko seeks to strike a balance between the particular labor of Ivan and the large patterns of work on the site, but Dovzhenko omits any indication of the role that Ivan's rail spur plays in the construction. We have no idea exactly what contribution his work makes. We never see Ivan in one of the sequences of integrated jobs. His labor is never linked with that of the others. Ivan's work seems to proceed separately, and this separation points up his isolation.

The question of Ivan's individual significance develops in a passage centering on his working skills. We see him at work, driving spikes at a prodigious rate. When he pauses to rest, a number of off-screen voices are heard as fellow workers express admiration of his effort and suggest that he enroll in a workers' school. But Ivan fails to act on the opportunity, choosing instead to rely entirely on his innate strength and energy. When we find him back on the job some time later, we witness the repercussions of his decision. He becomes involved in a socialist competition with another young worker who also drives spikes. When the race begins, Ivan starts out working frantically. His opponent, on the other hand, casually lights a cigarette and then works at a much more leisurely pace. The opponent wins the competition by doing more work with less effort. Ivan finally scratches from the race and from any hope of entering the shock worker elite when he bends a spike and has to stop to pull it out. As Ivan stands in frustration, Dovzhenko frames him from the waist down, and we see Ivan with a wrench in his hand shaking it in anger. The moment stands in formal counterpoint to the previous sequence in which he had basked in praise in a full shot. Now he can only shout at his opponent, asking him for his secret. "It's no secret," comes the reply. "I know my business." Ivan requires more than strength and energy. He needs to acquire the new skills of the modern industrial system, skills which are alien to his peasant background.

Dovzhenko counters Ivan's temporary failure by invoking several celebrated shock workers on the project, again playing his single hero off against larger groups. From the shot of Ivan's frustration Dovzhenko cuts to a series of awards for productivity. The sequence consists of individual close shots of workers with outstanding work records alternating with intertitles of their award certificates. The workers' particular achievements are carefully documented. The honored men perform various tasks. Among the workers we see an organizer, a teacher, an engineer. One man is honored for improving "American methods" for the manufacture of turbines. This labor cross section reminds us of the myriad activities involved in the construction project, and it highlights Ivan's alienation.[20]

In comic counterpoint, Dovzhenko completes the cross section by including a slacker. Stepan Guba appears in the middle of the awards sequence and interrupts the rather solemn proceedings by interjecting a farcical note of self-congratulation. Guba has from the beginning of the film filled the role of token slacker. He volunteers to leave his village for Dneprostroi, not out of a commitment to socialist construction, but only because he anticipates that he will make more money at the Dnieper site. At the end of one sequence detailing the variety of labors involved in the construction, Dovzhenko shows Guba fishing in the river on company time. Dovzhenko cuts from a shot of a crane lowering a basket of cement to a shot of Guba dangling his fishing line in the river, a visual pun which marks the difference between the two activities.

When Guba appears in the middle of the ceremonies, he authors a parody of the shock worker awards. Guba faces the camera in a medium close-up as the others had done. The others had professional titles and

Figure 15. *Ivan*

certificates of honor; Guba can claim neither of these and has to impro-
vise. He introduces himself verbally to the audience; since in his case
there is no written document to preserve the measure of his achievements, he must praise himself. The shock workers won titles—Hero,
Organizer, Engineer; Guba can only assign himself the label of
"Slacker" *(Ia progulshchik)*. The shock workers had their achievements
spelled out in their awards; Guba has performed no service, so he can
only rattle on about himself. He speaks not of work but of his physical
characteristics. He tells the audience about his neck, profile, back, and
gait. Since he performs no labor, there is nothing beyond his body to
identify him. He doesn't *do;* he simply *is.* (fig. 15)

In the Soviet version of work rewards, ironically, Guba serves a useful
function simply by being. The slacker was as important to Soviet mythology as the shock worker. Soviet officials needed negative as well as
positive incentives to encourage productivity. If one could hope to be labelled a shock worker by exceeding quotas, one also ran the risk of being
labelled a slacker by falling short of those same quotas. If the shock

Figure 16. *Ivan*

worker could expect public esteem, the slacker received public humiliation. The rituals of disgrace were just as codified as those of honor.
Shortly after the award ceremony, Guba goes center stage for a scene
which acknowledges those calculated humiliations. He reports to the
"black till," an isolated black booth reserved for slackers, in order to
draw his pay. (fig. 16) Guba responds to the embarrassment of the moment with a comic coyness. He stalks and sneaks around the small, isolated wooden booth for some time before finally screwing his courage to
the sticking place and venturing up to the pay window. There, a mysterious hand extends from the window to issue him his cash while the
sound track remains silent. But as Guba stands and counts his money, he
hears a sharp whistle emanating from the booth. He leans over to investigate. The hand again extends from the booth, reaching out gingerly to
stroke Guba's hand.

Then a comic nightmare begins. The mysterious hand grabs Guba vi-
olently and holds him rooted in place. He finally pulls loose and tumbles
to the ground. His initial suspicion of the ominous black booth seems
confirmed; the money simply is not worth the trouble. Guba runs away
to find an appropriate place to hide his shame, but another form of pun-

ishment is in store. A loudspeaker attached to the booth begins denouncing him by name. In a series of discontinuous shots, we see Guba
running from one location to another on the construction site. But no
matter where he goes, the voice from the loudspeaker follows him; the
volume of the voice never varies. He seems pursued by the voice; it remains with him like the sound equivalent of a thief's brand. This highly
distended and ritualized scene of Guba's humiliation speaks to the formal incentive system of the new Soviet economy, the currency of which
was public attention rather than cash.

The slacker was not the only stock villain of Five-Year Plan fiction.
The government also condemned skeptics and "cosmopolitans" who
questioned the personal sacrifices demanded on behalf of the plan. The
character of the intellectual who fills that role in *Ivan* seems to be the
worthy successor of the nepman of an earlier era. Concerned only with
his immediate well-being, he concentrates on amenities rather than on
long-range economic prospects. While the workers at the dam endure a
spartan existence, he lives with a frivolous wife in a comfortable home.
As part of his affectation, he carries a briefcase and spouts theoretical
gibberish whenever he finds an audience. When he and his wife are at
home listening to the radio and happen to tune in a political speech by a
Soviet official, his philistine wife insists that they turn to the popular mu-
sic played by a foreign station.

Within the ideological system which accompanied industrialization,
this character is faulted for his insistence on valuing immediate material
comforts. He wants to live in comfortable circumstances, and he sees no
merit in sacrificing short-term contentment for long-range construction.
Indeed, his fixation on present economic conditions causes him to denounce publicly the entire Five-Year Plan. In one scene, some workers
are quietly assembled in the mess hall, reading papers, stirring their tea,
or otherwise relaxing. The intellectual stands to address the workers and
launches into an abrasive speech which disturbs the quiet of the hall. He
fumes over current food prices and calls the rationale of the Five-Year
Plan "dialectical nonsense." More important, he proclaims that the
conditions of the Five-Year Plan destroy the individual, wiping out the
separate personalities of the workers. "There are no individuals" *(cheloveka net)*, he asserts.

These are strong accusations, and the film cannot let them stand un-
answered. But the best Dovzhenko can offer by way of a retort at that
point is to have one of the workers in the mess hall refute the intellectual
succinctly and forcefully. "No individuals?" he asks indignantly. "And
what of me?" *(Cheloveka net? A ia?)* That's all it takes apparently. The

worker reminds us that he considers himself an individual, and that simple act of faith must serve, for the moment at least, as a persuasive counter to the intellectual's accusation. The intellectual hangs his head and slips out of the mess hall in humiliation. He tries to escape the indignation of the worker just as Guba had sought to escape the sinister voice from the loudspeaker. Appropriately, the intellectual and Guba run into each other at a crossroad as they make their respective getaways. Dovzhenko brings them together at this point because they represent two forms of weakness: laziness and skepticism. A simple blind faith in the Five-Year Plan and a willingness to conform to its goals seems to be the only acceptable alternative.

Nevertheless, the intellectual's claims about the worth of the individual will not go away that easily. Dovzhenko must find a stronger argument to deal with the moral weight of that problem. He does so by invoking the specter of death, the loss of an individual. In this film in which workers make sacrifices for the overall project, we are asked to confront the moral implications of the ultimate sacrifice when a worker is killed on the job.

The matter is raised in a stunning sequence which merits careful description. In the middle of one of several scenes where the work proceeds routinely, we see cranes lowering baskets of cement. Something goes awry unexpectedly. A basket is lowered directly over the camera until the entire screen goes black. At the same instant the familiar background noises on the sound track are pierced by an abrupt scream which could easily be another train whistle but which turns out to be a human shriek. That cry is cut off abruptly, and all sound ceases. Only then do we realize that we have seen a subjective view of death. The camera has registered a point-of-view shot of a worker being crushed to death by the cement basket, and that aborted scream was his last breath. We soon witness several workers carrying the broken body of the dead man to a clearing and laying it down. Then the dead man's mother stands motionless over the body. (fig. 17) In a series of jump cuts we see her standing, then kneeling, then standing again over the body. As in Opanas's vigil over Vasyl in *Earth,* which was interrupted by two slow fades, she seems to remain indefinitely over the dead man. Finally she turns her head away from the body and stares off screen. For the first time she notices the activity of construction around her, and appropriately, the familiar construction noises gradually reenter the hitherto silent sound track. We realize that the silence represented her temporary refusal to hear or acknowledge the continued work around her. But now we follow her gaze with an eyeline match and see men again shovelling cement.

Figure 17. *Ivan*

The scene is calculated to isolate her in her grief and to mark the fact that the tragedy does not interrupt the work of others. This personal loss, devastating as it is to the mother, pales before the magnitude of the whole construction project.

The mother seems shocked that the death could mean so little. She bolts off in a mad dash which contrasts with her stoic vigil over the body. She makes a frantic run through the construction site, seeming constantly to challenge its enormous machines to kill her. She dashes from one machine to another and places herself in harm's way each time. Finally she ceases tempting death and chooses a course of action. She runs in a straight line, heading for the office of the director of the construction. A series of tracking shots interrupted several times by jump cuts traces the apparently limitless terrain she has to cover to reach her boss. The boss's distance from the workers is hinted at in another way as well. When she finally reaches the building housing the director's office, she has to pass through a series of doors. In a few seconds of screen time, in nine separate jump cuts, she runs through nine sets of double doors. This implies that an extraordinary office bureaucracy separates the mother from her son's boss. She finally bursts into the director's office, agitated by what she has been through, but if we were expecting her to encounter an aloof, remote bureaucrat in the manner of Eisenstein's *Old and New,* we are in for a surprise. When she finally confronts the director, he is on the phone to an assistant, inquiring about the death, angrily insisting that more care be taken to prevent accidents, and arranging for the dead man to be honored. As she overhears the instructions, the mother quickly relaxes, and her agitation disappears. Finally the director turns to the woman. "What do you want?" he asks. "Nothing," comes her firm response. She realizes that the death of her son does matter.

The sequence is built on a calculated anticlimax. Its elaborate representation of the death and of the mother's anger gives way to her quick reconciliation to her loss as she recognizes the value of the project's overall goal. Like the fiancée's temporary hysteria in *Earth,* the initial anger of the mother passes. She develops an equanimity based on a deeper appreciation of her son's contribution to the general welfare. She now has the moral authority to confront the issue of personal sacrifice which was left so inadequately answered after the intellectual's speech.

Her final appearance in the film is in clear contrast to the long sequence showing her earlier rash behavior. She appears at the end of the film to speak before the assembly of construction workers. She enters the hall without invitation and interrupts the proceedings, but the instant she makes her entrance in the back of the auditorium, all activity stops; the men and women gathered there respectfully turn their eyes toward her. Her long, deliberate walk down the center aisle to the podium is drawn out slowly, and it contrasts with her race through the construction site. There she raced frantically about, and the sequence was fragmented into scores of brief shots, some as short as a few frames. Her march through the hall is extended through several long tracking shots. Dovzhenko draws out the ritual of the entrance to provide the maximum weight to the mother's actions and words, which are now so measured. When she finally speaks, she proclaims that her son died in a worthy cause, and she calls on those assembled to redouble their efforts on behalf of the Five-Year Plan. Her acceptance of the sacrifice is offered as a moral guide. The loss of a single individual comes to seem a necessary and honorable sacrifice, not unlike a casualty of war.

That is more than a passing analogy. Dovzhenko needs a powerful correlative to argue for the submergence of the individual for the good of society. A sense of national commitment associated with war provides that. In *Zvenigora* and *Arsenal* he condemns the specter of war because it perverts human energy and wastes resources. But in *Ivan* the war analogy is supposed to summon up the strength and unity to achieve the tasks of the Five-Year Plan. A similar rhetorical strategy was used by the government to rationalize its effort to supervise the lives of individuals. Under the first Five-Year Plan, as one historian has noted, "the whole country underwent a quasi-military reorganization," and every realm of life and work was closely regimented.[21]

Not coincidentally, several elements in *Ivan* parallel the military experience. A recruiter travels around the country asking for volunteers to serve in a national task. That the workers live in sexually segregated huts and eat in a common mess hall suggests a barracks life. Some workers are singled out for efforts above and beyond the call of duty and are awarded medals. And occasionally a worker dies in the line of duty.

Up to the last reel of the film, the military analogy is left implicit. We recognize it in the constant rigor and regimentation of life on the project. But the analogy becomes manifest near the end of the film. While the workers are assembled in the lecture hall, a message comes through that a section of the dam is endangered. This emergency galvanizes the workers into a cohesive force, and they instantly charge out of the hall to meet the challenge.

In the original script for *Ivan*, Dovzhenko had planned to portray the effort of the workers to save the dam from failure as a desperate battle reminiscent of all-out war. Images of battle and labor were to merge in the scene. The shock workers were to summon up the legacy of fighting Cossacks to inspire their comrades. "I, too, am a Zaparozhian [Cossack]," a worker shouts as he pitches in to save the dam.[22] In the finished film, however, the matter is handled somewhat differently. The military analogy is made explicit by the sudden insertion of a martial parade at the time when the dam is in jeopardy. When the workers rush out of the hall to save the dam, we are not shown the work they actually do. Instead Dovzhenko cuts away to a lengthy parade of uniformed Red Army troops with their ordnance. After several minutes of the parade and troop maneuvers, we return to the lecture hall. The workers rush back into their seats, their efforts at salvaging the dam successful, though not represented in the film.

The confusion between militarism and patriotism, so common in the modern world, is exploited here. By conjuring up the image of military order, the film suggests a model for the civilian population to emulate under the rigors of the Five-Year Plan. It poses the need to produce as a

matter of national urgency, even national security. Historians have
noted that Soviet officials saw their crash industrialization program as
crucial to the USSR's survival. The successful promotion of productive
forces seemed the only way the Soviet system could survive in a hostile
capitalist world. To diverge from the prescribed path, when it was so defined, would be an act bordering on treason.[23]

What about Ivan's dissension, then, a seemingly serious matter given
these high rhetorical stakes? The film has tried to shift periodically between Ivan's story and the general work on the construction project.
Ivan chafes at the work system, with its regimentation, and at his own
sense of insignificance, and he listens to the complaints of the intellectual
who denounces the Five-Year Plan. In the script, Dovzhenko had
planned to reconcile Ivan to the collective enterprise in the scene of the
desperate effort to save the dam. In the heat of the moment, Ivan was to
lose his self- doubts and pitch in. He was literally to submerge himself in
the effort, plunging into the river with a spade to perform a crucial task.
He was then to emerge a changed, perhaps a cleansed man after a variant of baptism: "Ivan stands, wet from his legs to his head, with a spade.
Ivan stumbles. Ivan is happy."[24]

The final film, however, omits that dramatic transformation. We have
no idea from the film what role Ivan might have played in the salvage effort. Instead Ivan is granted his own epilogue. In the last scene Ivan is
being admitted to a workers' school. The opportunity that he had failed
to take earlier in the film is finally granted him. He walks proudly down
the aisle to take a seat in the front of the classroom, and the film ends
with a title that attempts to generalize from Ivan's momentary satisfaction: "Comrade professors. Give all the Ivans everything you have."
We are to presume that the knowledge Ivan will receive in the school will
assist him in future labor. No longer will he need to rely simply on brute
strength. He will, in the words of the rival shock worker, "know his business."

Dovzhenko finally concedes to Ivan a personal victory. In the final
analysis, Ivan is not required to accept his lowly station. In fact, Ivan is
never fully reconciled to the mass labor system of the Dnieper Dam. We
do not see him back on the line and have no idea what his future contribution will be. We leave him as he enjoys the special reward of education
and the prospect of personal promotion. To the very end, Ivan's story
has developed distinctly from that of the dam. Despite Dovzhenko's effort to fuse the two strains, they remain separate, if not equal.
Dovzhenko's failure to submerge Ivan into the faceless mass perhaps betrays a nagging doubt about the state's management of private life under

the first Five-Year Plan. Despite Dovzhenko's public protestation that his Ivan was merely "a component part of a great industrial collective, a great biography,"[25] the character refuses to disappear into collective anonymity.

All this represents a far cry from the pat formulas mandated by Soviet realism, formulas in which contented workers toiled away at their appointed tasks secure in the knowledge that they were building nothing less than the future. Dovzhenko frets and worries over the new Soviet economy's cost to worker self-esteem, a cost that may well have offset any coincidental rise in the gross national product. Dovzhenko would have us measure economic progress in something other than raw statistics.

VIII
Aerograd

THE SOVIET PRESS notices which greeted *Aerograd* deserve sampling in part for their political rhetoric.

> The merit of the picture is that...it shows the enemy as he is, not lessening his strength and danger, but revealing...his historical doom. (*Vecherniaia Moskva*, 9 November 1935)

> The picture enlists the spectator in the defense of socialism against the conspiracies of foreign adventurers and enraged enemies of the working class...Socialist realism gives [Dovzhenko] the creative power to bring to light...the beastly features and heinous souls of our enemies. (*Izvestiia TsIK*, 5 November 1935)

> A great feeling of hatred for the enemy is aroused....We want to run with [the hero] Stepan and smash the skulls of the enemy. (*Pravda*, 5 November 1935)

These reviews are representative of the film's reception, and in the atmosphere of Stalinist Russia of the 1930s, such strong remarks constituted praise and began the brief period of Dovzhenko's political rehabilitation.

For once Dovzhenko had released a film to the unanimous approval of the USSR's official critical establishment. But what were the terms of that approval? They consisted of claims that *Aerograd* denounced the Soviet Union's enemies, revealing their "beastly features" and "heinous souls" and encouraging audiences to "smash the skulls" of those enemies. As we have seen, the criticism mounted against *Earth* and *Ivan* quickly descended into the realm of the ad hominem, and Dovzhenko found his political judgment and even his patriotism called into question through ominous suggestions that his work gave aid and comfort to the USSR's enemies. It hardly seems coincidental that the praise for *Aero-*

grad centered on Dovzhenko's alleged representation of state enemies, especially when one recalls the concern with enemies, real and imagined, that dominated Soviet public discourse in the middle and late thirties. This was the era of the so-called Great Terror, the time of purges, labor camps, and enforced obedience to the state. In Stalinist Russia, anxiety was more than an unfortunate by-product of a nation in transition. Fear served as a policy tool, and the level of fear could be raised and lowered on command like a prime interest rate. A casual remark on a street, a subquota performance on the job, or an arbitrary denunciation could mean deportation to the camps. And the Soviet cinema, more than ever under the direct control of the state, was often used to propagate anxiety, to advance tales of wreckers, saboteurs, spies, Trotskyites, and foreign opponents.[1]

We still may ask how a sensitive artist like Dovzhenko came to direct a film that could inspire the rhetoric of hatred that we find in the reviews. And more important, what political aspects of Stalin's Russia produced a situation in which the highest compliment due a film was the claim that it inspired fear and loathing? An analysis of *Aerograd* in the context of the purge period will reveal something about the ways in which the anxieties of the Great Terror assumed tangible form and how presumed enemies of the Soviet Union were constructed and presented to its population.

Aerograd takes the form of a frontier adventure with the Soviet Far East as its setting. The narrative centers on the activities of the veteran hunter Stepan Glushak and his band of old revolutionary partisans, who are involved in an effort to rid the Far East of saboteurs so that the ultramodern city of Aerograd can be constructed. Glushak ambushes a group of Russian and Japanese saboteurs early in the film and then tracks a Japanese officer to the hut of Vasil Khudiakov, Glushak's oldest friend. Khudiakov harbors the foreigner and lies to Glushak to cover his treason. Meanwhile a counterrevolutionary Russian named Shabanov persuades a village of Old Believers, part of a reactionary religious sect, to form a paramilitary unit to resist Soviet settlement of the area, and the villagers join forces with Khudiakov and the Japanese infiltrator. Glushak's pro-Soviet partisans, including Glushak's aviator son Vladimir and his Oriental friend Van Lin, attack the village and stop the sedition. Glushak executes Khudiakov, and the way is cleared for Aerograd to be built.

As this synopsis already indicates, *Aerograd* treats several matters of concern to Soviet leaders in the 1930s: the settlement of the Far East, native resistance to Soviet authority in remote areas, and the growing fear of foreign (especially Japanese) and domestic enemies of the USSR. To appreciate the film's debt to Stalinism, we must explore these concerns in some detail and then determine how they are incorporated into *Aerograd* in fictional form.

Economic and security issues dominate the narrative of *Aerograd* and are often presented as being inseparable. *Aerograd* evidences the conflation of militarism and economic development that we find in *Ivan*.[2] In doing so it seizes on an economic program of particular strategic importance undertaken during the 1930s, the development of the Soviet Far East. This was a virgin land rich in resources, but its remoteness from Soviet population centers and its rugged terrain impeded developmental efforts. Moreover, the reluctance of conservative Far Eastern native populations to cooperate with Soviet authority posed a security threat. This problem was aggravated by Soviet disputes with China over the Chinese Eastern Railway and over White Russian partisans operating from Manchurian sanctuaries. The Japanese invasion of Manchuria in 1931 and the eventual Japanese alliance with Nazi Germany reaffirmed the USSR's need to protect its eastern borders.[3]

When economics are tied to security, economic setbacks become tantamount to military defeats. In Stalin's Russia the rhetoric of war was applied to the economy. In the "battle" against backwardness, the entire country was "mobilized." In such a climate, poor productivity could easily seem to result from lack of patriotism or from outright treason. An industrial planner or plant supervisor who had the bad fortune to be involved in a failing industry could expect to be accused of subversion. The insidious work of "wreckers" and "saboteurs" served to explain bugs in the Five-Year Plans. It was claimed that foreign agents and Russian traitors acting on orders from Hitler, Roosevelt, Trotsky, et al. kept industry from reaching the stated quotas.

On a gloomy December afternoon in 1934, a young man with a revolver slipped up behind Leningrad Communist party chief Sergei Kirov and shot him once in the back. Investigations directed by Stalin accused prominent Communist party members of the crime, and within a year the machinery of the purges was in full gear. The Kirov assassination initiated the Great Terror of the 1930s, which culminated in the spectacular show trials of 1936 and 1938, when scores of veteran Bolsheviks were "unmasked" and "revealed" to have been Axis spies planning to cede large tracts of Soviet territory to Germany and Japan. But Stalin had established the precedent of purging "wreckers" and "saboteurs" in the early 1930s with a series of trials and executions of less prominent figures. The Industrial party purge of 1930, the Menshevik trial of 1931, and the Metro-Vickers trial of 1933, among others, anticipated the formulas of the later show trials; all the accused, Stalin's investigators insisted, acted on orders from foreign powers to undermine the Soviet economy and Soviet security.[4]

Japanese infiltrators and Russian subversives in the Far East did not derive simply from Stalin's imagination. Many White Russian groups on the Manchurian side of the border did enjoy the protection first of Chinese and then of Japanese authorities. A Russian Fascist league, bankrolled in part by the Japanese, set up shop in Manchuria and occasionally carried out cross-border raids. But the cultural and diplomatic isolation of the USSR in the 1930s gave rise to intense xenophobia and paranoia. Soviet citizens literally could not pick up a newspaper without reading about subversion. Everyone was at once suspicious and suspect at a time when one could even face imprisonment for failing to denounce a family member who seemed disloyal.[5]

The subject of *Aerograd*—the preparation for constructing a modern city in the Far East—takes for its immediate source the building of Komsomolsk-on-Amur, an eastern industrial center. The city went up as part of the Five-Year Plan and served as a major air base. Young Komsomols, members of the USSR's Communist youth group, supplied the original labor for the center's construction and populated the city in the early years, sleeping in tents and in makeshift barracks. The party recruited volunteers by appealing to a pioneer spirit in a go-east-young-Komsomol campaign, and Komsomolsk-on-Amur grew from a small outpost to a thriving industrial center of 70,000 inhabitants by the end of the decade. Dovzhenko visited the city on expeditions to the Far East during the planning of *Aerograd*.[6]

When Dovzhenko publicly commented on *Aerograd* he displayed a bellicosity similar to the press reviews we have already sampled, claiming that he sought "to mobilize the defense of the USSR," which was "on the threshold of a new imperialist war."[7] In fact, he made the film in part to assure his political rehabilitation after going through the recent period of intense criticism and public disgrace. Weary from the press attacks on *Earth* and *Ivan,* he watched silently as his old associates in Ukrainian arts and letters chose between prison and artistic submission to authority. He saw himself "relegated to the camp of the sterile bourgeoisie as a talented but politically limited fellow traveller."[8] He had to do something to save his career and perhaps his life.

He made an important move when he initiated *Aerograd:* for the first time in his career he worked outside the Ukraine, leaving the familiar confines of the Ukrainfilm studio in Kiev to work at Moscow's Mosfilm facilities under the direct auspices of Great Russian authorities. He rationalized the move by claiming that he was escaping the site of recent artistic failure and that a change of venue portended a change of fortune. He took on the *Aerograd* project as a "safe" item, one far removed from the suspect nationalism of Ukrainian culture, and he collaborated with the Russian screenwriter Alexander Fadeev, a "safe" figure by virtue of the fact that he was an official in the powerful Union of Soviet Writers and a writer with impeccable Stalinist credentials.[9]

Dovzhenko nursed the project through the Soviet film industry's recently codified process of preproduction censorship designed to enforce ideological uniformity. He initiated the project in 1933 with a synopsis he submitted at the film industry's conference on "thematic planning" in Moscow. Immediately after he won permission to proceed with the project, he travelled to the Far East to explore the area and develop his ideas. After returning to Moscow in 1934 he submitted a full scenario to the Union of Soviet Writers in accordance with review procedures and received the USW's endorsement. At one point in the process Dovzhenko met with Stalin and several government officials in the Kremlin to get their sanction for the scenario. Dovzhenko returned to the Far East in July 1934 for several months of location filming and finished shooting at the Mosfilm studio in 1935.[10]

A party-line scenarist, the state apparatus, and Stalin himself played important roles in the creation of *Aerograd*. It should be no surprise that the principal concerns of the government became the central issues of the finished film. *Aerograd* opened in November 1935, when Soviets were celebrating the eighteenth anniversary of their revolution, but also at a time when purges, the threat of war, and the prospect of finishing out one's life in the Gulag concerned every Soviet citizen. An analysis of the narrative of *Aerograd* will demonstrate how Dovzhenko gave such dark concerns fictional form.

Aerograd begins with a prologue which explores the extraordinary expanse of the Far East's hilly, wooded taiga and its rough, nearly unnavigable character. As in many Dovzhenko films, an acknowledgment of the natural terrain precedes all other matters. The land in Dovzhenko's work exists a priori as the richest natural resource. But an airplane is introduced simultaneously and with it the potential to overcome the inhospitable nature of the taiga through technology. Airpower, Dovzhenko implies, will shorten the vast distances of the USSR and hasten the day of Soviet dominance of the land. Dovzhenko consciously exploits the old Slavic meaning of the name of the pilot Vladimir—roughly "ruler over the world."[11] And the rustic old partisans of Glushak's band are played off against young Vladimir, a too handsome, too blond, too ideal version of the "new Soviet man." The partisans are in awe of the ease with which Vladimir covers distances that their provincial minds cannot fathom. Vladimir explains that he will transport a downed American flyer back to the United States in a few hours, and the partisans exclaim that Vladimir can travel "faster than the sun."

The second theme established in the prologue is the central concern of the film, that of national security. After the single airplane is introduced, several air squadrons fill the sky. When the prologue moves to the seacoast, we see a group of small Soviet seacraft patrolling the shore. The Far East, we discover in the film, is especially vulnerable to enemies, both foreign and domestic. We are to understand that the proximity of Japan is the external threat, that the rich land of the taiga is coveted by Japanese expansionists, hitherto confined to a crowded island. The taiga, we soon discover, also harbors domestic subversives. They are regressive types who resist Soviet authority and economic change: people like Khudiakov, who holds onto his single farm in the age of collectivization, and people like the Old Believers, who live in another century. They will all join forces in the film. When economic progress becomes linked to security, the alliance suggests, those who resist development are really no different from foreign agents.

The narrative of *Aerograd* concentrates not on building but on purgation. It presumes the elimination of enemies to be the essential preliminary step in the development of the Far East. The chief agent in this task is Glushak, a rough-hewn hunter in the manner of Natty Bumppo. Glushak's name takes its root from the word *glush'*, which refers to a remote area or backwoods region. In addition, his prowess as a marksman and hunter has won him the nickname Tiger's Death in recognition of the many Siberian tigers he has tracked down and killed. Everything about him signifies a homespun integrity. Quick to smile, he enjoys the respect and esteem of the community of taiga partisans.

Early in the film Glushak demonstrates his marksmanship, his good manners, and—not to be ignored—his cold-bloodedness. He discovers a group of eight saboteurs moving through the forest and promptly disposes of five of them with five shots. Two of the figures who escape are Japanese infiltrators, whom Glushak pursues through the forest. Dovzhenko cuts back and forth between the hunter and his game, contrasting Glushak's graceful, measured movements with the desperate, frightened flight of the Japanese. When Glushak captures one of the Japanese, he permits the prisoner a last statement, and the infiltrator, rather than asking for mercy, unleashes a vitriolic verbal attack on Glushak and his countrymen, denouncing Russia with all the histrionics he can summon. He claims that the small island nation of Japan envies Russia its open landscape, its plentiful resources, and—significantly—its sense of national unity and purpose. He tells Glushak that he detests "your calm and your cheerful Soviet collective labor." During this entire diatribe Glushak displays nothing but calm and good cheer. He smiles benevolently at this prisoner—right up to the moment he executes him. Glushak's good-natured manner seems calculated to deflect attention from the grim role that he plays in the narrative, that of executioner. He is such an open, warm character, that we may lose track of the moral implications of the purges that appear in the film, especially when Glushak liquidates his old friend Khudiakov.

The film preys on Soviet fears of Japanese military adventurism. A priest tells the village of Old Believers that their salvation will lie with a Japanese invasion, and he predicts that "in the north—in the west—in the south, the red star will surely perish from the east wind." At one point in the film the Japanese officer who allies himself with the Old Believers steps into the forest by himself to practice an elaborate dance ritual with his samurai sword. But the sequence has none of the quiet beauty of the analogous moment in Kurosawa's *Seven Samurai*. The infiltrator is just awkward enough and overplays the moment sufficiently to seem ridiculous. Dovzhenko makes a point that the character is quite out of place in this environment and that his affection for ritual makes him an anachronism in the modern Soviet context. The Japanese officer insists on being called a samurai when he is finally caught by partisans, a fact which amuses the Russians. He also insists on being allowed to commit suicide. When he begins an elaborate suicide ritual, he provokes a boisterous laugh from one of his Russian captors. This hearty Russian finds a prescribed ritual of death slightly ridiculous, and he refuses to understand why anyone would welcome death.

To offset the traces of racism in the portrayal of the Japanese and to evoke an image of Soviet racial unity, Dovzhenko includes Asian characters in Glushak's circle. Glushak's friend and comrade in the partisan detachment is Van Lin, a Soviet of Chinese descent. While Vladimir is a tall, blond figure who seemingly could have stepped out of a poster for the Soviet air force, his wife is Korean, and the arrival of their new son is treated as a moment of general celebration.

The scene of the celebration over the newborn child occupies a central position in the film and helps differentiate the sense of community enjoyed by the partisans from the disharmony of the Old Believer village.

The sequence opens with a medium close-up of the mother holding the child. She and the baby are dressed in white and are surrounded by white bedclothes and curtains so that they seem to radiate a bright light. The shot abstracts the woman and child from any spatial context and appears as an archetypal image of motherhood in the tradition of a madonna icon. The second shot of the sequence reveals that she and the baby are located in Glushak's home and are surrounded by admiring friends and neighbors. More of the space is revealed in the third shot; the camera is positioned just outside the door of Glushak's hut, and looks into the home. The deep-focus composition shows various adults lining the path from the door to the far end of the room, where the woman and child sit in the extreme background but still in the center of the scene. In the foreground children from the village are ushered in. They will proceed between the two rows of adults to pay respects to the mother and child at the other end of the room.

The series of shots thus begins by focusing on mother and child and then gradually reveals more space around them. The mother and child always remain prominent in the area of white in the center of the frame. The sequence is literally constructed around them, and the action of the sequence reveals that the whole community is drawn to them. Children and adults, men and women, gather in a general celebration of birth, and the scene presents the mother and child as a social magnet which provides the community considerable cohesiveness. The village seems almost an extension of the family.

Glushak's home serves as a community center of sorts, housing a social celebration. It also is the site of a political meeting. Before the evening of celebration is over, the men gathered under Glushak's roof turn their attention to the grim business of dealing with current subversion. They decide to regroup their partisan band to attack the village of Old Believers. The social cohesiveness provided by the mother and child gives way to military matters, affirming the notion that social unity provides the only safeguard against foreign and domestic threats. Glushak's hut houses both military and civilian functions; in the version of national purpose represented throughout *Aerograd,* the two are hard to differentiate.

Dovzhenko juxtaposes the scene at Glushak's hut with scenes of the Old Believer village, and several significant contrasts appear between the two models of community. The Old Believers are depicted as pious religious fanatics who share none of the good-natured openness of Glushak and his friends. Shabanov's return to his village contrasts sharply with the joyous scene at Glushak's home. Shabanov has been away from the village for five years, and he now brings news of Bolshevik advances in the taiga. He exhorts the villagers to join with the Japanese in opposition to the Bolsheviks. In fact, he is apparently the single Russian of the original band of saboteurs to escape Glushak's ambush. Shabanov's return causes a ripple of anxiety to pass through the village; he is preceded by the fearful mention of his name, to which the villagers react in near panic. An intense, fanatical figure, he comes literally as death's messenger, informing several women in the village that their husbands have been shot by Glushak. The unifying role of the family figures prominently in the scene at Glushak's; the sequences at the Old Believer village stress familial dissension. A father berates his son for daring to show sympathy for the Soviets. Shabanov is utterly alienated from this wife and children because of his long absence and because of his monomania of anti-Bolshevism. At one point he even considers shooting his children to "save" them from the advance of Soviet settlement.

The Old Believers could be dismissed as incorrigibles, dedicated to backwardness and antisocial behavior as part of their creed. But the basic moral dilemma treated in the film is the story of Khudiakov's treason. His name comes from the Russian word *khudo,* which has as one of its meanings "mean" or "evil." In other Dovzhenko films the kulaks, nepmen, and shirkers who sap the strength of Soviet society are all treated comically, dismissed by being made the objects of ridicule. But in the grim climate of Stalinism in the thirties, sterner measures were called for; Khudiakov becomes a victim of the purges.

Dovzhenko's problem is to create a dramatic situation and a moral touchstone by which to justify the execution of Khudiakov. He does so by focusing on the Khudiakov-Glushak friendship and by making the betrayal the most solemn material of the film. The audience is then drawn into the moral problems of that betrayal by being specifically addressed. Characters frequently turn and speak to the camera. At such moments the characters, in effect, call on the audience to take note of some detail. Yet, in the development of the Khudiakov-Glushak relationship, this technique is no Brechtian distancing device. Rather, it implicates the audience directly in the action depicted. The first sign of this comes at the very beginning of the narrative: when Glushak first flushes out the saboteurs he turns, looks directly at the camera, and explains, "Now we will kill them." He uses the first person plural to draw the audience into the enterprise. Glushak will do the actual killing, but Dovzhenko asks us to consider that Glushak acts as a proxy for a larger group. This is reiterated when Glushak tracks one of the saboteurs to

Khudiakov's hut. He pauses outside his old friend's home, checks his rifle, and addresses the audience again: "We will enter and kill." He includes the audience in the hunt.

This sequence contains the narrative's first encounter between Khudiakov and Glushak. Glushak stands outside the hut and shouts at the top of his voice, "Come out!" Dovzhenko cuts to the inside of the cabin, and we see the hanging furs and curtains in the cabin shake from the force of the shout, as if disturbed by a gust of wind.

Khudiakov scampers out of the hut to confront Glushak, who asks if Khudiakov has seen any foreigners. Khudiakov's denial is protracted to emphasize the gravity of the lie. At this point he makes the fatal decision to harbor the enemy, and his lie to Glushsk seals his fate. When Glushak poses the question, Dovzhenko cuts to a long shot of Khudiakov, and we hear a very soft "no" on the sound track. This is followed by an abrupt jump cut to a medium close-up of Khudiakov, who faces the camera and repeats "no," this time somewhat louder. Dovzhenko then cuts to a long shot of Glushak standing several yards away from Khudiakov. Glushak shouts a lengthy speech to his friend which almost begs him to reconsider his answer: "Vasil Petrovich! Remember when we were still boys? I killed my fifth tiger and saved your life? Since then the natives have called me Tiger's Death. Soon my son will fly here from Moscow. He writes that 10,000 kilometers is already a short distance. Youth is breaking new paths to the ocean, and on the shore where I killed the tiger. . . Remember? They are building the city, Aerograd. That city will determine what happens both to us and to the Pacific Ocean." Glushak's speech invokes the long history of their friendship and then points to the rapid historical change going on around them. It implies that they find themselves at a turning point, the moment when modernization will overtake the Far East, and this is the moment of decision in their personal relationship as well. In the wake of this heartfelt speech Glushak asks again if Khudiakov has seen any foreigners, and in an extreme long shot, we see Khudiakov with his arms spread wide firmly shouting, "No!" Three times Khudiakov denies the truth.

Glushak chooses to accept Khudiakov's resolute denial. As Glushak moves back into the woods, he shouts a last piece of advice to Khudiakov, telling him to give up his private farm and join the nearby collective because this is not "the time for small farms." As Glushak's speech continues on the sound track, Khudiakov looks out into the woods, but Glushak has disappeared. Glushak has left the space, but his voice remains behind. The sequence begins and ends with Glushak's powerful voice penetrating Khudiakov's hut. Khudiakov seems haunted by the resonance of Glushak's calls as a reminder of his guilt, just as Guba was pursued by the bodiless voice in *Ivan*.

When Khudiakov goes back into his hut, the Japanese infiltrator is indeed there. Khudiakov's guilt is confirmed with the audience, even though Glushak at this point is left ignorant. The scene ends with Khudiakov and the Japanese posed next to each other. The samurai sharpens his sword and stares intently into the camera. Khudiakov sits facing the camera but never looks directly into it. He holds his head in his hands in shame, refusing to acknowledge the camera's presence.

In this film, the inability to return the camera's gaze indicates guilt. As we have seen, characters often acknowledge the audience represented by the camera. As a young Chukcha journeys to the future site of Aerograd, for example, he pauses for a moment to speak to the camera. When Glushak's wife lovingly mocks him by calling him an "old forest dog," he turns to the camera and asks, "Why did I marry such a tiger?" But why is it so important that Khudiakov's eyes avoid the camera when his guilt is established? The answer emerges in an anecdote Glushak tells a child. The child asks Glushak about his adventures as a tiger hunter, and Glushak claims that the secret lies in the fact that "a tiger cannot look a man in the eye." The tiger roars and springs at a hunter, but if the man looks it squarely in the eye, it hesitates just before the kill. That is when the hunter must kill it. "Just think of what power a man has in his eye," Glushak says in conclusion to his little story.

The ability to look an opponent in the eye is made a sign of power; the ability to look directly into the camera becomes a sign of integrity. When the partisans at Glushak's home suggest that Khudiakov is in league with the enemy, Glushak refuses to believe them. Dovzhenko cuts into the scene an insert which is a testament to Glushak and Khudiakov's mutual loyalty. The insert shows Glushak and Khudiakov standing next to each other in the middle of a forest. (fig. 18) In a single long take, they look directly into the camera and recite in perfect unison a long vow of friendship. "For fifty years our friendship has lasted here in the taiga and seems to have rushed by like a single day. Each day I look and look again and I ask myself if anywhere in the world there is such a beautiful and rich place. No place in the world is so beautiful and rich." This insert does not function as a narrative flashback. Rather, it stands as an abstract proclamation of trust made between the two men. Significantly, the vow is delivered directly to the camera.

The insert is motivated by the accusation against Khudiakov and by Glushak's stubborn loyalty to his friend. After the insert, Dovzhenko returns to Glushak's home at the moment when Glushak responds to the

Figure 18. *Aerograd*

accusation. Glushak denies that Khudiakov could be implicated in sub-version. He says "no" three times to those gathered, echoing the three denials made earlier by Khudiakov.

But Khudiakov's deceit is more than a betrayal of Glushak's trust. The vow was made to the camera, to the audience. Since Khudiakov betrays the audience, it is no wonder he cannot answer the camera's stare. When Khudiakov is captured by the partisans in the attack on the Old Believer village, Glushak confronts him for the second time.

> *Glushak:* "Vasil, you?"
> *Khudiakov:* "Me—me, Stepan—me."

Khudiakov confesses three times to offset the three denials of their first encounter. We recall that Glushak has been delegated to serve as executioner on behalf of the audience. "We will enter and kill," he had said during the early scene outside of Khudiakov's hut. Now that prediction comes true. Glushak must execute an enemy of the Soviet Union. Glushak will not kill Khudiakov in the presence of the other partisans. He leads Khudiakov away from the eyes of the others to the dense, iso-

Figure 19. *Aerograd*

lated part of the forest where the earlier vow of friendship had been made. But Khudiakov cannot escape the camera's eye; it follows them every step as they march into the forest. And in a stunning moment, as Khudiakov passes in front of the camera, he shields his face with his hand. (fig. 19) So profound is his shame, he hides his face from the audience he has betrayed. When he is shot by Glushak, he is framed from the waist down so that he does not have to face the camera at the moment of death.

Khudiakov cannot face the camera, but Glushak must do so in order to reaffirm his authority. Just before the execution, Glushak turns to the camera and proclaims: "I am killing a traitor and an enemy of the working class, my friend Vasil Petrovich Khudiakov, sixty years old. Be witness to my grief." The audience is brought fully into the act again. It will be "witness" to Glushak's grief, just as it had been witness to Khudiakov's crime. The sequence also apes the ritual of an official trial. The charges against Khudiakov are spelled out in a formal speech. The guilty man is fully identified with his crimes and condemned before the camera and the audience.

At the very end of the film Glushak addresses the audience for the last time. He stands on the site where Aerograd will be built and, facing the camera, calls upon future generations to build socialism in the taiga. Part of his speech is a near-perfect recapitulation of the oath of friendship he and Khudiakov had recited earlier: "Fifty years of my life have gone by in the taiga and it seems like only a day. Every day I look and I look again and I ask myself if anywhere else in the world is so rich and beautiful." But there is one very significant omission distinguishing this speech from the first: the reference to Khudiakov's friendship is gone. Now the discourse is only between Glushak and the audience. Khudiakov has been removed, liquidated. References to his existence disappear the moment he dies; he becomes a "nonperson."

Dovzhenko has been at great pains to justify the killing in the film and to justify Glushak's function as executioner. Glushak is made such a lovable old character it is easy to lose sight of the grim role he has undertaken. And the execution of Khudiakov is presented as the inevitable outcome of Khudiakov's betrayal of sacred trusts. The film ends with a stern warning on the consequences of disloyalty. Glushak calls on the audience to be ever more wary of future subversion. If any future enemy should appear, Glushak warns, one must "strike him in the eye" (again the eye!) and "strike him in the heart." In Stalin's Russia there was no relief from such vigilance.

The elimination of enemies in the narrative clears the way for settlement of the Far East. In an elaborate epilogue, we finally return to the ostensible interest of the film, Aerograd itself. In several Dovzhenko films, including *Earth* and *Ivan,* the honoring of a martyr becomes the occasion for a general renewal of will to work at the task of building socialism. The martyr in this case is Van Lin, killed by Khudiakov during the battle. The scene begins with an incongruity. Van Lin dies in the Old Believer village, the site of the battle. Khudiakov is captured there, and Glushak leads him into a distant part of the forest for execution. But when Glushak emerges from the forest to join his men in the village, he carries Van Lin's body. The logistics of the exchange seem impossible; yet the inconsistency could be significant. Glushak goes into the forest with a traitor and emerges with a martyr. Note again that when Khudiakov dies, he literally disappears from the film. There is no posthumous reference made to him. He is left in some isolated spot in the taiga.

The attention shifts to Van Lin and to the hero's funeral he receives. Glushak carries Van Lin to Vladimir's airplane. His body is then borne aloft in an obvious effort toward apotheosis. Van Lin and the airplane climb into the sky and soar over the taiga. But soon the sky is filled with

Soviet planes. Vladimir's machine gives way to scores of planes which seem to pour out of the clouds.

The epilogue finally takes up the theme of migration east. We discover that the planes carry thousands of volunteers who come to work on the building of Aerograd. In a spectacular show, they parachute to the ground. Van Lin's body is carried from the earth to the sky while the new recruits reverse that movement. One form of Soviet hero, the rugged, homespun partisan and civil war veteran, is replaced by a new breed of scrubbed, young regular troops.

The epilogue can only be called an orgy of militarism. Not only do airplanes and paratroops fill the sky, but columns of Red Army troops march through the taiga. They all converge on the site of the future city of Aerograd. A long series of intertitles informs us that the volunteers are coming to Aerograd from dozens of Soviet cities. Significantly, they all seem to be regimented troops despite the fact that one of the titles refers to Komsomols, members of the civilian youth corps.

The military provided the rhetorical model for Soviet discipline and unity under the Five-Year Plans of the thirties. The military model helped define the terms of national development for Soviet citizens, and the entire nation underwent a form of regimentation in a period when there seemed little difference between economic progress and national security. In *Aerograd,* saber rattling seems to take precedent over the economic promise of Far Eastern settlement, and the potential of socialist construction gives way to bellicose rhetoric. The gravity of the issues addressed in the film and the politics of the Terror may have precluded anything less.

IX
Shchors

THE INCIDENT could well have served to epitomize Stalinism, so trenchantly did it illustrate the general secretary's personal authority over Soviet artistic policy. Stalin decided to grace a state function in 1935 at which Dovzhenko and other prominent Soviet filmmakers were gathered. Much of the casual conversation at the meeting concerned the recent Soviet film *Chapaev,* a lionizing account of the Red Army commander and civil war hero. During the ceremonies Stalin suggested to Dovzhenko that he direct a "Ukrainian *Chapaev.*" That recommendation soon assumed the proportions of an official mandate, and the production machinery for a Ukrainian version of Stalin's favorite movie was soon set in motion. After *Aerograd* opened to favorable reviews, Dovzhenko was dispatched back to the Ukrainfilm studio to carry through on the suggestion. Stalin later asserted that he had only spoken in jest, somewhat disingenuously ignoring the fact that his merest whim could function as government fiat. The final outcome of Stalin's chance remark was Dovzhenko's *Shchors,* an account of the exploits of the Ukrainian civil war partisan under whom Dovzhenko had served and who, like Chapaev, died in battle and promptly entered the pantheon of Soviet heroes.[1]

The account of the film's genesis in Stalin's suggestion represents more than a telling anecdote about the Soviet ruler's special brand of persuasiveness. Indeed, the specter of Stalinism looms over the finished film, as it did over much of the Soviet cinematic product of the middle and late 1930s. For this was the period the "cult of personality," when countless Soviet films, plays, and literary works featured heroic and nearly infallible central characters who served as Stalin surrogates and who gave popular form to the state's various rationalizations of one-man rule.

In the manner of much Stalinist art, the title character dominates the narrative of Dovzhenko's *Shchors*. The film opens during the 1918 German intervention in the Ukrainian civil war. Ukrainian partisans form a brigade known as the Boguns under the command of young Nikolai Shchors, and they join with the Tarashchansk regiment, headed by the earthy old peasant Vasyl Bozhenko, to oppose German and Rada forces. German soldiers hope to return home after the Kaiser's abdication, but their officers resist. Shchors responds with a policy of fraternization between Ukrainian and German enlisted men which overwhelms the German officer corps and clears the way for the German evacuation. After Petliura takes command of the Rada forces, Shchors defeats him at Chernigov and soon liberates Kiev. A Rada counteroffensive forces Shchors back, and he is wounded in a desperate nine-day battle at Berdichev which momentarily halts Petliura's advance. Shchors recuperates with other wounded partisans, who discuss with him their dreams of the future. When word comes that Bozhenko's wife has been murdered by White agents, Shchors consoles the grieving Bozhenko. The two leaders regroup and lead a rout of Polish invaders. In the summer of 1919, however, Petliura's troops sweep across the Ukraine. Bozhenko is mortally wounded in the Rada assault, and his men carry him to his grave, where Shchors delivers the eulogy. The film ends with Shchors reviewing the troops at his newly established school for Red Army officers.

This synopsis should provide a sense of the narrative's somewhat disjointed nature, a feature that owes much to the unwieldy machinery of the Soviet creative establishment in the 1930s. *Shchors* was three years in production, during which time it underwent constant review by the film industry's ever-more-exacting censorship committees. During this interval Soviet historians were kept busy rewriting the official history of the revolution and civil war, erasing the contributions of recent purge victims and filling the newly created gaps with expanded claims about the individual roles played by Lenin and Stalin. Dovzhenko's project was inexorably caught in this revisionist process; sequences were arbitrarily altered to conform to the latest amendments in the official record. Whatever dramatic unity the original script may have had was sacrificed to countless revisions ordered by capricious outside auditors.[2]

In lieu of sound narrative continuity, the film offers the particular prominence of a central character who dominates the action, and it surrounds that figure with an aura of omnipotence. When *Shchors* finally appeared in 1939, it joined a genre of idolatrous films about powerful individuals from Russian and Soviet history, all of which were designed to provide precedent and legitimation for Stalin's authority. *Shchors* does not precisely refer to a contemporary situation. Rather, it was enveloped by a pervasive intellectual system associated with the cult of personality. Among other tactics, Stalin identified himself with Lenin and other revered historical figures and presented himself as their quasi-ordained successor. "If absolute monarchs had ruled by the Grace of God," noted Isaac Deutscher, "he [Stalin] ruled by the Grace of History; and he was worshipped as the demiurge of history."[3] Contributing to this phenomenon was a series of films of the 1930s which revived and extolled the memory of past leaders: such features as *Peter I, Alexander Nevsky,* and, most important, *Chapaev* assigned to historical figures a measure of wisdom and authority commensurate with that of Stalin. *Chapaev* enjoyed special salience. The most widely seen Soviet feature of the decade, reportedly finding some fifty million Soviet viewers within five years, the film became a favorite of the party leadership and was designated as a model for subsequent productions.[4]

Dovzhenko's "Ukrainian *Chapaev*" represented the first project since *Arsenal* in 1929 in which Dovzhenko turned away from the exigent phases of Soviet economic development for a historical reevaluation of the revolutionary period. And he followed current formulas by revising the account of the revolution that he had put forward a decade before. In *Arsenal* Dovzhenko ignored the role of Bolshevik leaders, concentrating instead on the hardships visited on the population at large, thereby earning an official admonishment for lack of *partiinost'*.[5] He more than compensated for this in *Shchors* by concentrating on a single figure who seems to represent the essence of party authority and who was created to mouth the party's calls for greater discipline and sacrifice in the face of continued foreign and domestic security threats.

Dovzhenko's revisionism also took its cue from prevailing practices. The strictly utilitarian definition of truth that underpinned the concept of historical reality obtained in Soviet historiography as much as it did in other ideological arenas. The past had to be rewritten periodically to make it serve current and pending state policies. And much of the historical record of the revolutionary period, as well as many of the original participants, fell victim to the purges. As veteran Bolsheviks disappeared into the camps or issued fantastic confessions of myriad capital crimes, their contributions to the Soviet system were struck from the record. Stalin personally supervised the writing of the Communist party's latest official history, *Short History of the Communist Party of the Soviet Union,* a text which reshaped the past to conform to the "revelations" of the purge trials.[6]

The purges touched Dovzhenko's film in a more immediate way than merely fostering a general climate of revisionism.[7] While the film was in production, the purges caught up with the Red Army. In the Kiev military district alone in 1937 and 1938, between six hundred and seven hundred officers were arrested, and the Ukrainian officer corps virtually ceased to exist. This grim turn encroached directly on the production of *Shchors*. Dovzhenko had planned to represent the principal members of Shchors's old regiment in the film and had enlisted some of the participants to serve as historical advisors on the set. But when the purges overtook the Red Army, one Bogun veteran after another disappeared from sight and, not coincidentally, from Dovzhenko's script. The most serious crisis on the film set occurred when Shchor's old lieutenant and Dovzhenko's friend from civil war days, Ivan Dubovoi, was arrested and shot in July 1938. Dovzhenko had retained Dubovoi as a consultant on the film, and the execution left Dovzhenko so distraught that he suffered a heart attack and had to postpone production for several months while he recovered.

Since so many Bogun veterans were rapidly being transformed into "nonpersons," Dovzhenko had to abandon plans to populate the film with re-creations of the original civil war partisans, surrounding the central character instead with a group of largely fictionalized composite figures. The only historical personages represented in the finished film are the title character and Vasyl Bozhenko of the Tarashchansk regiment. Both men died in combat in 1919 and were promptly lionized as Soviet martyrs, thereby achieving immunity from purge-era deletions in the historical record.

From its initial conception through its long, ill-starred production history, *Shchors* represents a product of thirties revisionism. Dovzhenko's Nikolai Shchors seems less a civil war figure than a representative of social relations in the 1930s. Dovzhenko relies on what was known about the life and career of Shchors in building his characterization, but he interprets the material in light of the ground that the USSR had covered in the two decades since Shchors had fought and died. Dovzhenko requires his film, which is set in 1919, to acknowledge that its audience exists in 1939. Not able simply to recount the events of the civil war, he incorporates into the narrative the changes, real and imagined, effected in the Soviet Union in the succeeding decades. His new version of the revolution has the social formations of thirties Stalinism already present *ab initio*. *Shchors* constitutes Dovzhenko's own small contribution to Soviet revisionism.

In *Arsenal* Dovzhenko concentrates to a large extent on the consequences of armed struggle, on land made sterile and people numbed by the war.

But *Shchors* looks to the nature of military command and regimentation, largely ignoring the effects of war on the indigenous population. In fact, the land and the civilians show none of the indelible battle scars evident in *Arsenal*. *Shchors* alternates between battle scenes and intervals of peace, but we find little indication of the residue of battle during the peaceful passages. The fields and landscapes remain rich and fertile, a far cry from the wasteland of *Arsenal*. The only enduring sign of war's presence is the smoke which lingers in the mise-en-scène. Smoke clouds appear frequently in the background of shots even during the peaceful scenes, as when the German authorities confront the population of a Ukrainian village or when Shchors addresses the prisoners. The smoke serves as a reminder of the battle recently fought, and it substitutes for the more graphic illustrations of war's toll that we recall from *Arsenal*. The landscape in *Shchors* remains suspiciously pristine and fertile, apparently immune from the damage of armed conflict.

Dovzhenko is almost as cautious in portraying war's impact on the population. When the Germans invade, we witness villagers fleeing with their belongings. When Petliura captures Berdichev later in the film, we see Jews in the village cowering from the first stages of a Petliurist pogrom. But these images of disrupted society seem tame in comparison with *Arsenal*. The civilians in *Shchors* hardly resemble the dehumanized specimens of the earlier film. When the Germans massacre the villagers, Dovzhenko shows a German machine gunner fire on the peasants, but, instead of providing an image of bloodshed, Dovzhenko cuts to a shot of a single, fatally wounded villager staggering to his hut. Dovzhenko omits any full view of the carnage, the severity of which we can only infer. Compare this with *Arsenal*'s pattern of focusing on victims.

In fact, the civilians in *Shchors* show remarkable resilience. They seem able to carry on with their lives rather easily despite the ongoing conflict. A peasant marriage party holds a celebration in the village streets while a battle rages around them. The celebrants ride through the streets and sing gaily even as Petliura's artillery barrage rains on the village; they seem as fully immune from death and destruction as the natural terrain. One of Shchors's soldiers accepts a wedding invitation while directing the operation of a howitzer. Several of Shchors's men break in on the wedding feast and stage an impromptu sword dance. A few moments earlier we had witnessed a genuine, fatal sword fight between Bolshevik and Petliurist troops. As this parallel suggests, the military and civilian realms seem to fuse in the civil war experience that is represented here, with the combat failing to break the normal routine of life.

In one scene Shchors and his men are honored by a group of villagers

Figure 20. *Shchors*

with an enormous feast. Healthy, smiling peasants turn out in their best
attire, and long tables are laden with harvest. (fig. 20) This is hardly the
ravaged peasant population that lived with famine throughout the real
civil war. Rather, this cheery image seems to be inspired by the countless
thirties posters and paintings showing the supposed outcome of Soviet
economic progress, with groups of contented, well-fed peasants celebrating their happy lot. This film is no more willing to acknowledge the en-
demic suffering of the civil war than Stalin was to acknowledge the
famines of the 1930s. Such omissions, like so many others we have noted
in Dovzhenko's work, bear consideration. In leaving out signs of serious
damage to the land and population, Dovzhenko makes his own deletions
in the historical record. Soviet realism, that special combination of fantasy and perceived necessity, had expunged want from the USSR's representation of itself, and Dovzhenko obliges by applying the modern
Soviet Union's idealized self-image retroactively to the civil war period.

While civilians fare decently in this version of the war experience, the
effect of war on the population is not the film's chief concern. Rather, it
attempts to present an ideal model of social organization and authority,
and in so doing, it develops the military motifs introduced in *Ivan* and
Aerograd. Dovzhenko offers a model of government vested in a combat

command structure and of a society defined as a disciplined military regiment.

The film significantly delays the introduction of genuine authority to heighten its import. The title character, who will become the instrument of that authority, does not appear until several minutes into the film. *Shchors* opens in medias res with a battle already under way. We discover that it is a quite uncentered battle—a series of apparently miscellaneous barrages and hand-to-hand encounters. It entails no definable strategy, and it ends in a debacle for the Ukrainians, as if Shchors's absence assures chaos.

After the battle we see the effect of German occupation. Dovzhenko shows a German sentry manning an outpost at night. The opening shot of the sequence is framed so that we see only his German helmet, his rifle, and a bilingual sign which says "Ukrainian Empire" in both German and Ukrainian *(Ukrainisches Reich / Ukrainska Derzhava)*. This formal image is offered as a shorthand representation of government by colonial rule. Order is imposed from outside. The film is setting the stage for the introduction of a homegrown authority.

We soon see Ukrainians slipping past the sentry and through a swamp to gather at Shchors's campsite. As a Bolshevik sentry stops them, they announce that they are partisans coming to join Shchors. They arrive from Ukrainian regions as widely diverse as Uman and Poltava. Shchors is still absent, but his name is invoked as a force which draws Ukrainians together like a powerful magnet. His name and his mystique precede his physical presence.

Shchors's Ukrainian sentry stops one small group of partisans in the same sequence and asks for their documents. He is told: "We have all kinds of documents, comrade. From Petliura, from the Poles, from the Germans." The chaos of the Ukrainian political system has rendered government papers meaningless. Formal, printed documents serve little purpose in this situation. One partisan tells the sentry that his documents are German. The partisan then turns and bares his back, telling the sentry to "read" the lash marks recorded there. This finally convinces the sentry to let them pass. The lash marks apparently function as persuasive documentation of the political situation of the country, one marked by anarchy.

Shchors is finally introduced as the remedy. We meet him as he is greeting his new volunteers. He assures them, "Today you will rest and tomorrow you will march, according to all the rules of military discipline." Much of the ensuing narrative will depict his efforts to institute that announced goal of establishing the "rules of military discipline."

Unlike the title character of *Chapaev*, who lacks erudition and polish, Shchors is represented from the start as a sophisticate and intellectual, and Dovzhenko will not let us forget it, frequently including reminders of Shchors's learning. The commander quotes Shevchenko to his prisoners of war, and he keeps portraits of Pushkin and Shevchenko in his quarters. The film also notes that Shchors was trained in medicine; we see him give a full medical examination to a goldbricking White officer. Dovzhenko offers Bozhenko as a friendly foil to the more cerebral Shchors. Bozhenko operates from more instinctive skills, lacking formal training and officer credentials. The boisterous peasant is a far cry from the ascetic, reticent Shchors, who neither drinks nor smokes and discourages those practices in others.

Here we find the most significant internal tension in the text. Dovzhenko wants to endear Shchors and his comrades to us by stripping them of pomp and affectation. They are presented as honest, homespun types who go to the front out of an innate sense of patriotism. Yet the film also tries to erect an image of infallible authority in Shchors, and it assigns him the task of making his motley crew over into a modern, ordered military unit, one in which the partisans' spontaneity is tempered and contained.

We are to note with pleasure the informality of Shchors's following throughout the narrative. The officer corps operates largely on the basis of first names or nicknames, and Shchors himself is called Nikolai or even Kolia. Bozhenko is known throughout the brigade as Batko, a Ukrainian term of endearment usually reserved for one's own grandfather. The salute is practically unknown in this group.

By way of contrast, the commanders of the German occupation force observe military rituals to a comic degree. When the German officers are confronted by their superior with the news that the Kaiser has abdicated, some of them take the noble course and promptly shoot themselves. The others neatly step over the bodies to close up ranks in the formation. Such formality extends to other Soviet enemies. Petliura opens himself to a devastating ambush because he insists on holding a parade to celebrate the archbishop's birthday. His shining regiment marches down the main street of Chernigov in their best blue uniforms with a full brass band, falling into Shchors's trap. Shchors's motley troops, on the other hand, forego ritual, spontaneously singing Ukrainian folk songs when they march or travel cross-country.

Bozhenko, more than any other character, manifests a basic distaste for formal military order. Cantankerous, blustering, but always forthright, he remains the only character in the film permitted to question

Shchors's decisions, though, significantly, he always obeys them. Bozhenko commands by gut instinct rather than by prescribed strategy. In the presence of the entire officer staff he is forced to admit that he cannot read a map when he fails to spot Vinnitsa, a town he is assigned to capture. But Bozhenko lets it be known that he can make his way to Vinnitsa well enough without the aid of any map. Ultimately Shchors confirms that Bozhenko reads a map "in his own way," that he can find any spot in the Ukraine and move his troops there rapidly from a more primal knowledge of the land.

As we can see, Dovzhenko has gone to much trouble to portray Shchors's brigade sympathetically by making them such open, unaffected types. Their disregard for pomp and circumstance is offered as their most positive characteristic. Yet he also wants to show us the process of establishing a modern military regimen, and Shchors represents the agent of that process. Throughout the film Shchors attempts to instill in his men a sense of discipline that runs counter to their spontaneous natures. Ultimately Shchors emerges as something of a prude. He makes much of the fact that he does not drink. A peasant offers him spirits at the village celebration; Shchors declines, announcing that the Bolsheviks will win the war without the aid of liquor, as if that were a first in the annals of combat. Shchors even attempts, although unsuccessfully, to make Bozhenko swear off demon cognac. Shchors berates a fellow officer for smoking when news of the death of Bozhenko's wife comes, as if the act were disrespectful. And when he sends men to infiltrate the German ranks and fraternize, he even makes them pledge not to use swear words.

These small acts of personal temperance are offered as part of an ideal model of self-discipline during revolutionary struggle, and it soon extends to larger concerns: the men must deny themselves sexual fulfillment as well. There are no ideal families in *Shchors* as in *Aerograd,* providing comfort, companionship, and sexual partners. At one point Shchors addresses his men and orders them to sever family ties for the duration of the war. Shchors himself seems to have done so. His wife is absent from the film. Although he writes her, he never visits her, and he recuperates with his troops rather than with his wife when he is wounded. Even his letter to her seems curiously sterile. Shchors staggers into his quarters utterly exhausted after the nine-day battle at Berdichev, gazes around as if lost and confused, and then lets his gun and coat simply fall to the floor. He does not write the letter himself; he dictates it to an aide who sits at a typewriter in an adjoining room. And while he dictates the letter, he holds his head under a water tap and douses himself with cold water! The sense of alienation suggested in this staging complements the coldness of the letter, which is less a personal note than a military communiqué describing the battle ("He [Petliura] had five armored cars and thirty-two cannons"). The scene may have been calculated to reveal a sensitive, personal side to the commander, but it, in fact, betrays Shchors's isolation. He sacrifices all to the war, and it so drains him of emotion that none is left for his wife.

Even Bozhenko's wife, who is also kept absent, is described less as a spouse than as an abstract maternal force. When Bozhenko learns of her death, he behaves as if he has lost a mother. He announces to his men that he and they are all orphans now. He calls her "Matka," an endearing term for a mother, and tells the men that they will no longer have anyone to brew their tea and mend their shirts.

Military commitment even displaces private love at one point. When Shchors's troops enter the village wedding festivities, the young bride forsakes her new husband to join the Bolshevik partisans. She berates the groom for choosing to remain politically neutral, and her cutting remark that he is "neither hot nor cold" even seems to associate political neutrality with sexual dysfunction. She turns instead to Shchors's trusted lieutenant, Petro, announcing that she fell in love with him "the first moment [she] laid eyes on him." That moment came, not coincidentally, when Petro was directing an artillery barrage. She is drawn to him because of his conduct as a soldier, and she promptly enlists in Shchors's brigade.

The text posits all of these examples of self-denial as part of the fundamental order necessary to establish an effective military machine. Shchors imposes a much more serious discipline on his men by tempering their impulsiveness. Bozhenko's instinctive aggression in combat contains a dose of what Shchors characterizes as "anarchism." Bozhenko is ready to kill his prisoners without a hint of regret, and he is incredulous when Shchors proposes rehabilitating the White officers instead and using them to staff the proposed military school. When Bozhenko learns that spies in Kiev have killed his wife, he proposes taking his Tarashchansk regiment to sack the city until Shchors solemnly vows to intercept Bozhenko's regiment with his own Bogun troops and personally to kill Bozhenko. Later Shchors has to order Bozhenko not to allow his men to cross the Polish border in pursuit of Petliura's troops. "Not even a bird" will be permitted to violate Polish territory, Shchors warns. It is important that Bozhenko submits to Shchors's decisions even though they frequently defy Bozhenko's innate impulses. The film insists that authority must be respected and suggests that Bozhenko fails to see beyond the apparent reality of his situation. He simply reacts to immediate appearances, and it is left to Shchors to explain the long-term consequences of strategy, to see through immediate, ephemeral appearances to the future. Bozhenko assumes that Bolsheviks never retreat willingly. But Shchors orders Bozhenko to pull back from terrain that he had fought hard to win, knowing that a momentary retreat will aid in the eventual defense of Kiev. The same foresight informs Shchors's decision to use veteran White officers in his school. Bozhenko cannot accept the idea of rehabilitating enemies. But Shchors looks ahead and recognizes that the school will profit the Red Army for generations and that the short-term concessions are worth the long-range investment. Shchors seems to possess transcendent knowledge of the future.

Indeed, the narrative invokes the future, and the film even acknowledges its status as a document of the 1930s. Shchors professes to recognize the impact of the partisans' exploits on future generations. When Bozhenko hears of his wife's death, he falls into a deep depression. One of the devices that Shchors uses to bring Bozhenko out is an appeal to Bozhenko's place in history. "Remember, Batko," he says, "our names are already recorded in history in golden letters." Shchors persuades Bozhenko to conduct himself stoically by invoking history, contending, in effect, that Bozhenko must maintain his composure to conform to the image history has foreordained for him. A more blunt appeal to future generations occurs when Bozhenko is laid to rest. Shchors's brief eulogy over Bozhenko's body notes that they are in the midst of battle and have no time for an elaborate ceremony. He postpones the memorial, promising, "We will remember you [Bozhenko] in twenty years." Shchors makes the memorial for Bozhenko a phenomenon of 1939, the year that the film appeared. Thus, the film owns up to its status as a product of the 1930s by invoking its release date and, by extension, its 1939 audience.

The film's most glaring omission constitutes its most important concession to the imperatives of thirties revisionism. The real Nikolai Shchors died in battle on 30 August 1919. And, as all Soviet audiences would have known, Shchors's trusted comrade Bozhenko died only days prior to that, on 21 August. Despite the fact that *Chapaev,* the prototype film for Dovzhenko, ends with the title character's death, and that Shchors was popularly remembered for his martyrdom, *Shchors* completely omits any reference to the title character's fated end. The film's elaborate lament for Bozhenko seems to dispense with the issue of martyrdom. After Bozhenko's funeral, the film moves to an epilogue showing Shchors reviewing a parade of officers at his school for Red Army commanders. A literal reading of the ending would suggest that Shchors

Figure 21. *Shchors*

must have established a school in the week between Bozhenko's death
and his own. But Soviet audiences would have been aware of the historical impossibility of that sequence. Shchors was involved in a desperate
fight against a Rada counteroffensive at that time, a fact which renders
Dovzhenko's conclusion chronologically impossible.[8]

Why did Dovzhenko devise an ending which seems, inexplicably, to
omit Shchors's martyrdom from an account of the last months of an en-
shrined Soviet martyr? In part, Dovzhenko had to bow to purge politics.
We recall that Dovzhenko was stunned by the arrest and execution of his
old friend Dubovoi, who had served with Shchors and who was a consultant on the film. Dovzhenko complained impotently to his diary
about the dilemma posed by "the new version of Shchors's death." That
new version, in fact, involved an ugly frame-up of Dubovoi; before being executed he was forced to sign an incredible confession, professing to
have assassinated Shchors.[9] One can imagine the untenable position in
which Dovzhenko found himself. His own military consultant was
pulled away from the film in the middle of production and "unmasked"
as the murderer of the film's title character. Dovzhenko clearly could not
incorporate this version into his film. The only way for him to deal with
Shchors's death was to deny it.

He leaves the narrative open by leaving Shchors conspicuously alive.

Figure 22. *Shchors*

But the epilogue does more than this. It assigns to Shchors a curious brand of immortality. We see Shchors standing at the window of a small, wooden barracks, reviewing troops at his school for Red Army commanders as the graduates pass by in snappy parade maneuvers. (figs. 21 and 22) This scene could not have happened in the time and space of the narrative and still remain faithful to the history of Shchors's life and death. What is more, when we look at the troops marching past, they do not at all resemble the partisans we have followed throughout the film. They are a smart, crack unit, a far cry from Shchors's ragtag comrades. In fact they are not civil war troops at all: although they carry the banner of Shchors's band of Boguns, their uniforms and weapons clearly identify them as regular Red Army troops of the 1930s.[10] To highlight the contrast between the original Boguns and this slick outfit, Dovzhenko has some men from Shchors's old partisan band standing behind him in their rough, makeshift uniforms. Shchors is lifted out of 1919 and represented in the 1930s. Or rather, a character in 1919, Shchors, gazes out a window and sees 1939. The concept of historical reality finds precise dramatic form in this juxtaposition. Shchors can literally see and discern distant historical goals. Like Lincoln Steffens, he has seen the future, and it works.

Or more precisely, it marches. For this is a crack, polished military formation, showing the order and precision that Shchors has advocated. Shchors's old partisans, however, have won our loyalty through their informality, through their very lack of polish. Dovzhenko buries that old-style partisan with Bozhenko, and he lets Shchors survive into the future as the forerunner of the modern military establishment realized in the military school. Shchors and his Boguns mediate between military heroics of the past (their regimental name alludes to the Cossacks) and the up-to-date professional army of the Stalin years.

Shchors's final speech to the parade troops adds another dimension. We see him in a medium shot leaning slightly out the barracks window gazing onto the parade ground. He does not look directly into the camera as he speaks but slightly to one side of and past it. By now the military parade and portentious closing speech have become familiar in Dovzhenko films, having already concluded *Ivan* and *Aerograd*. But here Shchors, instead of addressing an ideal audience represented by the camera, clearly is speaking to the soldiers on the parade ground. In a sense, that military regiment has supplanted the audience which was addressed so forthrightly in *Aerograd*. The military is now presented as the ideal audience, one that will recognize and answer to authority. The only image of post-civil war Soviet society we have is this regiment, and it is offered at a time when the military model of social organization dominated the nation.

Fittingly, Shchors's final speech invokes supreme authority. He tells the troops to "hate slavery like death" and to "love revolution like life." But Shchors does not mouth these sentiments on his own initiative. He cites his source: "I, Shchors, tell you that, and Lenin told it to me." Shchors is represented as the spokesman for Lenin's will. In fact, several times in the film Shchors appeals to Lenin's authority to justify his own measures. When Shchors's associates prove skeptical about his methods, Shchors has only to mention that Lenin supports him to stifle any dissent, and Shchors is the only character in the film permitted to speak Lenin's sacred name. We are to discern that Shchors's military skill results from his direct line to Lenin. And in a sense, Shchors's immortality at the film's end stems from the fact that he is vested with the infallible power and wisdom of Lenin. Again, the contrast with *Arsenal* is illuminating. *Arsenal* also ends with an immortal figure. But Timosh rises from the common ranks to attain his invulnerability. Shchors claims extraordinary power by appealing to the mystique of Lenin and, by extension, to the ideology of *partiinost'*. The device not only honors the memory of Lenin; it justifies Shchors's every action. That justification was well-known and often employed in the atmosphere of the personality cult.

X

Michurin

IN STALIN'S RUSSIA it was referred to loftily as the "Michurin path." Now we assign it the more prosaic label of "Lysenko cult," and we try to comprehend how the charlatan T. D. Lysenko (1898–1976) gained personal control over Soviet genetics. The Lysenko movement was one of the most contradictory phenomena in Soviet history. Its supporters insisted that it was the first genuine "materialist science," the first scientific school to dispose entirely of any vestige of religious mysticism or superstition. Yet the movement flourished in large part because of a calculated campaign to establish a personal aura around Lysenko which deflected attention from legitimate scientific investigation. What transpired in the laboratory and greenhouse was often less significant for Lysenko than what went on in Soviet political circles and in the Soviet media. Speeches, pamphlets, novels, poems, songs, plays, and films promoted Lysenko's image and made him a cult figure.

Dovzhenko's last film, *Michurin,* was a part of the campaign. An idealized screen biography of the Russian horticulturist Ivan Michurin (1855–1935), the film appeared at the height of the Lysenko movement and contributed to the cult. Lysenko often pointed to Michurin as his immediate precursor, and he actively promoted Michurin's memory. Stalin arranged to have Lysenko and Michurin literally celebrated in legend and song. Poems with reference to "the eternal glory of the academician Lysenko" who "walks the Michurin path" became fashionable.[1] Other works portrayed Michurin as a prophet crying out in the wilderness and preparing the way for Lysenko. The two scientists assumed mystical qualities as this carefully planned and orchestrated legend developed. Dovzhenko's *Michurin* similarly glorifies the title character, assigning to him almost magical rather than purely rational powers and thus unwittingly betraying the contradiction of a "materialist" science built on popular mystification.

Dovzhenko's rather episodic narrative seizes on particular passages of Michurin's life. It opens in the late nineteenth century with two wealthy Americans, Byrd and Meyer, visiting Michurin's nursery and making him extravagant offers to work in America. Michurin refuses, choosing instead to serve his own country. He carries on in Kozlov although his work remains unappreciated by Russian officials, and Father Christopher, a local priest, even denounces Michurin's "meddling" in God's natural order. Michurin receives some consolation from a small, enlightened group gathered to celebrate the arrival of the new year 1900. During the World War Michurin suffers a personal blow from the death of his wife, Alexandra, but the success of the 1917 revolution lifts his depression and clears the way for his research to be recognized across the new Russia. The Revolutionary Committee governing the province secures funds to support Michurin's research, and his nursery becomes a national showcase. He faces a final crisis in 1924, when his orchards are threatened by a particularly harsh winter, but the trees survive and blossom in the spring. Michurin finally becomes a recognized Soviet hero and is honored in a celebration to mark his eightieth birthday.

The film derives from the legends and polemics of Lysenkoism. The Lysenko movement generally grew out of real problems within the Soviet agricultural sector.[2] The USSR required increased harvests to feed the legions of former peasants who had been transferred to industry, and Lysenko promised immediate gains in agricultural production. His exaggerated claims seemed to serve the historical reality of Soviet economic development and could thus find justification under Stalin's functional definition of truth. With the initiation of the collectivization program Stalin cracked down on "bourgeois specialists" in genetics and horticulture who expressed doubt about the feasibility of government agricultural quotas. This opened the way for Lysenko, a homespun Ukrainian agriculturist who "worked by intuition and press release,"[3] and who claimed to hold the key to a form of Marxist biology that would, in effect, require nature to submit to Soviet government policy. His inflated claims were accepted as the route to long-term gains in Soviet agriculture and thus were consistent with the definition of historical truth.

At a time when the government demanded that all science must "finally defend and develop dialectical and historical materialism" and "uphold the purity of the principles of Marxism-Leninism,"[4] Lysenko helped his case by appealing to the work of Marx, Engels (especially *Dialectics of Nature,* a seminal book in the USSR), and Lenin. He claimed that his methods, which stressed environment over heredity, were consistent with Marxism and promised greater control over crops. He mastered the appropriate Stalinist rhetoric: chromosome theory was "reactionary, idealist, metaphysical and barren," and it showed dangerous signs of "formalism." He denied the existence of genes, holding that they were idealist constructs with no place in materialist biology. He accused his critics of being Trotskyites and agents out to sabotage Soviet science. He even discredited the discipline of genetics by linking it with the racist theories of Hitler.[5]

Lysenko's favorite scapegoats were the founders of genetics: the German biologist August Weismann (1834–1914), the American zoologist Thomas Hunt Morgan (1866–1943), and especially the influential Gregor Mendel (1822–84), who had the particularly poor judgment to have been a member of a religious order. Lysenko and his followers devised an ingenious morality play in which the sinister Weismann-Morgan-Mendel line dominated bourgeois science with the support of a superstition-ridden church and craven, wealthy capitalists intent upon withholding practical knowledge of nature from the proletariat. Enter such men of vision as Michurin and Lysenko, who are discovered by Soviet leaders Lenin and Stalin and who, with the help of the Soviet rulers, unmask the bourgeois conspiracy in the sciences. Soviet scientists and writers began to parrot the condemnation of the "reactionary pseudo-scientific theory invented by the bourgeois pseudo-scientists, Weismannists, Mendelists, and Morganists."[6]

Ivan Michurin turned out to be an appropriate supporting actor in Lysenko's production. While Michurin never openly endorsed Lysenko, his ideas had much in common with those of Lysenko. Michurin worked in Kozlov, a small town northeast of Moscow. He lacked formal education, and his research in horticulture began as a simple hobby while he worked full time as a railway clerk and signal repairman. When he turned in earnest to horticultural research, he had to support himself by operating a watch repair shop. After the 1917 revolution his experiments won some supporters in the new Soviet regime, and he began to receive financial backing from the government. In 1919 his modest nursery was put under the direction of the Commissariat of Agriculture. In September 1922 the government official Mikhail Kalinin visited Michurin, after which government appropriations for Michurin's research increased substantially. Ultimately Michurin received the Order of Lenin, the Order of the Red Banner, and during an official eightieth birthday party for the horticulturist, a celebrated cable of congratulations from Stalin.[7]

As David Joravsky has shown, however, Michurin profited from a talent for public relations comparable to that of Lysenko.[8] Michurin played the role of a simple man from humble origins who suffered through years of tireless, unappreciated labor. He made his lack of education an asset; he claimed to rely on pragmatism and common sense, and he railed against established scientists for being theoretical obscurantists. Michurin attacked the scientific establishment before the Lysenko vogue because the majority of Russian scientists dismissed his findings. They had good reason. Michurin claimed to have started hundreds of new strains of fruits and berries, but his methods of breeding were so careless that none of the strains proved stable from one generation to the next. By 1931, only one of his new fruit varieties was found suitable for use in commercial orchards.

Michurin embellished the facts of his life as part of his publicity campaign. In one tale he was fond of repeating, he told how American agents constantly journeyed to his door and offered him riches to emigrate to the United States. He exploited this story to drum up government support for his research, leaving the clear impression that he might take up the American offer if the Soviet government did not ante up. But his version was largely fiction. Although Frank Meyer of the United States Department of Agriculture did make two trips to Kozlov, he never attempted to entice Michurin away from his home. Meyer wanted only to purchase some of Michurin's plants, and when Michurin's price proved too high, the deal fell through.

Michurin's biggest asset was his appreciation of the rules of Stalin's personality cult. He discerned that the best way to receive official praise was to give credit to Lenin and Stalin. Michurin's own account of his life had him struggling under the old regime against backwardness and superstition in the manner of Galileo. He claimed that Lenin and Stalin discovered him and brought to public light the worth of his research. In a letter to Stalin he portrayed himself before the Soviet revolution as a "lone experimenter, unrecognized and ridiculed by official savants and bureaucrats of the tsarist Department of Agriculture." Came the revolution and all that changed, owing to the wisdom and justice of "the Soviet system and party which you [Stalin] lead."[9]

In return for official support, Michurin promised Soviet rulers that he would find the means to improve Russia's food supply. Michurin advocated that environment be stressed over heredity in plant breeding so that humans could speed up the evolutionary process by adapting plants to new environments without waiting for nature to take its course. "We cannot wait for favors from nature: we must wrest them from her," became his motto.[10]

Michurin's contention that human intervention could completely determine plant evolution found favor when Lysenko came to power. Michurin never actively campaigned for the Lysenko school although Lysenko approached him for an endorsement. But Lysenko and Soviet leaders systematically built up Michurin's reputation with public ceremonies and awards. After Michurin died in 1935, Lysenko proved happy to portray Michurin as a courageous pioneer who had paved the way for Lysenko's own theories. In the summer of 1948, a special meeting of the Soviet Union's Academy of Agricultural Sciences was convened to make official the infallibility of the Michurin-Lysenko school and to celebrate the success of the "struggle to expose and to rout ideologically Mendelism-Morganism" under "the banner of Michurin's materialist biology."[11] The Michurin doctrine was now the "sole correct line in the biological sciences."[12]

Lysenko gained power in the Russian scientific community in part through the suppression of balanced empirical investigation. What mattered to Soviet officials was the "historical necessity" of Lysenko's movement. Lysenko and Michurin became subjects of countless panegyrics. Their deification forestalled scrutiny of their dubious theories. When Lysenko addressed the Academy at that crucial 1948 meeting, he credited Stalin with inspiring his work and making possible his triumph.[13] For once he told the truth.

This was the context in which Dovzhenko fashioned his version of Michurin's life. Dovzhenko, an avid naturalist and Michurin admirer, though no expert in horticultural science, became interested in working on Michurin in 1944 in the wake of one of the most serious of countless scrapes with Soviet officialdom. Dovzhenko's always tenuous relations with the *apparat* were aggravated when Stalin himself scuttled Dovzhenko's war project *Ukraine in Flames,* and Dovzhenko was summoned to Moscow for a severe reprimand by no less than Lavrenti Beria, the notorious head of the secret police. One party spokesman complained that Dovzhenko had failed to honor "the Leader" in any of his films. "You couldn't spare ten meters of film for the Leader," Mikhail Chiaurelli railed. To work again Dovzhenko needed an ideologically safe subject, one that showed no "nationalist tendencies." Once again he had to opt for a non-Ukrainian subject, and again he left his home studio in Kiev to work in Moscow at the Mosfilm facility. A film on Michurin seemed "a cozy retreat": "The subject doesn't seem to go with my 'nationalism': after all, it's Russian."[14]

Nevertheless, the film was years in production because of government intervention. Although Dovzhenko started the project during the war, the script received so many revisions that the film did not appear until the beginning of 1949. The progress of the scenario was checked at every stage by the film industry's proliferating committees of censors. In December 1945 Dovzhenko suffered a minor heart attack after one especially rancorous conference with censors. He finally finished a presentable draft in the spring of 1946. This version he opened up to general scrutiny in March with a public reading and publication of the text.[15]

And even though the scenario was approved, his troubles with the film project continued. After much work, in the spring of 1948 Dovzhenko presented to authorities what he assumed would be a final version of the film, but after the preview, film industry chief Ivan Bolshakov labelled it a "mediocre, colorless, and uninteresting film," apparently unaware that the bureaucracy's labyrinthine review procedure fostered mediocrity and colorlessness. Bolshakov insisted on a number of deletions until the film seemed to Dovzhenko "completely cut up and naked." But the most unkindest cut came from Stalin, who rejected the film outright. After the ordeal Dovzhenko retreated to a sanatorium for three weeks to recover from a near breakdown.[16]

All of this meddling was designed to bring *Michurin* into line with the official version of Michurin's career and with the latest polemics on biology by Soviet scientists of the Lysenko school. For example, Dovzhenko was ordered to insert the fictional character of Professor Kartashov into the film as a token of the professional opposition to Michurin. Kartashov was to mouth the line of the hated Weismann-Morgan-Mendel school.[17]

The revised revision of the early revisions was finally deemed acceptable for public consumption, and the film premiered in January 1949. The constant external pressure and meddling had delayed completion of the film until after the 1948 conference of the Academy of Agricultural Sciences. The Lysenkoist public relations effort which followed the 1948 conference eclipsed all the preceding campaigns. Dovzhenko's *Michurin* opened in Moscow with tremendous fanfare as part of the celebration of the triumph of Lysenko. The government made every effort to find the largest audience possible for *Michurin*. Despite the fact that it was a color film and that copies were expensive, Soiuzkino manufactured and distributed 1,500 prints, an unusually high number. Moscow was plastered with *Michurin* posters. The film industry even experimented with what was a new promotional device in the USSR, running *Michurin* trailers in various cinemas weeks prior to the film's opening.[18]

The preproduction censorship mill ground slowly but exceedingly fine. So exacting was the control process that the finished, approved *Mi-*

churin could be considered a near-perfect interpretation of the now-sacred Lysenko line and thus above reproach. Reviews of *Michurin* were less aesthetic evaluations than additional contributions to Lysenko publicity; some reviewers spent less time on the intrinsic characteristics of the movie than on the virtues of Lysenkoism. One reviewer praised Dovzhenko for manifesting *partiinost'*, a rare such compliment in Dovzhenko's troubled career.[19] Another critic delighted in the way the film exposed "reactionary theorists Weismann, Mendel, and Morgan." Better yet, *Michurin* succeeded admirably in "showing the personal merits of Lenin and Stalin in revealing Michurin to the people, to the country, while showing all the relevance of his theories to the matter of socialism."[20] The catch phrases came trippingly off the official tongue. The Michurin-Lysenko cult was a problem for more than just Soviet scientists to cope with. It was inflicted upon the entire Soviet population.

On New Year's Day 1949 T. D. Lysenko, president of the Academy of Agricultural Sciences, forecast to the Soviet public that his methods would bring "limitless growth in harvests." On that same day Dovzhenko's *Michurin* opened in Soviet cinemas.[21]

The narrative of *Michurin* is constructed around a single direct opposition: the distinction between the prerevolutionary and postrevolutionary periods in Michurin's life. The former phase is characterized by a series of denials and hardships for Michurin: refusal of support from government, the scorn of the established church, the death of wife Alexandra. The narrative's second phase presents Michurin with a series of rewards and fulfillments: the support of the new Soviet government, honor in official ceremonies, the energy and enthusiasm of a group of young workers who flock to the Kozlov nursery and provide a compensation for the loss of Alexandra. Dovzhenko asks us to contrast a period of darkness with a period of enlightenment, and he suggests that Michurin deserves the rewards of this enlightenment for his years of lonely work.

Significantly, Michurin's theories do not change from the first half of the film to the second. We do not see him develop a set of tentative ideas into a mature science; he does not struggle with any vexing questions. Rather, he is imbued with infallible wisdom from his first appearance to his last. *He* understands nature fully. The only question the film poses is whether the world will come to its senses and recognize the virtues of the Michurin line. This is settled when the revolution creates the intellectual climate which permits Michurin's work to be understood. Michurin does not change; the society around him does, thanks to the advent of communism. Michurin's knowledge of nature is innate and immutable;

he does not so much pursue investigations as issue pronouncements.

As the narrative proceeds we witness particular isolated moments in Michurin's life, and dates are ticked off to keep us oriented in history: 1900, the coming of the World War, the 1917 revolution, the death of Lenin. The meticulous record of time is significant, and the issue of the passage of time is raised frequently in the narrative. Michurin seems obsessed with time. He constantly complains that his work is so pressing that he has no time for diversions. He fears he will grow old and die before he has time to complete his experiments. He surrounds himself with scores of clocks in his home. Their constant ticking dominates the sound track and reminds us of the time that is slipping away. The prominent clocks signify several matters. At the most basic level the clocks remind us that the real Michurin supplemented his income in the early years by repairing timepieces; we even see Michurin accept a commission from Father Christopher in the film. Furthermore, the clocks represent Michurin's obsession with the loss of valuable time to inevitable old age and death. He feels the passing of each hour as time lost in a race because he can think only of the great amount of work that remains to be done.

Most important, however, is the fact that Michurin wants to alter the very essence of the natural realm and to change the way that humans perceive time. He opposes the idea that significant changes occur in nature over thousands of years, and he challenges man's passive acceptance of nature's slow evolutionary process. He calls for a human intervention in nature to control evolution, making shifts in nature a matter of a few years rather than a millennium. He tells Professor Kartashov that changes in an apple blossom normally take a thousand years; Michurin can effect change in only five. "We must not wait for nature's favors," he says at another point, paraphrasing the slogan of the actual Michurin. "To take them from her—that is the problem."

This is emphasized in Michurin's confrontation with Father Christopher early in the film. Michurin has been commissioned to repair a clock for the priest. Father Christopher visits Michurin, ostensibly to check the progress of the repairs but actually to criticize Michurin's horticultural work. Michurin finally ejects the priest from his home in anger, saying, "You do not need clocks. For you time does not move. You are eternal like stagnation." We are reminded of this meeting later when Michurin attends the New Year's Eve party marking the advent of the twentieth century. When the clocks chime midnight, they hark back to the moment when Michurin's clocks sounded during his confrontation with Father Christopher. In the former meeting the chimes motivate Michurin to denounce Father Christopher as a man without time. In the

New Year's Eve gathering the chimes inspire Michurin's first proclamation of what he hopes will be the future of Russia. He tells those present that the twentieth century will witness man's successful efforts to transform the world according to rational plans and asserts that he will "create change in nature after my own wish." This prophecy is fulfilled, of course, with the coming of the revolution. The Soviets go about changing the social realm rapidly by planned efforts, and Michurin claims that equivalent efforts will also enable them to manipulate the natural realm.

Father Christopher is designed to represent moral objections to Michurin's research. The priest considers human intervention in nature a blasphemous act. According to the official version of Michurin's life, the church did everything possible to discourage his work. Clergymen were supposed to have railed: "Don't commit blasphemy! Don't turn God's garden into a brothel!"[22] Father Christopher refers to Michurin's garden as Sodom and Gomorrah, and he associates crossbreeding with infidelity. By making the priest an amateur gardener and having him openly defend Mendel, Dovzhenko links the church with Mendelism. The fact that Mendel was a monk was not lost on the Lysenkoites, and the film suggests that religious conservatism was behind Mendelist genetics. When Michurin denounces Mendel, Father Christopher makes the sign of the cross, as if criticism of Mendel were a sacrilege. The film answers the analogy of sexual promiscuity mouthed by Father Christopher by invoking the institution of the family. Ivan and Alexandra Michurin treat their work as a family affair. They are a childless couple, but they refer to their young trees as their children. At one point Michurin tells of a dream in which he has a daughter who appears in the form of a cherry tree.

Dovzhenko presents Michurin as a character lacking the eloquence to promote his theories. Though Michurin often cannot persuade skeptics in debate, he can convince them with hard evidence—a specimen from his garden. When confronted by an opponent who doubts his work, the scientist produces a new item which inevitably astounds the learned detractor. He impresses his American visitors, Byrd and Meyer, with a lily of pleasant fragrance after Meyer claims that lilies have no smell. He reaches into a desk drawer and produces a peach grown in Kozlov, to the astonishment of Father Christopher, who insists that peaches cannot grow so far north. To win favor with the young members of the Revolutionary Committee, Michurin presents them with huge, tasty apples; apparently the apples persuade them of the value of Michurin's experiments, and they allocate funds for the nursery. Professor Kartashov tells Michurin that it is impossible to cross an apple with a pear; Michurin

Figure 23. *Michurin*

defeats him by promptly handing him such a fruit. There is a touch of
the magician about Michurin. Whenever his ideas are challenged, he
reaches into a pocket or a desk drawer and almost magically produces a
splendid specimen that deflates the opposition. Such dramatic gestures
often quash theoretical scrutiny of his work.

The one time that Michurin expresses any self-doubt comes during
the prerevolutionary period when he loses his only genuine family. Alexandra's death sends him into a prolonged malaise and isolation that em-
phasizes his alienation from a society that does not value his work and
raises the question of whether his research will ever benefit anyone. The
film solves this problem by providing a surrogate family to replace Alexandra—the young people of the revolution. Michurin's meeting with the
bright young members of the Revolutionary Committee brings him out
of his malaise, and he establishes a new family of sorts with the young
Soviets; he even sports his frock coat at the meeting and announces he is
wearing it for the first time since his wedding, thus reinforcing the association. This second "marriage" is made with young people who will
promote the social utility of Michurin's work. (fig. 23) In the second half
of the film, politics replaces religion as the practice which characterizes
society; Father Christopher disappears entirely from the film. And in the

Figure 24. *Michurin*

Soviet period, young people replace the elderly among principal characters. The old, conservative skeptics of the first half give way to a cadre of
fresh, excited disciples, and Michurin shifts roles from maverick to patriarch.

Only one test remains for Michurin after the revolution, and once
again it is a challenge posed by death. This occurs in the sequence in
which Michurin learns about Lenin's death. The scene is set in the winter of 1924 during a devastating blizzard. Michurin's assistants build
fires in the orchard in a desperate effort to save the trees from the cold.
Michurin emerges from the house to inform them of Lenin's death. He
treats the death as an omen and instructs his assistants to cease their efforts to warm the trees. He will let winter do its damage, and if the trees
survive, he will know that his breeding schemes are a success.

This scene parallels the scene of Alexandra's death from the tsarist
period. Both deaths are linked with winter; both are challenges to Michurin. Alexandra's death is portrayed as a personal loss; Lenin's, as a
worldwide tragedy. After Alexandra's death, society compensates Michurin by providing the young disciples; with Lenin's death the orchard
itself—nature—seems determined to compensate Michurin. After Michurin announces he will let the frost do its worst, we see the trees survive the winter. When spring finally arrives, there is a sequence
documenting the beautiful blooming of the garden. In a long, lyrical

passage, Michurin stands on a ladder in the orchard waving his arms like an orchestra conductor. (fig. 24) The camera tracks this way and that as if following the instructions of his conducting. And everywhere the camera turns, it reveals new blossoms emerging on the branches. The trees have survived the natural disaster. More important, Michurin seems to be personally orchestrating the spring regeneration. I have noted that he occasionally behaves like a conjurer and that the source of his wisdom remains rather mysterious. In this passage, he seems to possess an almost supernatural authority to manipulate the physical world. Magical powers rather than reasoned scientific inquiries characterize the figure. He is the scientist as magician.

The film concludes appropriately with Michurin's enshrinement as a cult figure. The last scene invokes his historical eightieth birthday celebration. This episode is offered as compensation for all the abuse Michurin received from officialdom in the first half of the film. And in the last speech in the film Michurin acknowledges the source of his good fortune: "Bless the work of the people. And bless the names of the ones who put me on this platform—Lenin and Stalin." Michurin's strength, we are to understand, is acquired by virtue of a direct line to the source of all wisdom, the party leadership. Though the film wants to debunk religious mysticism, it ends with an almost religious reverie. And in his last film Dovzhenko acknowledges the existence of Joseph Vissarionovich Stalin—the Leader.

Mysticism and wonder triumph over scientific exactness in *Michurin*. The film that is supposed to disdain the old forces of mysticism in the scientific community—that was the accusation lodged against the Mendelists—succeeds only in surrounding Michurin with an even more fantastic aura. His theories are not developed. Michurin simply possesses them like the sign of a special vision. The film does not ask us to scrutinize those theories but only to wonder at the greatness of the bearer. Such was the fundamental contradiction in the whole Lysenko movement. The so-called materialist theories of Lysenko were in fact popularized through a mystical cult. Lysenko could fulminate rather than experiment, Dovzhenko's film could mystify rather than educate, because of the "historical reality" of Soviet agricultural development and because of the peculiar notion of veracity that governed works of Soviet realism.

In praise of the historical Michurin a Lysenkoist academic proclaimed: "Like the magician of the fairy tale Michurin scattered over the vast expanses of the Soviet Union green massifs of fruit orchards and decorated them with hitherto unseen varieties."[23] Michurin waves his arm, and the land turns green. The passage could be describing the spring blossoming scene in Dovzhenko's film, a film in which a magician (Michurin) appears in a fairy tale (Lysenkoist mystification). In lieu of careful scientific documentation, Lysenko and his followers offered incantations about the universality of dialectical materialism and the innate wisdom of great men—Lenin, Stalin, and, of course, Ivan Michurin.

Through such tactics the Lysenkoists remained in power for years. Their legacy, however, was a series of agricultural setbacks stemming from Lysenko's wrong-headed reforms. Nature, never prone to follow cults and apparently insensitive to the subtleties of "historical reality," steadfastly refused to obey the dictates of Lysenko's materialist biology.

XI
Conclusion

W HEN DOVZHENKO DIED in November 1956, a victim finally
of the heart condition that had afflicted him for decades, he had waited
almost eight years for permission to direct a new film. Since the completion of *Michurin,* proposal after proposal and script after script had gone
before review committees and had been turned down. Ironically, when
death came, Dovzhenko was only one day away from the start of shooting on a new feature, *Poem of an Inland Sea.* He had invested nearly two
years in developing the script and had won permission to carry through
on the production thanks to the easing of controls in the post-Stalin
"thaw" of the middle and late 1950s.[1]

This tragic end nevertheless seemed to possess an eerie appropriate-
ness. Literally to his last day, Dovzhenko's creative impulses were subor-
dinated to the vagaries of state conduct. The circumstances of his final
years remind us once again of the extent to which the shape of his career
was determined by forces beyond his control, and they bring us back to
the original thesis of this study: far from representing the projection of
private visions, his work entailed a reaction to public policy and a contribution to the public discourse surrounding those policies. His creative
labor was more in the nature of an ongoing career in public service than
an expression of the essential inner man.

Indeed, in the Soviet system, art is viewed as a public trust rather than
an exercise in personal expression. The creative process inevitably involves a form of compromise between the individual artist and the government's artistic bureaucracy, with the balance occasionally shifting
from the one to the other. In Dovzhenko's experience that balance was
affected by several external factors. In the early phase of his career he
worked under the relative leniency of the Communist party's 1925 resolution on literature, and he enjoyed the benefits of a diverse, competitive
film industry which granted considerable autonomy to the national stu-

148

dios like the Ukraine's VUFKU. But the ambiguities of the Kremlin's policy on the nationalities complicated his situation, even during the early years of comparative freedom. Lenin's original position on self-determination ostensibly granted to the empire's national republics the permission to retain separate identities, but it also left the central Soviet government with the option to crush separatist tendencies. Firm criteria for what constituted legitimate national identity and what betrayed unacceptable "nationalist deviation" never emerged, leaving Stalin and his minions free to interfere in Ukrainian cultural and political affairs on any pretext. This they did with increasing frequency and severity, beginning with the campaign against VAPLITE. And while Dovzhenko may have escaped this initial crisis, it had ramifications for his eventual career in cinema as he became the target of the same criticisms once marshalled against his old Kharkov associates.

The most significant shift in the balance between individual and collective control of the artistic product resulted from the social regimentation effected in the 1930s. The entire artistic bureaucracy was overhauled to solidify state control of the arts, and the attendant film industry consolidation of the early 1930s obliged the national studios to surrender much of their sovereignty. As the bureaucracy grew at once larger and more intransigent through the 1930s and 1940s, Dovzhenko and his fellow filmmakers found their creative energies progressively consumed by the procedural rigors of the preproduction review. By the late 1940s the film industry virtually calcified, so thoroughly did the stolid bureaucracy frustrate creative initiative. The lessons of Dovzhenko's late career might tempt one to update Kempis: Man proposes, but the *apparat* disposes.

The traditional tack of Dovzhenko's Western admirers—to isolate his work from history by ascribing it to his special regard for the "eternal themes" of life, death, and nature's pervasiveness and to praise his work as lyrical while neglecting to say that it is also thoroughly topical—runs up against the hard reality of these creative constraints. This received critical opinion should find even less comfort in the historical readings of the films put forward in this study. Rather than dwelling on the romantic clichés about Dovzhenko as the lyric poet who sings praises to eternal nature, we should confront a more compelling issue: few filmmakers from the Soviet or any other cinema showed such concern for shifts in national policy and fashioned such a referential collection of works.

Consider, for example, how frequently external conditions occasioned Dovzhenko's choices of genre and subject matter. He entered VUFKU with an interest in comedy and with credentials as a satirist, and his first labors, *Vasia the Reformer* and *Love's Berry,* drew from contemporary comic formulas and addressed the nagging problems of greed and hypocrisy evidenced during NEP. *Diplomatic Pouch* also appropriated popular cinematic conventions—in this case foreign borrowings hastily transmuted into the hybrid genre of the "red detective"—and applied them to the complex international relations which surrounded the Nette affair and simultaneous tensions with Great Britain. His two accounts of the Ukrainian revolution, *Zvenigora* and *Arsenal,* owed their existence to the official commemorations marking the USSR's decade of progress. The late 1920s and early 1930s saw the Soviet Union commence its monumental industrialization program. Dovzhenko responded by examining the program's effect on various sectors: *Earth* and agriculture, *Ivan* and heavy industry, *Aerograd* and virgin lands development in the Soviet Far East. His two biographical projects were inspired by Stalinist glorification of major historical figures: *Shchors* drew on the revisionist versions of the revolution mandated by the cult of personality, and *Michurin*'s representation of its title character derived from the mystification of Lysenkoism.

We find an impressive range in this catalogue of subjects, a range that certainly cannot be explained through simple appeal to Dovzhenko's individual instincts. If we group the films generally by period and genre, we discover a compelling logic of evolution that followed broad trends of Soviet historical development. The earliest productions betoken the nation's coming to grips with the novelty of its socialist system, one without historical precedent and one that gave rise to new problems in both domestic *(Vasia, Love's Berry)* and foreign relations *(Diplomatic Pouch)*. The commemorations of the revolution *(Zvenigora, Arsenal)* denote the Soviet Union's effort to establish a celebratory mythology about its own origins, an effort evidenced as well in such films as *October* and *End of St. Petersburg.* The effort itself marked a threshold of achieved maturity as the Soviet Union recorded a successful first decade of existence and prepared to abandon its transitional NEP phase. Dovzhenko turned to pending matters of economic transition *(Earth, Ivan, Aerograd)* during his nation's next historical phase, that of planned development. And his efforts at historical biography *(Shchors, Michurin)* show the orchestrated hero worship which afflicted the USSR during the period of "high Stalinism."

By thus grouping the films chronologically, we willy-nilly appeal to the most impersonal forces to explain the corpus's general shape. What of those qualities of Dovzhenko's work that clearly stem from his personal life—the interest in Ukrainian peasant culture and the respect for its traditions? These features are emphasized in the existing critical literature, and there is certainly no denying that they are present in the oeuvre nor that they enrich it enormously, a fact often acknowledged in this study. And as we recall, Dovzhenko liked to portray the films as strictly autobiographical works. But even as we concede that he drew heavily on his origins, we can also appreciate that larger historical determinants entered as proximate causes. Dovzhenko's biography is itself, of course, a product of history. His class and national origins, his fortuitous introduction to revolutionary politics, and his association with VAPLITE formed the historical subject we identify as Alexander Dovzhenko, and thus at one level of remove, they shaped the films that bear Dovzhenko's signature. In light of this we can define Dovzhenko the author, not as an unfettered creative imagination, but as a social being who existed at the junction of a particular set of historical forces. Such a definition permits us to recognize him as singular but not necessarily idiosyncratic, for many of the forces that forged his biography altered the very shape of his society. His signal contribution to that society was the skill with which he interpreted those forces and gave them coherent dramatic form in his work.

It seems clear from all this that he did not bring a formed Weltanschauung to his work. Rather, it appears that he possessed a keen sensitivity to the social changes taking place around him, and he drew on that asset. Careful observation rather than private inspiration comprised the measure of his artistic imagination. This helps account for the oeuvre's variety and topicality. His was a deft gaze, not a fixed world view.

Jean-Paul Sartre's concept of the "project"—an individual's willful, determined response to the objective preconditions of his or her historical situation—obtains in Dovzhenko's case.[2] Dovzhenko's project was to analyze the ferment around him, to reduce it to a set of distinct fictions, and to present it back to the members of that society in the more vivid, comprehensible form of narrative. He seized on the social contradictions inherent in a society in transition, fashioned them into tales which incorporated these contradictions into manageable dramatic forms, and sought to impose on them a narrative resolution. He endeavored—wisely or not, successfully or not—to contain social conflict through his narratives and to lessen the threat posed by change. His project was to cushion the shock of the new.

By appealing to the concept of the individual's project we can finally begin to trace the Ariadne's thread that runs through Dovzhenko's varied career. It exists in the very fact of his ongoing concern with change. Even as the subject matter of his films shifts with the passing issues of the moment, his continued interest in social transformation constitutes, in itself, a form of continuity. In topics ranging from the novelty of NEP to the neoteric discipline of Lysenkoism, Dovzhenko treats the effects of social progress, and he constructs his narratives around characters who must deal with a changing world.

As such, Dovzhenko's work might be characterized as unified without being uniform, its unity deriving from consistent structures representing the processes and effects of change. Ultimately that representation harks back to the USSR's modernization effort. All of Dovzhenko's films, in one manner or another, concern the Soviet Union's historical development, and in so doing, they betoken its overdetermined nature. In this "most advanced and most backward" of nations, to recall Althusser's epithetical phrase, a progressive, ruthless political elite was prepared to force change on a backward, often recalcitrant population. This central conflict resonated through every social sector, generating the related antagonisms that made the Soviet modernization effort so difficult and painful. These antagonisms pervaded Soviet society as it struggled with its developmental agenda, and they provided the sources of narrative conflict for Dovzhenko's films. That he could deal with such a wide range of topics upholds the very definition of overdetermination: The central contradiction of the overdetermined society never appears in perfect, recondite form in any given sector of the society; it is never distilled into some neatly observable whole. Rather it takes the shape of smaller, local tensions distributed through countless individual social formations. In the nine discrete social formations which constitute the extant fiction films of Alexander Dozvhenko, we can recognize the fact of overdetermination in the various narrative conflicts pitting conservative social instincts against changing social conditions. The specific components of the model mutate from narrative to narrative, but the strategy persists.

That strategy proves sufficiently malleable to accommodate the different issues which came to the fore at particular moments, issues ranging from sexual politics, to industrialization, to scientific policy. We recall, for example, that Dovzhenko tends to organize his fictions around a limited, generally unified social unit (a family, a military regiment, a village, etc.) which is faced with the prospect of imminent change. The narrative then predicates the necessity of the group's bending to change while nevertheless protecting its original integrity and status. Much of the ensuing narrative account entails a difficult negotiation between these progressive and conservative impulses. In implementing this strategy, Dovzhenko occasionally creates opposing characters to embody the conflicting impulses and then situates the adversaries within the primary group to measure the tensions afflicting it. The complex character relationships of *Zvenigora* epitomize that tactic. There Dovzhenko designates the extended family as the threatened social unit and enlists individual family members to personify progressivism and reaction. His preliminary scenario puts forth a tidy generational split. Grandfather assumes the role of the Neanderthal blinded by the mystification of legend, while Timosh develops into a modern rationalist. The triangular relationship emerging in the finished version of the film proves the more nuanced. There, Dovzhenko retains Timosh as the advocate of progress and makes brother Pavlo the reactionary. With the primary conflict preserved, albeit in a variant, Dovzhenko could use Grandfather to mediate between the two extremes. The character maintains ties with the past in the legends he recounts, but he endures the changes of the Soviet era and, in the film's conclusion, wins acceptance into the modern Soviet system.

Variations on the model of a community threatened by division appear in several subsequent films. In *Earth* a single family again feels the pressure of social conflicts as the family members confront the choice of participation in the new collective or continued allegiance to an inherited farming system. Again the split occurs along generational lines. Young Vasyl casts his lot enthusiastically with the future while his father Opanas hesitates to abandon the security of a familiar agricultural order. The mechanism of reconciliation between alternatives is provided by a narrative event rather than by a mediating figure as in *Zvenigora*. Vasyl's martyrdom is felt across the generations, and it unites Opanas with the young advocates of the collective.

The pattern varies even more in *Aerograd*. The small partisan band of the Siberian village replaces the extended family as the central community. This isolated group is steeped in its own history. All the group members are veterans of civil war battles which transpired many years prior to the time of the story, and Glushak often speaks nostalgically of experiences dating back a half century. Yet this tradition-rich band encounters the prospect of changes wrought by air travel which will end their geographical isolation and hasten full development of their territory, a fact mandated by the plans to build the modern city Aerograd. In this case the divided response to change crystallizes in the Glushak-Khudiakov relationship. Although not blood relatives, the two men often behave like brothers and trace their friendship back to childhood, giving their union something of the familial quality of the two previously mentioned films. When the two friends split over the issue of modernization, however, there is no opportunity for a mutual accommodation of their differences. Khudiakov's decision to resist progress devolves into simple treason and seals his fate. The Great Terror of the 1930s pre-scribed purgation.

The differences within the regiment in *Shchors* involve far less of a sense of crisis. Instead they take the form of a friendly competition be-tween the old-style partisan Bozhenko and the young forward-looking (recall that he literally sees into the future) commander Shchors, and they never quite break into open conflict. Within this military regiment—which behaves like a family and in which officers are ad-dressed by first names or by such friendly sobriquets as Batko (Grandfa-ther)—the relationship between Bozhenko and Shchors is not unlike that of father and son. In this case, however, the child is father of the man in that Shchors must discipline the often childlike impetuousness of Bozhenko. That their squabbles never threaten the integrity of the larger group of soldiers whose fate they control speaks to the success of Shchors's effort to instill unity and discipline in the troop and, in a larger context, to the policy of regimentation that gripped the Soviet Union in the late 1930s.

These selections from different stages of Dovzhenko's career suggest at once the consistency and flexibility of his response to social change. His tactic of representing contradiction through mutual antagonists within a given group would extend to his representation of various social institutions. The institution enjoying the greatest prominence in Dovzhenko's work is the family, to the extent, as we have seen, that members of nonfamilial organizations occasionally seem to behave like immediate relatives. The family proper serves Dovzhenko as a neatly condensed record of the society's recent history, in the manner of a time line, with the older generations holding on to the past while younger generations look optimistically forward. Children come to stand for the promise of the nation's future in this schema, and the arrival of infants into the community assumes the dramatic weight of a national rite of passage. Consider the birth scenes in *Earth* and *Aerograd*. When Vasyl's mother gives birth during the extended funeral sequence at the end of *Earth,* we recognize that this moment compensates for the death of Vasyl. The birth also distinguishes the collective, with its future thus assured, from the kulaks, who are never identified with such fertility. In *Aerograd* Vladimir's son draws the community together, as indicated in the scene where the entire village turns out to honor the mother and child. In both instances birth solidifies the primary group by assuring its continuity.

The exceptions to this pattern do not necessarily subvert it. The baby in *Love's Berry* certainly inspires no such beneficent response among the characters who come in contact with it. Quite the contrary, the most petty personal motives surface at each character's first encounter with the infant. But Dovzhenko uses these reactions to point up what he represents throughout the film as the selfishness catered to by NEP. These characters live for themselves and for the moment, and they make no commitment to the Soviet Union's future. Hence their cynical responses to the child, who represents no future promise but only an immediate problem. Even greater irony tinges the sequence in *Arsenal* where each veteran returning from the World War confronts an unfaithful wife and an illegitimate offspring. Here again Dovzhenko invokes birth only to identify a social failing, a perversion of the natural reproductive process brought about by a corrupt political system. In certain films, such as *Shchors* and *Michurin,* we may remark on the very absence of children. The adult fraternity at the center of *Shchors* consists of men who have forsaken the bonds of family in favor of regimental loyalty. The future in that film takes form not in the presence of children but in the modern army unit on parade at the film's end. Nature's process of regeneration, birth, has given way to an image of a new generation seemingly born at officers' candidate school, yet another sign of social regimentation within the Soviet system. Similarly, although Michurin and his wife do not produce offspring, the social reorganization effected around Michurin after the revolution seems to bear surrogate children. The energetic young communists who materialize in the second half of the film to work in Michurin's orchard substitute for direct descendants, but, significantly, they seem to be from revolution rather than from woman born. Such variations suggest the value placed on social continuity in Dovzhenko's work, as he finds measures even in military and political spheres to substitute for the natural ritual of childbirth.

But the function of the family for Dovzhenko is not simply to perpetuate the species. The family often represents a previously constituted, functioning unit which can perform public works when called upon to do so. Dovzhenko thus associates the family, an institution with the most venerated tradition, with the vital political activity that will encourage future change. The British railworker's family in *Diplomatic Pouch* work and act more like members of a revolutionary cell than of a civilian household. They reveal unflagging loyalty to communism, and they carry out their subversive work with considerable skill and determination. Opanas's family in *Earth* finally subordinate their kinship loyalties to an expanded allegiance to the collective at the film's end. The collective even seems to supplant the family as the primary social unit, or more precisely, the collective becomes something like a grand extension of the family. A not dissimilar leap is made between the family and the military establishment in *Aerograd*. The ritual gathering in which the villagers honor Vladimir's child is quickly transformed into the partisan troop's strategy session. Glushak's hut thus serves as both home and command post, and Vladimir is both Glushak's son and the point man for his assault force. This move from familial to political responsibility evolves to its logical conclusion in *Shchors*. The men in Shchors's unit, on orders from their commander, abandon their families for the duration of the war, and Shchors's own alienation from his wife is measured in the oddly cold letter he sends her, their only form of contact.

These examples trace a movement toward a greater sense of social rather than interpersonal obligation assumed by the films' characters, a pattern which answered to the gradual socialization of privacy that accompanied Soviet development. Dovzhenko's succession of central characters follows this pattern. In the NEP satire *Love's Berry* the principal characters recognize no larger ideal and manifest no sense of the greater national good. But as the Soviet Union entered its period of planned economic development, Dovzhenko began to fashion central characters willing to forego individual satisfaction on behalf of distant, shared goals. *Ivan* is the transitional work in this regard. The title character is torn between public commitments and private instincts. He willingly leaves his home to participate in an industrialization effort that stresses broad societal rather than individual rewards. Yet he also resists being swallowed up by the leviathan of the Soviet mass-labor system, and he tenaciously holds on to his inherited sense of self-worth. By the time we come to *Shchors*, however, even this ambivalence has disappeared. Dovzhenko creates a moral system in that film which honors the men around Shchors who give up all claim to personal gratification. They are called upon to lead ascetic lives, down to Shchors's insistence that they temper such petty vices as drinking, and they work in pursuit of military objectives that are often beyond their understanding. Theirs is the supreme faith in the inherent worth of the Soviet revolution. Michurin might be the worthy civilian successor to Shchors. So obsessed is he with his work and the brighter future it promises for all that he barely maintains a distinct private life. His home is hard to distinguish from his laboratory, and his wife seems to be as much a research assistant as a spouse.

This trend toward loyalty to larger, more abstract causes runs parallel to an evolving image of authority. As Dovzhenko's secondary characters progressively surrender their claims to individual pleasure and autonomy, more and more powerful authority figures emerge to assume greater control. Not coincidentally, these figures are identified with the state, often harking up the image of Stalinist power. In the early films state influence plays little part at best. The policemen and magistrate appear as minor comic figures in *Love's Berry,* and significantly, they provide no enlightened policy but only embrace the piety which is the object of ridicule throughout the film. In *Diplomatic Pouch* and *Arsenal* the rank and file prove capable of upholding the cause of revolution on their own. The proletarians in *Diplomatic Pouch* form an exemplary grass-roots movement, working effectively without recourse to official guidance. *Arsenal* utterly omits the role played by the Bolshevik chiefdom in the Ukrainian revolution. The arsenal defenders even seem to fight without benefit of a command hierarchy. Timosh assumes a nominal leadership role, but he is very much of the men whom he commands; he is primus inter pares. We find officialdom in *Ivan* in the person of the project director who is confronted by the dead worker's mother. In this case authority seems remote—witness the obstacle course the mother runs to reach his office—but benevolent. Of greater consequence is the fact that he and his ilk are not much in evidence elsewhere in the project. The daily work proceeds without close supervision. With *Shchors,* however, the emphasis switches entirely to the nature of command. Shchors dominates the activities of his compatriots, and the film promotes a social model in which submission to a power elite becomes the general order, a model which betokens the expanded power of the Soviet government.

One institution associated with that power is the Soviet military establishment. The army receives much attention in Dovzhenko's work, but again its image evolves from film to film. In keeping with the egalitarian sentiments expressed in *Arsenal* and *Zvenigora,* the Bolshevik troops in these films operate with a casual sense of discipline at best. More important, the Red Army enjoys no strategic success in either film. The Bolshevik campaign suffers a crushing defeat in *Arsenal,* and the only compensation offered in the wake of the loss is the sudden invincibility Timosh achieves at the film's end. The Red Army also suffers defeat in *Zvenigora,* but in this case the revolutionary effort is salvaged by the energetic industrial production undertaken by the civilian population. This connection between economic and military power develops in the films of the 1930s. The civilian work force at Dneprostroi in *Ivan* lives a quasi-military, barracks life, and Dovzhenko even inserts a martial parade into the film's climax to make the association between economic growth and national strength explicit. Dovzhenko further conflates economic and military power in *Aerograd* by tying the development of the Soviet Far East with the area's security. *Shchors* extends the military ethic to the entire society, and the crack unit we observe at the film's end seems a far cry from the casual, spontaneous fighters serving with Timosh in *Arsenal.*

The characters in Dovzhenko's films are not just subjects of the state;

they are also workers, and Dovzhenko's version of the Soviet labor system alters with time as well. In its mocking of NEP, *Love's Berry* contains no image of sustained, directed labor, only the indolence of a bourgeoisie at perpetual leisure. The only work shown comes from soft service jobs catering to the bourgeoisie. This changes when Dovzhenko takes up the first phase of organized development in *Earth,* wherein we see the agricultural sector modernized through the reorganization of working procedures and the introduction of machines. But as the film's harvest sequence suggests, these changes do not disrupt the peasants' lives but only improve working efficiency. Adjustment to new methods proves more difficult for the title character of *Ivan.* His case speaks to the profound sense of dislocation experienced by the "new proletarians" of the 1930s who were uprooted from the comfort and security of their villages.

Besides the labor system, Dovzhenko's extended review of Soviet modernization gives much attention to new technology as a catalyst of economic development. When we look at *Arsenal* we find technology serving no productive function. Exploited for the art of war, the machines of that film are sinister and destructive, and they consistently defy human control. In *Earth,* by contrast, the new agricultural equipment is introduced to the village for the benefit of its inhabitants as part of programmatic innovation, and it poses no threat to the peasantry's world. The villagers adjust quickly to the presence of the farm implements, working in perfect synchrony with their new tools in the harvest sequence and barely altering their time-honored methods of growing and gathering grain.

Dovzhenko's most sophisticated study of the peasantry's adaption to new technology appears in *Ivan.* The peasants who assume new lives at Dneprostroi must work with enormous machines ranging from trains to cranes and earth movers. By and large, the workers manage the equipment skillfully enough, but occasionally these outsized tools threaten to dominate their users. In one case, we recall, they take a human life, and in the following sequence, the implements seem to threaten the mother's safety when she runs through the work site, crossing paths with one great machine after another. This bifurcated view of technology, as working partner and as alien menace, evokes the peasants' ambivalent attitude toward their new situation: a willingness to enter the modern working order tinged with a Luddite-like suspicion of the most prominent symbol of that order, the machine.

That expression of reservation disappears, however, by the time Dovzhenko makes *Aerograd,* where state-of-the-art technology is present in the form of aircraft. Vladimir's airplane assumes a special aura. It is a graceful, majestic machine that soars over the landscape and inspires awe among the earthbound characters of Glushak's village, a respect cogently expressed in the villagers' childlike wonder at Vladimir's ability to travel "faster than the sun." Significantly, this technological innovation does not serve simply as a producer good like the construction tools in *Ivan* introduced as a preliminary stage of industrialization. Rather, the airplane is the measure of the Soviet Union's achievement. It is the result as much as the agent of progress, and it signifies the gains the Soviets have made. Like the other images of technology in Dovzhenko's work, it serves as a milestone along the Soviet Union's long road to modernity.

But what happens when the machines enter the garden? How are the natural settings so prominent in Dovzhenko's films affected by modernization? Western critics like to give much weight to the pastoral nature of Dovzhenko's work, and they often assert that he is honoring an eternal natural beauty somewhat in the manner of the romantic poets. They may be drawn to this conclusion because of the particular renown of *Earth*, Dovzhenko's most widely seen and respected film. In that example, to be sure, Dovzhenko equates nature with stability and appeals to a timeless life cycle. Nor does the introduction of technology disrupt the land's serenity in that particular film. But these elements are specific to *Earth*, serving as rhetorical devices calculated to naturalize the changes in village life.

The natural realm does not remain pristine in other films; on the contrary, it frequently submits to human manipulation. In *Arsenal* Dovzhenko invokes nature principally to measure the destructiveness of humans engaged in armed conflict. War ravages the natural terrain, and the scarred land reminds us of social crisis. Famous parts of the natural landscape are central to *Ivan* and *Aerograd*—specifically, the Dnieper River and the Siberian taiga. Both films, in fact, open with lengthy, lyrical prologues portraying these two natural sites in their primeval form. We are shown the powerful currents of the Dnieper in the first reel of *Ivan* and the vast, forbidding terrain of the taiga in *Aerograd*. But in both cases the passages are present precisely to anticipate the changes that will occur when the hand of man enters. We are to understand that the Dneprostroi will tame the treacherous river and that the city Aerograd will promote full development of the taiga region. In neither case will Soviet progress submit to some immutable ideal of the natural realm. The Soviets set out to subdue the earth. *Michurin* presents the culmination of this faith in man's ability to conquer nature. The infallible central character of that film is committed to establishing absolute human control over nature's activities, and only his benighted antagonists express any belief in an inviolate natural order.

If belief in progress takes precedent over reliance on nature's bounty for Dovzhenko, what about his celebrated uses of anthropomorphism? Western critics have concluded from them that Dovzhenko simply conflates nature and human endeavor in yet another indication of his romantic sensibility. In fact, the anthropomorphic passages are specific to particular dramatic situations and have limited functions. Horses speak in *Arsenal*, but the moments serve merely to condemn or validate individual actions. On the first occasion, a horse chastises a man for a senseless act of violence; on the second, the horses confirm their unity with their Bolshevik masters in a scene which celebrates revolutionary action. We have noted how components of the natural realm assume the same emotions as humans in *Earth*, but these instances only serve that film's specific tactic of justifying collectivization. And when the trees seem to respond to the title character's immediate directions in the famous blossoming scene of *Michurin*, the device merely enhances the image of the old scientist as the possessor of preternatural powers. It owes more to the sophistry of Lysenkoism than to any innate predilection on Dovzhenko's part.

Even when Dovzhenko employs motifs from ancient folkloristic sources, he is not so much baring his "peasant's soul" as rationalizing twentieth-century phenomena. The Roksana legend, which plays such an important part in *Zvenigora*, functions as an allegory which tellingly parallels events in modern sections. In *Arsenal* Dovzhenko summons up the image of the invincible hero of folklore at the film's conclusion, but he does so in order to overcome the decidedly modern moral dilemmas posed by revolutionary struggle. When he appeals to the past, then, he does far more than acknowledge his peasant background; he appropriates the past to establish a historical warrant for the present.

This was certainly in keeping with his project. As these protean themes indicate, he did not simply deploy a fixed set of motifs across a body of films. Rather, over the course of a career spanning more than two decades, he monitored the relentless advance of Soviet history. He mapped and remapped a perpetually shifting social terrain rather than a constant natural terrain. The received opinion about Dovzhenko—that he projected an unfading image which locked nature and human nature into one invariable routine—seems long overdue for substantial revision. Certainly his effort to honor the past, even as he depicted the Soviet Union's double-time march into the future, distinguished his project. But the romantic notion that Dovzhenko embodied the essence of the peasantry, with its permanent attachment to the past and to the land, tells only part of the story. His films also remind us constantly of their moment.

Perhaps we do not need to dispense entirely with the familiar characterizations of Dovzhenko as the pastoral poet who summoned up bucolic images from the depths of his peasant's soul. But we can put them into perspective by remembering the most banal and most profound fact of Dovzhenko's career: he drew a paycheck from an industry that operated under state control, and in turn he worked to produce films that spoke to state policy. We surely do him no injustice by recalling that he labored in the service of the state. The nature of that service answered to conflicting historical sources as distant as his rural origins and as immediate as his employers' most capricious policy shifts.

Born of a society that often seemed to be frozen in time, reared into an age that seemed to know only upheaval and change, Dovzhenko existed at the site of historical conflict. His project entailed a troubled effort at reconciliation. It is precisely the troubled nature of his effort that most deserves our continued attention and study.

Appendices

Notes

Bibliography

Index

Appendix 1: A Dovzhenko Chronology

12 September 1894

Alexander Dovzhenko is born into a peasant household in the Chernigov region of northeast Ukraine.

1914

Dovzhenko completes elementary and secondary school. He commences a brief career in teaching and develops his initial interest in art.

1917

Dovzhenko continues his education in Kiev. He becomes involved in radical politics during the revolutionary upheavals of 1917.

January 1918

Ukrainian nationalists, under the rubric of the Central Rada, split with the Russian Bolsheviks, calling for an autonomous Ukraine. Fighting ensues between Rada troops and the Red Army as civil war sweeps across the Ukraine.

February 1918

The Red Army captures Kiev and forces the Rada into a retreat. The Rada effects an alliance with invading German troops, and Germany soon establishes a puppet regime under the Ukrainian Paul Skoropadsky.

1918

Dovzhenko organizes an anti-Skoropadsky rally in Kiev, an event that draws him more firmly into leftist politics.

November 1918

Germany withdraws from the Ukraine, leading to Skoropadsky's overthrow. Simon Petliura takes command of Rada forces and continues the fight against Bolshevik rule.

1919–20

Dovzhenko aligns himself with pro-Bolshevik factions in the Ukraine. He joins the Ukrainian Red Army, serving for a time with Nikolai Shchors's brigade.

1920

Petliura is forced into exile, and the Bolsheviks consolidate power throughout the Ukraine.

1920–22

Dovzhenko is rewarded for his services to the Bolshevik cause with an appointment to the foreign service of the new Soviet Ukraine. Posted in Berlin in 1922, he studies art under Erik Heckel.

1923–26

Dovzhenko works as a political cartoonist in Kharkov, where he associates with the literary organization VAPLITE. He leaves the movement just prior to a Bolshevik crackdown on VAPLITE for signs of alleged Ukrainian nationalism.

June 1926

Dovzhenko moves to Odessa to enter the Ukrainian film organization VUFKU, which is undergoing major expansion.

1926

Dovzhenko assists on the production of the comedy *Vasia the Reformer,* and he writes and directs the comedy *Love's Berry.*

1927

Dovzhenko directs the adventure melodrama *Diplomatic Pouch,* which takes its source from international tensions between Britain and the USSR.

1927–28

The USSR marks the tenth anniversary of the Soviet revolution. The nation's film industry commemorates the occasion with films on the revolution. Dovzhenko contributes the revolutionary epic *Zvenigora.*

1929

Dovzhenko completes another commemorative film, *Arsenal,* which concerns civil war conflicts between Bolshevik and Rada forces.

1928–30

The Soviet Union moves out of its semicapitalist NEP system and into the controlled economic system of the first Five-Year Plan. The new order entails rural collectivization and plans for a rapid industrialization of the economy.

1930

Dovzhenko takes up the issue of collectivization in *Earth.* The finished film receives harsh criticism in the official press.

1930–34

The Soviet film industry is consolidated and placed under tight ideological control. New film projects undergo exacting preproduction review by industry censors.

1932

Dovzhenko treats Soviet industrialization efforts in *Ivan.* The film is shot at the Dneprostroi hydroelectric complex, a showcase of the first Five-Year Plan. Party critics attack this film as well.

December 1934

The murder of Soviet official Sergei Kirov sets in motion the events leading to the Stalinist purges of the middle and late 1930s. The Soviet press regularly plays on the country's fear of spies and traitors as the USSR responds to threats posed by the Axis powers of Germany and Japan.

1935

Dovzhenko completes *Aerograd,* a film on the development of Soviet Siberia. The film also invokes concerns about internal subversion and Japanese-inspired sabotage in the Soviet Far East. The finished film is favorably reviewed by the Soviet press.

1935–39

At Stalin's suggestion, Dovzhenko undertakes a film biography of Soviet civil war martyr Nikolai Shchors. Constant censorship review protracts the film's production process. *Shchors* is altered several times prior to eventual completion in order to conform to Stalinist revisions of the historical record.

1941–45

Dovzhenko works on documentaries as part of the USSR's war effort.

1945–52

Party interference in the activities of the Soviet film industry becomes so exacting that film production gradually grinds to a near halt.

1944–48

Dovzhenko works on *Michurin,* a lionizing biography of the Russian horticulturalist Ivan Michurin. Script revision again delays the production as Dovzhenko must incorporate the most current tenets of Lysenkoist biology into his account. Because of its eventual fidelity to Lysenkoism, the film is hailed by the Soviet press.

1949–56

Dovzhenko has proposal after proposal for new film projects rejected by the *apparat.* He dies on 26 November 1956, one day before shooting is to begin on *Poem of an Inland Sea.*

Appendix 2: Dovzhenko Credits

Vasia the Reformer (6 reels: VUFKU, 1926)
> Director: F. Lopatinsky. Scriptwriter and assistant director: A. Dovzhenko. Camera operators: I. Rona and D. Demutsky.
> Cast: V. Liudvinsky, Iu. Chernyshev, Iu. Shumsky, N. Chernysheva, S. Shagaida.

Love's Berry (2 reels: VUFKU, 1926)
> Scriptwriter and director: A. Dovzhenko. Camera operators: I. Rona and D. Demutsky.
> Cast: N. Krushelnitsky, M. Chardynina-Barshaia, D. Kapka, I. Zamychkovsky, I. Zemgano, N. Nademsky.

Diplomatic Pouch (7 reels: VUFKU, 1928)
> Director: A. Dovzhenko. Scriptwriters: M. Zats and B. Shcharansky. Camera operator: N. Kozlovsky. Set designer: G. Baizengerts.
> Cast: A. Klimenko, G. Zelondzhev-Shipov, I. Penzo, I. Kapralov, O. Merlatti, A. Dovzhenko, K. Eggers, A. Belov.

Zvenigora (6 reels: VUFKU, 1928)
> Director: A. Dovzhenko. Scriptwriters: M. Johansen and I. Tiutiunnyk. Camera operator: B. Zavelev. Set designer: V. Krichevsky.
> Cast: N. Nademsky, S. Svashenko, A. Podorozhny, P. Skliar-Otava, A. Simonov, I. Seliuk, L. Barbe, G. Astafev.

Arsenal (7 reels: VUFKU, 1929)
> Scriptwriter and director: A. Dovzhenko. Camera operator: D. Demutsky. Set designers: N. Shpinel and V. Meller.
> Cast: S. Svashenko, A. Buchma, N. Nademsky, N. Kuchinsky, D. Erdman, O. Merlatti, A. Evdakov.

Earth (6 reels: VUFKU, 1930)
> Scriptwriter and director: A. Dovzhenko. Camera operator: D. Demutsky. Set designer: V. Krichevsky.
> Cast: N. Nademsky, S. Shkurat, S. Svashenko, Iu. Solntseva, E. Maksimova, P. Masokha, V. Mikhailov.

Ivan (7 reels: Ukrainfilm, 1932)
> Scriptwriter and director: A Dovzhenko. Camera operators: D. Demutsky, Iu. Ekelchik, M. Grider. Set designer: Iu. Khomoza. Music composers: Iu. Meitus, I. Belza, B. Liatoshinsky.
> Cast: P. Masokha, S. Shkurat, T. Iura, N. Nademsky, A. Khvylia.

Aerograd (8 reels: Mosfilm, 1935)
> Scriptwriter and director: A Dovzhenko. Camera operators: E. Tisse, M. Gindin, N. Smirnov. Set designers: A. Utkin, V. Panteleev. Music composer: D. Kabalevsky.
> Cast: S. Shagaida, S. Stoliarov, S. Shkurat, D. Dobronravov, N. Tabunasov, V. Uralsky.

Shchors (14 reels: Kiev Film Studio, 1939)
> Scriptwriter and director: A. Dovzhenko. Assistant director: Iu. Solntseva. Camera operator: Iu. Ekelchik. Set designer: M. Umansky. Music composer: D. Kabalevsky.
> Cast: E. Samoilov, I. Skuratov, A. Khvylia, P. Masokha, A. Buchma, G. Iura, N. Kriuchkov.

Michurin (10 reels: Mosfilm, 1948)
> Scriptwriter and director: A. Dovzhenko. Assistant director: Iu. Solntseva. Camera operators: L. Kosmatov, Iu. Kun. Music composer: D. Shostakovich. Set designers: M. Bogdanov, G. Miasnikov.
> Cast: G. Belov, A. Vasileva, V. Solovev, N. Shamin, M. Zharov, K. Nasonov.

Notes

CHAPTER I: INTRODUCTION

1 Viktor Shklovskii, *Za sorok let* (Moscow: Iskusstvo, 1965), p. 393.
2 For comprehensive bibliographies on Dovzhenko see Marco Carynnyk, *A Dovzhenko Bibliography* (Cambridge: MIT Press, 1973), and Iu. Rubinshtein, "Bibliograficheskii ukazatel' literaturnykh proizvedenii A.P. Dovzhenko i materialov o ego tvorchestve," *Iz istorii kino* 1 (1958): 149-95.
3 Dovzhenko, "Notebooks," in *Alexander Dovzhenko: The Poet as Filmmaker*, ed. and trans. Marco Carynnyk (Cambridge: MIT Press, 1973), p. 157.
4 Respectively: Ivor Montagu, "Dovzhenko: Poet of Life Eternal," *Sight and Sound* 27, no. 1 (1957): 45; Lewis Jacobs, "Dovzhenko," *The Left* 1, no. 1 (1931): 78; Charles Shibuck, "The Films of Alexander Dovzhenko," *New York Film Bulletin* 2, no. 11 (n.d.): n.pag.; Carynnyk, "Introduction," *Poet as Filmmaker*, pp. ix-lv; Herbert Marshall, *Masters of the Soviet Cinema* (London: Routlege & Kegan Paul, 1983), p. 159.
Although his conception of Dovzhenko's "mythopoeic vision" remains vague, Carynnyk's survey is by far the most valuable of those cited above, drawing as it does on the author's considerable knowledge of Ukrainian culture and Dovzhenko's career. See also P. Adams Sitney's thoughtful career survey, in which he attempts to equate Dovzhenko with symbolist poets ("Alexander Dovzhenko," in *Cinema: A Critical Dictionary*, ed. Richard Roud [New York: Viking Press, 1980], 1:279-91).
5 Nine of Dovzhenko's ten fiction films survive. His first film project, *Vasia the Reformer* (1926), is lost. He also directed or supervised four documentary films during the 1940s.
6 See Pierre Macherey, *A Theory of Literary Production*, trans. Geoffrey Wall (London: Routlege & Kegan Paul, 1978); idem, "The Problem of Reflection," *Sub-Stance*, no. 15 (1976), pp. 6-20; Terry Eagleton, *Criticism and Ideology* (London: New Left Books, 1976); and idem, "Pierre Macherey and the Theory of Literary Production," *Minnesota Review*, no. 4 (1975), pp. 134-44.
7 Eagleton, *Criticism and Ideology*, pp. 44-45.
8 Ibid., p. 163.
9 Macherey, *Literary Production*, pp. 85-90.
10 Terry Eagleton, *Marxism and Literary Criticism* (Berkeley and Los Angeles: University of California Press, 1976), p. 5.

11 Idem, *Criticism and Ideology,* p. 72.

12 Macherey, "Problem of Reflection," pp. 18–19.

13 Louis Althusser, *For Marx,* trans. Ben Brewster (London: Verso Editions, 1979), chap. 3 (Althusser's discussion of "overdetermined" societies) and p. 97.

14 Isaac Deutscher, *The Unfinished Revolution* (New York: Oxford University Press, 1967), pp. 27–28.

15 Ibid., pp. 37, 38.

CHAPTER II: THE FORMATIVE YEARS

1 Dovzhenko, "Autobiography," in *Poet as Filmmaker,* pp. 11–12.

2 See Eagleton, *Criticism and Ideology,* chap. 2.

3 John S. Reshetar, *The Ukrainian Revolution, 1917–1920* (Princeton: Princeton University Press, 1952), chap. 1.

4 George S. N. Luckyj, *Between Gogol' and Ševčenko* (Munich: Wilhelm Fink Verlag, 1971).

5 Except as otherwise noted, the following biographical summary draws from the following: Dovzhenko, "Autobiography," pp. 3–13; A. Mar'iamov, *Dovzhenko* (Moscow: Molodaia Gvardiia, 1968), chaps. 1–10; and M. V. Kutsenko, *Storinky zhyttia i tvorchosti O. P. Dovzhenka* (Kiev: Dnipro, 1975), pp. 7–42.

6 On the lot of such peasant households see Gerald Tanquary Robinson, *Rural Russia under the Old Regime* (1932; reprinted ed., Berkeley and Los Angeles: University of California Press, 1969), chap. 6.

7 On this aspect of peasant life see Marc Bloch, *The Historian's Craft,* trans. Peter Putnam (New York: Vintage Books, 1953), pp. 40–41.

8 The quotations are from Dovzhenko's autobiographical short story "The Enchanted Desna," trans. Eve Manning, *Soviet Literature,* 1958, no. 6, pp. 15 and 32.

9 T. V. Baimut, "Novye materialy k biografii A. P. Dovzhenko," *Iskusstvo kino,* 1959, no. 10, pp. 149–51.

10 Unless otherwise noted, the following summary of political and military events is based on Reshetar, *Ukrainian Revolution,* chaps. 2–6.

11 Stanley W. Page, "Lenin and Self-Determination," *Slavonic and East European Review* 28, no. 71 (1950): 342–58.

12 The following discussion of the Kharkov literary and artistic movement draws from George S. N. Luckyj, *Literary Politics in the Soviet Ukraine, 1917–1934* (New York: Columbia University Press, 1956), chaps. 3–7.

13 Many of Dovzhenko's drawings and cartoons from the period are collected in I. Zolotov and G. Konovalov, *Dovzhenko—Khudozhnyk* (Kiev: Mystetstvo, 1968).

14 See Richard Taylor, *The Politics of the Soviet Cinema, 1917–1929* (Cambridge: Cambridge University Press, 1979), chap. 2.

15 See Richard T. DeGeorge, *Patterns of Soviet Thought* (Ann Arbor: University of

Michigan Press, 1970), pp. 135-38; see also Lenin's seminal essay "Party Literature and Party Organization," in V. I. Lenin, *On Literature and Art* (Moscow: Progress Publishers, 1970), pp. 22-27.

16 See Marc Slonim, *Soviet Russian Literature* (New York: Oxford University Press, 1967), chap. 5; and Margaret Bullitt, "Toward a Theory of Marxist Aesthetics: The Development of Socialist Realism," *Russian Review* 35, no. 1 (1976): 62-63.

17 For the following discussion of the Soviet film industry I have used Taylor, *Soviet Cinema*, chap. 4-5; I. N. Vladimirtseva and A. M. Sandler, eds., *Istoriia sovetskogo kino, 1917-1967*, 4 vols. (Moscow: Iskusstvo, 1969-76), 1:14-32; Steven P. Hill, "A Quantitative View of Soviet Cinema," *Cinema Journal* 12, no. 2 (1972): 21; Paul Babitsky and John Rimberg, *The Soviet Film Industry* (New York: Praeger Publishers, 1955), chap. 1.

18 The following material on VUFKU and Dovzhenko's early experiences there draws from Vladimirtseva and Sandler, *Istoriia*, 1:543-55; Mar'iamov, *Dovzhenko*, chap. 8; Semen Svashenko, "Kluch k chelovecheskoi dushe," *Sovetskii ekran*, 1964, no. 17, p. 12.

19 Taylor, *Soviet Cinema*, chap. 6; Babitsky and Rimberg, *Soviet Film Industry*, p. 141.

CHAPTER III: EARLY EFFORTS

1 For Dovzhenko's opinion of his early work see editors' notes in A. P. Dovzhenko, *Sobranie sochinenii*, ed. Iu. Ia. Barabash et al., 4 vols. (Moscow: Iskusstvo, 1966-68), 1:334. Typical of subsequent critical evaluations are Barthélmy Amengual, *Alexandre Dovjenko* (Paris: Editions Seghers, 1970), p. 35, and Luda Schnitzer and Jean Schnitzer, *Alexandre Dovjenko* (Paris: Editions Universitaires, 1966), p. 32. See also David Robinson's effort to rehabilitate the early films: "Dovzhenko: Notes on the Director's Work before *Zvenigora*," *The Silent Picture*, no. 8 (1970), pp. 11-14.

2 Betty Kepley and Vance Kepley, "Foreign Films on Soviet Screens, 1921-1932," *Quarterly Review of Film Studies* 4, no. 4 (1979): 429-42.

3 Lev Kuleshov, *Kuleshov on Film*, ed. and trans. Ronald Levaco (Berkeley and Los Angeles: University of California Press, 1974), p. 128.

4 Dovzhenko, "Autobiography," in *Poet as Filmmaker*, p. 13; Mar'iamov, *Dovzhenko*, p. 42.

5 Rostislaw Jurenew, *Alexander Dowshenko* (Berlin: Henschelverlag, 1964), p. 16; Mar'iamov, *Dovzhenko*, pp. 72-79.

6 For a description of the film see A. V. Macheret et al., eds., *Sovetskie khudozhestvennye fil'my*, 3 vols. (Moscow: Iskusstvo, 1961), 1:126-27.

7 See, for example, the short satirical piece "Standard Types in Soviet Realist Films," reprinted in Jay Leyda, *Kino: A History of the Russian and Soviet Film*, 3d ed. (Princeton: Princeton University Press, 1983), p. 256.

8 See Leon Trotsky, "Vodka, the Church, and the Cinema," in *Problems of Everyday Life*, trans. Z. Vergerova (New York: Monad Press, 1973), pp. 31-35.

9 See James H. Billington, *The Icon and the Axe* (New York: Vintage Books, 1970), p. 492, and Gail Warshofsky Lapidus, *Women in Soviet Society* (Berkeley and Los Angeles: University of California Press, 1978), chap. 2. The quotations are reproduced in J. P. Nettl, *The Soviet Achievement* (New York: Harcourt, Brace & World, 1967), p. 110, and Theodore Von Laue, *Why Lenin? Why Stalin?* 2d ed. (Philadelphia: J. B. Lippincott, 1971), pp. 142–43, respectively.

10 On the *detektiv* genre see Sergei Iutkevich et al., eds., *Kinoslovar'*, 2 vols. (Moscow: Sovetskaia entsiklopediia, 1966–70), 1:447–48, and Babitsky and Rimberg, *Soviet Film Industry*, pp. 121–22.

11 Mar'iamov, *Dovzhenko*, pp.70–71; Jurenew, *Dowshenko*, p. 18. For the Mayakovsky poem see *Mayakovsky on Poetry*, ed. and trans. Herbert Marshall (London: Pilot Press, 1945), p. 125.

12 The following discussion of the Soviet Union's dealings with foreign leftists is drawn from several sources. The issue is exhaustively covered in volume 7 of E. H. Carr's *A History of Soviet Russia*, 14 vols. (London: Macmillan, 1954–78). For more pointed discussions see Leonard Schapiro, *The Communist Party of the Soviet Union* (New York: Vintage Books, 1964), pp. 196, 218–19, 354–55; Robert Conquest, *V. I. Lenin* (New York: Viking Press, 1972), pp. 109–11; and Nettl, *Soviet Achievement*, pp. 103–4. On the USSR's dealings with the British see Daniel F. Calhoun, *The United Front* (Cambridge: Cambridge University Press, 1976).

13 Deutscher, *Unfinished Revolution*, p. 69.

14 Hitchcock, interview in Charles Higham and Joel Greenberg, *The Celluloid Muse* (Chicago: Regnery, 1971), p. 92.

15 Extant prints of the film are missing the first two reels. It is possible that the content of the pouch is revealed in the missing segments, but surviving plot synopses based on the full, original version of the film give no indication that the documents are described in the missing reels. For a full plot synopsis see Macheret, *Sovetskie khudozhestvennye fil'my*, 1:228.

16 Mar'iamov, *Dovzhenko*, p. 85.

17 Quoted ibid., pp. 102–3.

18 *Iskusstvo i zhizn'* 7 (1928): 12.

CHAPTER IV: *ZVENIGORA*

1 Sergei Eisenstein, "The Birth of an Artist," in *Notes of a Film Director*, ed. and trans. X. Danko (New York: Dover Publications, 1970), p. 142.

2 Dovzhenko, *Sobranie sochinenii*, 1:253.

3 See, for example, Schnitzer and Schnitzer, *Dovjenko*, p. 43.

4 Mar'iamov, *Dovzhenko*, p. 116, and editors' notes in Dovzhenko, *Sobranie sochinenii*, 1:335.

5 See Y. M. Sokolov, *Russian Folklore*, trans. Catherine Ruth Smith (New York: Macmillan, 1950), pp. 342–68, 617–18.

6 Mar'iamov, *Dovzhenko*, pp. 58, 71–72, 112–15.

7 Dovzhenko, "Autobiography," in *Poet as Filmmaker,* p. 13.
8 Babitsky and Rimberg, *Soviet Film Industry,* p. 141.
9 Quoted in Mar'iamov, *Dovzhenko,* p. 109.
10 Quoted in editors' notes in Dovzhenko, *Sobranie sochinenii,* 1:343. On the jubilee and the films commissioned to celebrate it see Leyda, *Kino,* chap. 11.
11 Dovzhenko, "My Method," trans. K. Santor, *Experimental Cinema,* no. 5 (1934), p. 23.
12 Dovzhenko's scenario is published in Dovzhenko, *Sobranie sochinenii,* 1:59–86. Subsequent references to this source appear within the text as page citations.
13 On the invasion see Nicholas V. Riasanovsky, *A History of Russia,* 2d ed. (New York: Oxford University Press, 1969), pp. 25–26.
14 Cf. Shevchenko, "The Haydamaks," *The Poetical Works of Taras Shevchenko,* ed. and trans. C. H. Andrusyshen and Walter Kirkconnell (Toronto: University of Toronto Press, 1964), p. 101.
15 Kh. Khersonskii, "VUFKU na perelome," *Pravda,* 10 February 1928, p. 6.
16 Dovzhenko, *Sobranie sochinenii,* 1:254.
17 Mykola Bazhin quoted in Mar'iamov, *Dovzhenko,* p. 146.

CHAPTER V: *ARSENAL*

1 Reshetar, *Ukrainian Revolution,* pp. 106–15.
2 Dovzhenko, "Autobiography," in *Poet as Filmmaker,* p. 14.
3 Dovzhenko, *Sobranie sochinenii,* 1:255.
4 The Dovbush tale is quoted in M. P. Vlasov, *Geroi A. P. Dovzhenko i traditsii fol'klora* (Moscow: VGIK, 1962), p. 19.
5 Dovzhenko, *Sobranie sochinenii,* 1:256.

CHAPTER VI: *EARTH*

1 Mar'iamov, *Dovzhenko,* pp. 197–99.
2 Ibid., pp. 199–200.
3 P. Bliakhin, "Zemlia," *Pravda,* 29 March 1930, p. 4; Mar'iamov, *Dovzhenko,* pp. 200–202. Some journals sponsored open debates on the film. *Vecherniaia Moskva,* 1 April 1930, p. 2, for example, featured a series of pro and con editorials. The essay titles provide a sense of the controversy: "A great conquest, but also great defects"; "On a film one would want to see many times"; "Biology drove out sociology"; "Unquestionable mastery, but questionable content"; "Ancillary themes hid socialist content." For a fuller survey of the *Earth* controversy see Paul Burns, "Cultural Revolution, Collectivization, and Soviet Cinema: Eisenstein's *Old and New* and Dovzhenko's *Earth,*" *Film and History* 11, no. 4 (1981): 84–96.
4 Dem'ian Bednyi, "Filosofy," *Izvestiia,* 4 April 1930, p. 2.
5 See, for example, Marcel Oms, *Alexandre Dovjenko* (Lyons: Premier Plan, 1968), pp. 35–41; Ken Kelman, "Classic Plastics and Total Tectonics," in *Film*

Culture Reader, ed. P. Adams Sitney (New York: Praeger Publishers, 1970), pp. 387–92; and Gilberto Perez, "All in the Foreground: A Study of Dovzhenko's *Earth,*" *Hudson Review* 28, no. 1 (1975): 67–86.

6 Lazar Bodyk, *Dzherela velykogo kino* (Kiev: Radianskyi pys'mennyk, 1965), p. 66.

7 Except as otherwise noted, the following summary of the agricultural situation draws from Robinson, *Rural Russia,* chaps. 5–8; Moshe Lewin, *Russian Peasants and Soviet Power: A Study of Collectivization,* trans. Irene Nove (New York: Norton, 1975); and Alec Nove, *An Economic History of the U.S.S.R.* (Harmondsworth, England: Pelican Books, 1972), chap. 7.

8 Quoted in Isaac Deutscher, *Stalin: A Political Biography,* 2d ed. (New York: Oxford University Press, 1966), p. 320.

9 W.E.D. Allen, *The Ukraine: A History* (Cambridge: Cambridge University Press, 1941), p. 324.

10 Dovzhenko quoted in Vlasov, *Geroi A. P. Dovzhenko,* p. 29.

11 Lewin, *Russian Peasants,* p. 499.

CHAPTER VII: *IVAN*

1 Dovzhenko, "Autobiography," in *Poet as Filmmaker,* p. 15.

2 Cf. Chapter 2 above for a discussion of the mode of production governing Dovzhenko's earlier films, and see Eagleton, *Criticism and Ideology,* chap. 2, on the general concept of an artistic mode of production.

3 On the nature of the USSR's industrialization effort in the 1930s see Nove, *Economic History,* chap. 8.

4 Herbert Marcuse, *Soviet Marxism* (New York: Vintage Books, 1961), chaps. 1–3.

5 Ibid., p. xiv.

6 Ibid., p. 72.

7 Ibid., pp. 70–71.

8 On the effect of Stalinism on the arts generally in the Soviet Union see Bullitt, "Theory of Marxist Aesthetics," pp. 66–76, and C. Vaughan James, *Soviet Socialist Realism* (New York: St. Martin's Press, 1973), chaps. 3–4. On changes within the film industry see Babitsky and Rimberg, *Soviet Film Industry,* pp. 38–44.

9 Babitsky and Rimberg, *Soviet Film Industry,* pp. 95–98, 159–62.

10 Ibid., p. 243; Hill, "Quantitative View," p. 21.

11 Babitsky and Rimberg, *Soviet Film Industry,* p. 143; Leyda, *Kino,* p. 291.

12 Dovzhenko, *Sobranie sochinenii,* 1:280.

13 The following discussion of industrialization and its effects on Soviet workers draws from Pierre Sorlin, *The Soviet People and Their Society: From 1917 to the Present,* trans. Daniel Weissbort (New York: Praeger Publishers, 1968), pp. 161–73; Deutscher, *Unfinished Revolution,* pp. 46–48; and Nettl, *Soviet Achievement,* pp. 119–29. On the Dneprostroi and its labor supply see Anne D.

Rassweiler, "Soviet Labor Policy in the First Five-Year Plan: The Dneprostroi Experience," *Slavic Review* 42, no. 2 (1983): 230–46.
14 Dovzhenko, "Autobiography," p. 16.
15 Idem, *Sobranie sochinenii,* 2:19.
16 Idem, "Autobiography," p. 16.
17 On the production's many problems see editors' notes in Dovzhenko, *Sobranie sochinenii,* 1:338; Mar'iamov, *Dovzhenko,* pp. 223, 228; Jurenew, *Dowshenko,* pp. 53–54; and Dovzhenko, "Autobiography," pp. 16–18.
18 Dovzhenko, *Sobranie sochinenii,* 1:154.
19 Nettl, *Soviet Achievement,* pp. 119–21.
20 Featured in the sequence are the actual laborers awarded shock worker certificates at Dneprostroi; see the full page of portraits of Dneprostroi shock workers in *Bol'shaia sovetskaia entsiklopediia,* 1st ed., 65 vols. (Moscow: Sovetskaia entsiklopediia, 1926–47), 22:780f.
21 Riasanovsky, *History of Russia,* p. 551.
22 Dovzhenko, *Sobranie sochinenii,* 1:153.
23 See Marcuse, *Soviet Marxism,* chap. 2.
24 Dovzhenko, *Sobranie sochinenii,* 1:154.
25 Ibid., 2:281.

CHAPTER VIII: *AEROGRAD*

1 For a history of the purges and their effect on the society generally see Robert Conquest, *The Great Terror,* rev. ed. (New York: Collier Books, 1973).
2 On the relationship between Soviet development and security see Marcuse, *Soviet Marxism,* chap. 2.
3 On problems of Soviet security in the Far East see George Alexander Lensen, *The Damned Inheritance: The Soviet Union and the Manchurian Crisis, 1924–1935* (Tallahassee, Fla.: Diplomatic Press, 1974).
4 Conquest, *Great Terror,* pp. 731–40.
5 On the subversion fostered by the Russian Fascist league see John J. Stephan, *The Russian Fascists* (New York: Harper & Row, 1978), esp. chaps. 4–6, 12–13. The law concerning the implication of family members was effected by Stalin's personal order (Deutscher, *Stalin,* p. 354).
6 See *Bol'shaia sovetskaia entsiklopediia,* 1st ed., 23:827; Dovzhenko, "Why I Created *Air-City,*" *New Masses,* 31 December 1936, p. 29; Mar'iamov, *Dovzhenko,* p. 233; Jurenew, *Dowshenko,* p. 63.
7 Dovzhenko, *Sobranie sochinenii,* 1:307.
8 Idem, "Autobiography," in *Poet as Filmmaker,* p. 16.
9 Ibid., p. 18; on Fadeev's background see Slonim, *Soviet Russian Literature,* pp. 174–77.
10 On the film's production history see Mar'iamov, *Dovzhenko,* chap. 16; editors' notes in Dovzhenko, *Sobranie sochinenii,* 1:399; Leyda, *Kino,* p. 353.
11 Mar'iamov, *Dovzhenko,* p. 240.

CHAPTER IX: *SHCHORS*

1 Dovzhenko describes the film's genesis in Dovzhenko, "Uchitel' i drug khudozhnika," *Pravda,* 5 November 1936, p. 3.
2 On the film's production history see editors' notes in Dovzhenko, *Sobranie sochinenii,* 1:339-41; cf. Dovzhenko's angry diary entry concerning outside interference during the production (Dovzhenko, "Notebooks," in *Poet as Filmmaker,* p. 106).
3 Deutscher, *Stalin,* p. 609. For a general discussion of the personality cult see ibid., pp. 609-14. Nina Tumarkin gives a detailed and fascinating account of the Soviet practice of exploiting Lenin's memory in *Lenin Lives! The Lenin Cult in Soviet Russia* (Cambridge: Harvard University Press, 1983).
4 John Rimberg, *The Motion Picture in the Soviet Union, 1919-1952* (New York: Arno Press, 1973), p. 202.
5 See Dovzhenko, *Sobranie sochinenii,* 1:256-57.
6 Deutscher, *Stalin,* pp. 381-82.
7 The following discussion of the Red Army purge draws from Conquest, *Great Terror,* chap. 7. For the purge's impact on Dovzhenko's *Shchors,* especially the impact of Dubovoi's death, see Mar'iamov, *Dovzhenko,* pp. 281-82.
8 On the lives and deaths of the real Shchors and Bozhenko see *Bol'shaia sovetskaia entsiklopediia,* 2d ed., 49 vols. (Moscow: Sovetskaia entsiklopediia, 1949-57), 48:277, and ibid., 3d ed., 31 vols. (Moscow: Sovetskaia entsiklopediia, 1970-81), 3:363-64.
9 Nikita Khrushchev describes the plot to accuse Dubovoi of Shchors's murder in Khrushchev, *Khrushchev Remembers,* ed. and trans. Strobe Talbot (Boston: Little, Brown, 1970), p. 80. Dovzhenko's diary quotation is from Dovzhenko, "Notebooks," p. 106.
10 See illustrations in K. F. Skorobogatkin, *50 let vooruzhennykh sil SSSR* (Moscow: Voennoe izdatel'stvo ministerstva oborony SSSR, 1968), for the evolution of Red Army uniforms.

CHAPTER X: *MICHURIN*

1 Quoted in Zhores A. Medvedev, *The Rise and Fall of T. D. Lysenko,* trans. I. Michael Lerner (Garden City, N.J.: Anchor Books, 1971), p. 130.
2 The most thorough and reliable study of Lysenkoism is David Jarovsky, *The Lysenko Affair* (Cambridge: Harvard University Press, 1970). Unless otherwise noted, my material on Lysenkoism draws from this source.
3 Ibid., p. 60.
4 Quoted in DeGeorge, *Soviet Thought,* p. 249, n. 3.
5 Medvedev, *Rise and Fall,* pp. 21-23, 49-50.
6 Lysenko as quoted in Theodosius Dobzhansky, "Russian Genetics," in *Soviet Science,* ed. Ruth C. Christman (Washington: American Association for the Advancement of Science, 1952), pp. 2-3.
7 The official version of Michurin's life and achievements is given in I. V. Mi-

churin, *Selected Works* (Moscow: Foreign Language Publishing House, 1949), pp. 1–15, and *Bol'shaia sovetskaia entsiklopediia*, 3d ed., 16:355.

8 The following summary of Michurin's self-fabricated legend is based on Jarovsky's discussion of the horticulturist in *Lysenko Affair*, pp. 40–54.

9 Michurin, *Works*, p. 14.

10 Ibid., p. 10.

11 P.N. Yakovlev, "Introduction," in Michurin, *Works*, p. xix.

12 Quoted in Dobzhansky, "Russian Genetics," p. 1.

13 Schapiro, *Communist Party*, p. 531.

14 Quotations from Dovzhenko, "Notebooks," pp. 233 and 102, respectively. For background on the film's production see Mar'iamov, *Dovzhenko*, chap. 19; and editors' notes in Dovzhenko, *Sobranie sochinenii*, 3:757–58.

15 Dovzhenko, "Notebooks," pp. 141, 144–46. Six versions of the scenario survive in the Dovzhenko archives, giving some idea of how extensive the revision process was (editors' notes in Dovzhenko, *Sobranie sochinenii*, 3:757).

16 Bolshakov as quoted in Babitsky and Rimberg, *Soviet Film Industry*, p. 190; Dovzhenko's response in "Notebooks," p. 158.

17 Mar'iamov, *Dovzhenko*, p. 329; and Jurenew, *Dowshenko*, p. 105.

18 *New York Times*, 3 January 1949, p. 14.

19 R. Iurenev, "Sbyvaetsia ego mechta," *Ogenek*, 1949, no. 5, p. 27.

20 D. Mikhailov, "Michurin," *Vecherniaia Moskva*, 7 January 1949, p. 3.

21 Lysenko as quoted in Jarovsky, *Lysenko Affair*, p. 143. For confirmation of the film's opening see Macheret, *Sovetskie khudozhestvennye fil'my*, 2:405.

22 Quoted in Yakovlev, "Introduction," p. xvii.

23 Ibid., p. xviii.

CHAPTER XI: CONCLUSION

1 On Dovzhenko's final years see Mar'iamov, *Dovzhenko*, chap. 11. Many of Dovzhenko's unrealized projects were filmed after his death by his widow Solntseva, an accomplished artist in her own right; on her career see Iutkevich, *Kinoslovar'*, 2:566–67.

2 Jean-Paul Sartre, *Search for a Method*, trans. Hazel E. Barnes (New York: Vintage, 1968), pp. 91–111.

Bibliography

Allen, W.E.D. *The Ukraine: A History.* Cambridge: Cambridge University Press, 1941.

Althusser, Louis. *For Marx.* Translated by Ben Brewster. London: Verso Editions, 1979.

Amengual, Barthélmy. *Alexandre Dovjenko.* Paris: Editions Seghers, 1970.

Babitsky, Paul, and Rimberg, John. *The Soviet Film Industry.* New York: Praeger Publishers, 1955.

Baimut, T. V. "Novye materialy k biografii A. P. Dovzhenko." *Iskusstvo kino,* 1959, no. 10, pp. 149-51.

Bednyi, Dem'ian. "Filosofy." *Izvestiia,* 4 April 1930, p. 2, and 6 April 1930, p. 2.

Billington, James H. *The Icon and the Axe: An Interpretive History of Russian Culture.* New York: Vintage Books, 1970.

Bliakhin, P. "Zemlia." *Pravda,* 29 March 1930, p. 4.

Bloch, Marc. *The Historian's Craft.* Translated by Peter Putnam. New York: Vintage Books, 1953.

Bodyk, Lazar. *Dzherela velykogo kino.* Kiev: Radianskyi pys'mennyk, 1965.

Bol'shaia sovetskaia entsiklopediia. 1st ed. 65 vols. Moscow: Sovetskaia entsiklopediia, 1926-47.

Bol'shaia sovetskaia entsiklopediia. 2d ed. 49 vols. Moscow: Sovetskaia entsiklopediia, 1949-57.

Bol'shaia sovetskaia entsiklopediia. 3d ed. 31 vols. Moscow: Sovetskaia entsiklopediia, 1970-81.

Bullitt, Margaret. "Toward a Theory of Marxist Aesthetics: The Development of Socialist Realism." *Russian Review* 35, no. 1 (1976): 53-76.

Burns, Paul. "Cultural Revolution, Collectivization, and Soviet Cinema: Eisenstein's *Old and New* and Dovzhenko's *Earth.*" *Film and History* 11, no. 4 (1981): 84-96.

Calhoun, Daniel F. *The United Front: The TUC and the Russians, 1923-1928.* Cambridge: Cambridge University Press, 1976.

Carr, E. H. *A History of Soviet Russia.* 14 vols. London: Macmillan, 1954-78.

Carynnyk, Marco. *A Dovzhenko Bibliography.* Cambridge: MIT Press, 1973.

Conquest, Robert. *The Great Terror: Stalin's Purges of the Thirties.* Rev. ed. New York: Collier Books, 1973.

Conquest, Robert. *V. I. Lenin.* New York: Viking Press, 1972.

DeGeorge, Richard T. *Patterns of Soviet Thought.* Ann Arbor: University of Michigan Press, 1970.

Deutscher, Isaac. *Stalin: A Political Biography.* 2d ed. New York: Oxford University Press, 1966.

Deutscher, Isaac. *The Unfinished Revolution: Russia, 1917–1967.* New York: Oxford University Press, 1967.

Dobzhansky, Theodosius. "Russian Genetics." In *Soviet Science,* edited by Ruth C. Christman, pp. 1–7. Washington, D.C.: American Association for the Advancement of Science, 1952.

Dovzhenko. A. P. *Alexander Dovzhenko: The Poet as Filmmaker.* Edited and translated by Marco Carynnyk. Cambridge: MIT Press, 1973.

Dovzhenko, A. P. "The Enchanted Desna." Translated by Eve Manning. *Soviet Literature,* 1958, no. 6, pp. 3–44.

Dovzhenko, A. P. "My Method." Translated by K. Santor. *Experimental Cinema,* no. 5 (1934), pp. 23–24.

Dovzhenko, A. P. *Sobranie sochinenii.* Edited by Iu. Ia. Barabash et al. 4 vols. Moscow: Iskusstvo, 1966–68.

Dovzhenko, A. P. "Uchitel' i drug khudozhnika." *Pravda,* 5 November 1936, p. 3.

Dovzhenko, A. P. "Why I Created *Air-City.*" *New Masses,* 31 December 1936, p. 29.

Eagleton, Terry. *Criticism and Ideology: A Study in Marxist Literary Theory.* London: New Left Books, 1976.

Eagleton, Terry. *Marxism and Literary Criticism.* Berkeley and Los Angeles: University of California Press, 1976.

Eagleton, Terry. "Pierre Macherey and the Theory of Literary Production." *Minnesota Review,* no. 4 (1975), pp. 134–44.

Eisenstein, Sergei. *Notes of a Film Director.* Edited and translated by X. Danko. New York: Dover Publications, 1970.

Higham, Charles, and Greenberg, Joel. *The Celluloid Muse: Hollywood Directors Speak.* Chicago: Regnery, 1971.

Hill, Steven P. "A Quantitative View of Soviet Cinema." *Cinema Journal* 12, no. 2 (1972): 18–25.

Iskusstvo i zhizn' 7 (1928): 12. [A review of *Diplomatic Pouch.*]

Iurenev, R. *Alexander Dowshenko.* See Jurenew, Rostislaw.

Iurenev, R. "Sbyvaetsia ego mechta." *Ogenek,* 1949, no. 5, p. 27.

Iutkevich, Sergei, et al., eds. *Kinoslovar'.* 2 vols. Moscow: Sovetskaia entsiklopediia, 1966–70.

Jacobs, Lewis. "Dovzhenko." *The Left* 1, no. 1 (1931): 78–79.

James, C. Vaughan. *Soviet Socialist Realism: Origins and Theory.* New York: St. Martin's Press, 1973.

Jarovsky, David. *The Lysenko Affair.* Cambridge: Harvard University Press, 1970.

Jurenew, Rostislaw. [R. Iurenev.] *Alexander Dowshenko.* Berlin: Henschelverlag, 1964.

Kelman, Ken. "Classic Plastics and Total Tectonics." In *Film Culture Reader,* edited by P. Adams Sitney, pp. 387-92. New York: Praeger Publishers, 1970.

Kepley, Betty, and Kepley, Vance. "Foreign Films on Soviet Screens, 1921-1932." *Quarterly Review of Film Studies* 4, no. 4 (1979): 429-42.

Khersonskii, Kh. "VUFKU na perelome." *Pravda,* 10 February 1928, p. 6.

Khrushchev, Nikita. *Khrushchev Remembers.* Edited and translated by Strobe Talbot. Boston: Little, Brown, 1970.

Kuleshov, Lev. *Kuleshov on Film.* Edited and translated by Ronald Levaco. Berkeley and Los Angeles: University of California Press, 1974.

Kutsenko, M. V. *Storinky zhyttia i tvorchosti O. P. Dovzhenka.* Kiev: Dnipro, 1975.

Lapidus, Gail Warshofsky. *Women in Soviet Society.* Berkeley and Los Angeles: University of California Press, 1978.

Lenin, V. I. *On Literature and Art.* Moscow: Progress Publishers, 1970.

Lensen, George Alexander. *The Damned Inheritance: The Soviet Union and the Manchurian Crisis, 1924-1935.* Tallahassee, Fla.: Diplomatic Press, 1974.

Lewin, Moshe. *Russian Peasants and Soviet Power: A Study of Collectivization.* Translated by Irene Nove. New York: Norton, 1975.

Leyda, Jay. *Kino: A History of the Russian and Soviet Film.* 3d ed. Princeton: Princeton University Press. 1983.

Luckyj, George S. N. *Between Gogol' and Ševčenko:* Polarity in the Literary Ukraine, *1789-1847.* Munich: Wilhelm Fink Verlag, 1971.

Luckyj, George S. N. *Literary Politics in the Soviet Ukraine, 1917-1934.* New York: Columbia University Press, 1956.

Macheret, A. V., et al., eds. *Sovetskie khudozhestvennye fil'my.* 3 vols. Moscow: Iskusstvo, 1961.

Macherey, Pierre. "The Problem of Reflection." Translated by Susan Sniader Lanser. *Sub-Stance,* no. 15 (1976), pp. 6-20.

Macherey, Pierre. *A Theory of Literary Production.* Translated by Geoffrey Wall. London: Routlege & Kegan Paul, 1978.

Marcuse, Herbert. *Soviet Marxism: A Critical Analysis.* New York: Vintage Books, 1961.

Marshall, Herbert. *Masters of the Soviet Cinema: Crippled Creative Biographies.* London: Routlege & Kegan Paul, 1983.

Mar'iamov, A. *Dovzhenko.* Moscow: Molodaia Gvardiia, 1968.

Mayakovsky, Vladimir. *Mayakovsky on Poetry.* Edited and translated by Herbert Marshall. London: Pilot Press, 1945.

Medvedev, Zhores A. *The Rise and Fall of T. D. Lysenko.* Translated by I. Michael Lerner. Garden City, N.J.: Anchor Books, 1971.

Michurin, I. V. *Selected Works.* Moscow: Foreign Language Publishing House, 1949.

Mikhailov, D. "Michurin." *Vecherniaia Moskva,* 7 January 1949, p. 3.

Montagu, Ivor. "Dovzhenko: Poet of Life Eternal." *Sight and Sound* 27, no. 1 (1957): 44-48.

Nettl, J. P. *The Soviet Achievement.* New York: Harcourt, Brace & World, 1967.

Nove, Alec. *An Economic History of the U.S.S.R.* Harmondsworth, England: Pelican Books, 1972.

Oms, Marcel. *Alexandre Dovjenko.* Lyons: Premier Plan, 1968.

Page, Stanley W. "Lenin and Self-Determination." *Slavonic and East European Review* 28, no. 71 (1950): 342-58.

Perez, Gilberto. "All in the Foreground: A Study of Dovzhenko's *Earth.*" *Hudson Review* 28, no. 1 (1975): 67-86.

Rassweiler, Anne D. "Soviet Labor Policy in the First Five-Year Plan: The Dneprostroi Experience." *Slavic Review* 42, no. 2 (1983): 230-46.

Reshetar, John S. *The Ukrainian Revolution, 1917-1920.* Princeton: Princeton University Press, 1952.

Riasanovsky, Nicholas V. *A History of Russia.* 2d ed. New York: Oxford University Press, 1969.

Rimberg, John. *The Motion Picture in the Soviet Union, 1919-1952.* New York: Arno Press, 1973.

Robinson, David. "Dovzhenko: Notes on the Director's Work before *Zvenigora.*" *The Silent Picture,* no. 8 (1970), pp. 11-14.

Robinson, Gerald Tanquary. *Rural Russia under the Old Regime.* 1932. Reprint. Berkeley and Los Angeles: University of California Press, 1969.

Rubinshtein, Iu. "Bibliograficheskii ukazatel' literaturnykh proizvedenii A. P. Dovzhenko i materialov o ego tvorchestve." *Iz istorii kino 1* (1958): 149-95.

Sartre, Jean-Paul. *Search for a Method.* Translated by Hazel E. Barnes. New York: Vintage Books, 1968.

Schapiro, Leonard. *The Communist Party of the Soviet Union.* New York: Vintage Books, 1964.

Schnitzer, Luda, and Schnitzer, Jean. *Alexandre Dovjenko.* Paris: Editions Universitaires, 1966.

Shevchenko, Taras. *The Poetical Works of Taras Shevchenko.* Edited and translated by C. H. Andrusyshen and Walter Kirkconnell. Toronto: University of Toronto Press, 1964.

Shibuck, Charles. "The Films of Alexander Dovzhenko." *New York Film Bulletin* 2, no. 11 (n.d.): n.pag.

Shklovskii, Viktor. *Za sorok let.* Moscow: Iskusstvo, 1965.

Sitney, P. Adams. "Alexander Dovzhenko." In *Cinema: A Critical Dictionary,* edited by Richard Roud, 2 vols., 1:279-91. New York: Viking Press, 1980.

Skorobogatkin, K. F. *50 let vooruzhennykh sil SSSR.* Moscow: Voennoe izdatel'stvo ministerstva oborony SSSR, 1968.

Slonim, Marc. *Soviet Russian Literature.* New York: Oxford University Press, 1967.

Sokolov, Y. M. *Russian Folklore.* Translated by Catherine Ruth Smith. New York: Macmillan, 1950.

Sorlin, Pierre. *The Soviet People and Their Society: From 1917 to the Present.* Translated by Daniel Weissbort. New York: Praeger Publishers, 1968.

Stephan, John J. *The Russian Fascists: Tragedy and Farce in Exile, 1925-1945.* New York: Harper & Row, 1978.

Svashenko, Semen. "Kluch k chelovecheskoi dushe." *Sovetskii ekran*, 1964, no. 17, p. 12.

Taylor, Richard. *The Politics of the Soviet Cinema, 1917–1929.* Cambridge: Cambridge University Press, 1979.

Trotsky, Leon. *Problems of Everyday Life.* Translated by Z. Vergerova. New York: Monad Press, 1973.

Tumarkin, Nina. *Lenin Lives! The Lenin Cult in Soviet Russia.* Cambridge: Harvard University Press, 1983.

Vecherniaia Moskva, 1 April 1930, p. 2. [A series of editorials on *Earth.*]

Vladimirtseva, I. N., and Sandler, A. M., eds. *Istoriia sovetskogo kino, 1917–1967.* 4 vols. Moscow: Iskusstvo, 1969–76.

Vlasov, M. P. *Geroi A. P. Dovzhenko i traditsii fol'klora.* Moscow: VGIK, 1962.

Von Laue, Theodore. *Why Lenin? Why Stalin?.* 2d ed. Philadelphia: J. P. Lippincott, 1971.

Zolotov, I., and Konovalov, G. *Dovzhenko—Khudozhnyk.* Kiev: Mystetstvo, 1968.

Index

DESIGNED BY BARBARA WERDEN
COMPOSED BY POINT WEST TYPESETTING
CAROL STREAM, ILLINOIS
MANUFACTURED BY THOMSON-SHORE, INC.
DEXTER, MICHIGAN
TEXT AND DISPLAY LINES ARE SET IN BASKERVILLE

Library of Congress Cataloging-in-Publication Data
Kepley, Vance, 1951–
In the service of the state.
Filmography: pp. 169–170.
Bibliography: pp. 181–185.
Includes index.
1. Dovzhenko, Oleksandr Petrovych, 1894–1956—
Criticism and interpretation. I. Title.
PN1998.A3D648   1986   791.43′0233′0924
86-40054   ISBN 0-299-10680-2